SOCIOLOGY AND MEDICINE

T0382896

Ashgate Classics in Sociology

Series Editors:
Robert Dingwall, University of Nottingham, UK
Alan Aldridge, University of Nottingham, UK
Tim Strandleman, London Metropolitan University, UK

This series is the successor to Cardiff Classics in Medical Sociology, expanding the publishing agenda of the original series to include reprints and revised editions of influential works accross the discipline of sociology and collections of key articles by well-known sociologists.

Also in the series:

Identifying Hyperactive Children
The Medicalization of Deviant Behavior Expanded Edition
Peter Conrad
ISBN 0 7546 4518 5

A Constant Burden
The Reconstitution of Family Life
Margaret Voysey Paun
ISBN 0 7546 4470 7

Essays on Professions
Robert Dingwall
ISBN 0 7546 4614 9

Sociology and Medicine
Selected Essays by P.M. Strong

Edited by
ANNE MURCOTT
University of Nottingham, UK

Routledge
Taylor & Francis Group

LONDON AND NEW YORK

First published 2006 by Ashgate Publishing

Reissued 2018 by Routledge
2 Park Square, Milton Park, Abingdon, Oxon OX14 4RN
711 Third Avenue, New York, NY 10017, USA

Routledge is an imprint of the Taylor & Francis Group, an informa business

First issued in paperback 2018

A Library of Congress record exists under LC control number: 2006009706

Notice:
Product or corporate names may be trademarks or registered trademarks,
and are used only for identification and explanation without intent to
infringe.

Publisher's Note
The publisher has gone to great lengths to ensure the quality of this reprint
but points out that some imperfections in the original copies may be
apparent.

Disclaimer
The publisher has made every effort to trace copyright holders and
welcomes correspondence from those they have been unable to contact.

ISBN 13: 978-0-815-39713-7 (hbk)
ISBN 13: 978-1-138-62061-2 (pbk)
ISBN 13: 978-1-351-14884-9 (ebk)

Contents

Preface

Anne Murcott

This book covers several enduring themes in sociology and medicine: encounters between doctors and patients; inter-occupational contrasts and tensions; sociological research approaches to vital topics in health; and what Everett Hughes long ago talked of as the chronically perilous condition of sociology poised between science and profession (Hughes 1971). These are also long-standing intellectual preoccupations of Philip M. Strong's[1] twenty-year contribution to the field – one which he, in turn, did much to shape. For his work coincides with the notably fertile and rapid period of growth in medical sociology/sociology of health and illness in Britain that began in the late 1960s, a period in which ethnography ('imported' from British social anthropology and North American symbolic interactionism) left an indelible mark. In this respect, the twelve chapters collected together here constitute not only prime examples of his contribution, but also offer a glimpse of this period in the history of the field itself.[2]

Strong was not quite fifty when he died in July 1995.[3] Three years before, he had mulled over the idea of editing a selection of his articles. By that earlier date he had already published thirty-two papers and a further three were forthcoming. But they had appeared in a wide scatter of journals and as chapters in a dozen different books,[4] several of which were no longer in print. If nothing else, bringing them together in a single book would be convenient, especially for students, notably those pursuing newly instituted courses in health studies needing new library resources. A contract researcher for virtually all of his career, by 1992 Strong was based at the London School of Hygiene and Tropical Medicine (LSHTM) working on a study of the public debate over the AIDS crisis and government AIDS

---

1 While known as Phil day-to-day, he varied the form of his name in print.

2 For an introductory history, as well as reference to other overviews of the field, see Murcott (2001).

3 For an appreciation of his work and career see Bloor (1996).

4 See bibliography of Strong's main contributions in this volume.

policy.[5] This was an innovative and also demanding study. Coupled with mounting management commitments, as well as some teaching and PhD supervision, it added up to work pressures which led him to set the editing project aside. It got no further than the handwritten contents page later re-discovered among his papers.

The present volume is not, however, the one he sketched. For his plan had been to move beyond simply sandwiching a group of articles between a pair of covers – however useful a service it may have been to re-publish them together. Instead, he was thinking of using the collection not only to expose continuities in his earlier contributions that ran through and into the AIDS project, but to take the work further by developing a discussion of the as yet undefined new directions in which he suspected those continuities promised to lead. Strong's untimely death left the AIDS project uncompleted[6] and those new directions uncharted.

Since this is a different collection from the one he planned, readers deserve a little explanation of the thinking that led to selecting the twelve pieces included here. I begin with comment on the editorial stance that has been adopted.

While an author introducing their *own* work may find themselves squirming uncomfortably lest they stand accused of vanity publishing, editing a collection of work by an author no longer able to express their intentions induces other kinds of unease. Chief of these is one akin to the dilemma facing a biographer.[7] Are they to confine themselves to extant documentary evidence – diaries, obituaries, letters and the like – about their subject? Or are they to allow a biographic imagination to create what have to be fictional (albeit well informed) conversations, thoughts and feelings that plausibly fill the gaps in the documentary record? In all probability, the quality of the resulting biography does not completely depend on the choice. But what can be good for biography may not necessarily serve the sciences anything like so satisfactorily – a thought it is as well to take seriously, especially when there is no space here for digressions on what counts as truth or what kind of science sociology is or is not to be.[8]

5   The project was part of an inter-disciplinary programme of studies concerning the social impact of AIDS on the UK, funded by the Nuffield Provincial Hospitals Trust (now The Nuffield Trust).

6   Chapters 11 and 12 reprinted in this volume arose from his work on the AIDS project, along with a series of other articles (for details, see the bibliography of Strong's work in this volume).

7   I am greatly indebted to Jude Mackrell for an illuminating conversation on these points.

8   The reader may, though, like to pick up Strong's judgement that Goffman saw himself as a scientist (see Chapter 3 of this volume).

Consequently, in putting this collection together I have sought to rely more firmly on published expressions of Strong's position, and to minimise (although not eliminate completely) drawing on his unpublished papers and on my or any other friends' and colleagues' recollections of seminars or conversations. In like vein, in describing the selection presented here, I have tried to avoid second guessing what he would himself have written as an introduction to his own work.

One of the main purposes of this collection is quite straightforward. It is simply to display elements of Strong's thinking that persisted throughout the twenty or so years he was publishing, but which would be evident only to those familiar with his *complete* output. That this is even an issue, results from a combination of, on the one hand, what Bloor describes as 'the peripatetic contract researcher's condition' (Bloor 1996: 554) with, on the other, the double-life that medical sociologists (among many others) may be obliged to lead, seeking to address medical, nursing and policy colleagues as well as those in the 'home' discipline.[9] These various audiences have their own preoccupations and with them, their own preferred journals and research genres. So it is hoped that a side effect of this collection may be that readers familiar with Strong's work in one sphere will not only recognise well known themes, but also follow his thinking into other realms and see those same themes from a fresh angle – never mind discover new ones. Not least, especially if they study the footnotes and references, readers will discover how different Strong's intellectual engagement was from that of a great many sociologists. His workaday reading beyond sociology was broad, taking him deep into social theory, philosophy, social history and political science. His leisure reading went wider still, routinely including yet more history (ancient as well as mediaeval, early modern and contemporary), fiction (notably Jane Austen and Anthony Powell,[10] both authors' entire output re-read several times), and poetry (his copies not just of Donne and Marvell, Auden and Larkin but also Robert Burns and Arthur Hugh Clough became increasingly well-worn).[11]

---

9 A state of affairs probably far more widespread now than for much of Strong's career, resulting instead from the much higher prominence that is being given to researchers' active and planned engagement with a wide variety of academic and non-academic 'users'. Correspondingly, it means that, at the time, his position in this respect was probably much more unusual.

10 Whose work he discusses in 'The Rivals', reprinted in this volume as Chapter 6.

11 Consider Strong's choice of titles for his academic articles, e.g. 'The Rivals' nods toward Sheridan and his obituary-appreciation of Goffman alludes, of course, to Oscar Wilde.

What becomes clear from the chapters collected here, however, is that although Strong described himself as a *medical* sociologist, his preoccupations extended to the more generally sociological, in that they could transcend the specifics of the medical settings in which his empirical research was located. At one point, he summarised this aspect of his work in three succinct questions:

> How can we begin to pin down some key features of the micro-social world? How far do our imperial ambitions – ambitions common to every trade – distort the analyses we offer? What reasons are there, if any, for faith in social science and in the particular methods it selects for its inquiry? (Strong 1986:4–5).

Stern perhaps, and certainly exacting, Strong's questions provide an intensely compressed recognition of sociology's core activities not just as thought-out (theorised), deliberate and methodical attention to investigating the social, but also demanding a sociologically informed reflection on those activities, together with a consciousness, via the warrant claimed for their authoritativeness, of the way they are to be received beyond the discipline's boundaries.

It would be a mistake, none the less, to think that Strong's concerns were indifferent to the distinctive character of the therapeutic settings of his investigations or the specifics of clinical work and patient experience. Observation of their work at very close quarters engendered in Strong a profound respect for doctors, albeit infrequently expressed, that acknowledged the intractabilities and sheer effort of their routine professional lives. In parallel, those same observations evinced compassion for their patients, albeit more likely to be concealed beneath irony and wit – as, for instance, in 'Aren't children wonderful?', the title of the paper re-published here as Chapter 1, and 'Workers' Playtime', a heading in the article included as Chapter 2.[12] Moreover, Strong's moral stance on social affairs became more evident in his later work on the uncompleted AIDS project. The enormity of epidemic disease and, if unchecked, the consequent complete social collapse, led him to a solemn reconsideration and resurrection of Thomas Hobbes' seventeenth-century urging that an authority of some sort is necessary to hold utter social disintegration at bay. Such engagement with the practical world of affairs achieved what is perhaps its most explicit expression in Strong's essay (first published posthumously) included as the final chapter in this collection.

---

12 This is a punning allusion to a Second World War radio programme (which was to run until the 1960s) on the BBC Home Service, an outside broadcast, daily, moving between the canteens of factories round the country, comprising 'sing-along' medleys of popular tunes and comedy routines, helping boost morale as part of the war effort.

If authors presenting their own work may well want to evade accusations of immodesty, an editor has the advantage of being freer fully to praise where due. In this instance, an edited collection seems an especially appropriate way of representing – as well as re-presenting – Strong's work. For, notwithstanding his qualities as a researcher, it is his tremendous flair as an exponent of the essay which is possibly the most distinctive element of his sociological legacy. As Bloor remarked in an appreciation of Strong's contribution in *Sociology of Health & Illness*,[13] 'his death robbed us of our most accomplished essayist' (Bloor, 1996: 551). Clarity mattered greatly to Strong, but so too did the aesthetics of literary style. He devoted a very considerable time and effort to drafting and revising – regularly advising others to follow his lead in checking their prose by reading sentences out loud as they write. So one of the grounds for selecting items for reprinting here, is an interest in illustrating Strong's style and the manner in which he so readably stretched the confines of a sociological journal article or an academic chapter into an essay.

Strong's affinity for the essay neatly comes together with his abiding admiration for, and absorption in, Erving Goffman's sociology. In a letter to Goffman[14] thanking him for sending a copy of *Forms of Talk*, Strong enclosed a copy of his review of it for *Sociology*,[15] commenting:

...I chickened out of reviewing the essays in the book. I could have reviewed one but not all of them – you put so much in. So I used the occasion to make some general remarks on the essay form in social science and your use of it (24 August 1982).

Complimenting Strong on the review, Goffman noted in his reply that it 'illustrat(es) in its very form what its content turns out to be' (7 September 1982). Continuing the recursion, Strong repeated this trick of writing in the form which he was discussing in his own obituary-cum-appreciation of Goffman (Strong 1983a), also in *Sociology of Health & Illness*.

Both pieces – review and appreciation – note that the very term essay, derives from Montaigne[16] 'who used it to describe his "attempts" to reflect on various aspects of his own life, hoping thereby to illuminate those of others' (Strong 1982: 454). And both include commentary on the essay form itself, the nub of which runs as follows:

---

13 A journal of whose Editorial Board Strong had been a member and which he served as Assistant Editor for a period in the early 1980s.

14 Their correspondence was sporadic and confined to the last two years of Goffman's life. Only three letters of their exchanges survive.

15 See bibliography of Strong's work in this volume.

16 Whose own essays Strong had read and re-read in both French and English.

The essay is a systematically personal enterprise, rooted in everyday experience. In it, the author seeks ardently for a slippery truth, but makes no claim to having necessarily found it. It is an exploratory and essentially open form in which one may use data from anyone: friends, journalists, novelists and social scientists alike ... Finally, precisely because it is so personal, the essayist is free to develop his or her own style, to make jokes, to be whimsical, to digress, to employ both the tragic and comic modes; to use, that is, all the literary devices which the writer of the scientific article can, at best, only smuggle in surreptitiously. Those who proclaim scientific truth must dress in sober apparel; essayists may wear whatever they choose (Strong 1983a: 348).

A knowledge of Strong's writings make it tempting to speculate that he was also musing on a style of working, thinking and writing, to which he himself seemed powerfully attracted. At the least, readers might find it illuminating to bear his remarks in mind when turning to the twelve chapters of the present volume.

These chapters are organised into three sections. The first two consist of pieces on major substantive topics in which Strong was especially interested – entitled here, 'Doctors, Patients and Encounters', and 'Professional Place, Occupational Boundary'. The third, under a composite heading of 'Models, Methods and Methodologies', groups together four pieces which, from rather different directions, tackle questions of how sociology may approach study of its subject matter (cf. also Murcott 1998). Beneath these broad headings a good many continuing substantive concerns in the sociology of medicine, health and illness are readily to be found: the implications for identity of medical screening; forms of consultation etiquette; divisions of health care labour and hierarchies; the intricate social concomitants of deviance from clinical norms; managers' viewpoint of the problems the nature of medicine and nursing posed when new organisational arrangements in health services (the case of the so-called Griffiths reforms) which were introduced general management to Britain's National Health Service in 1984; policy responses to the threat of major, and unprecedented disease, and more.

Perhaps, though, it will be Strong's methodological contributions which turn out to be the most long lasting element of his intellectual legacy. These contributions touch on concerns which even now, ten years after his death, continue to resonate in sociology, in research in health, policy, nursing and medical care, and in circles wider still. Yet they tend to appear either towards the margins of Strong's work or are integrated so seamlessly into the discussion of substantive matters that they can be easily missed. An early excursion is marginal by definition, appearing as 'A Methodological

Appendix'[17] (reprinted here as Chapter 9) to his book-length treatment of the observations of paediatric consultations (Strong 1979a). Unlike other examples, such as Whyte's venerable appendix to *Street Corner Society* (1966) which was written several years after its initial publication, Strong wrote the appendix to accompany the book's first appearance in print. Pre-dating the explosion of urgings to reflexivity which accompanied the rise of post-modernism, it presents clearly written reflections reporting the conduct of the research – reflections that manage to evade the twin dangers of narcissism and confession. Pre-dating more extensive and widely publicised discussion of rhetoric in ethnographic writing (Clifford and Marcus 1986, Atkinson 1990) the sharp-eyed reader will spot a secure, wryly expressed, grasp of the matter at the end of its section on 'Quantifying Qualitative Data'. And, at roughly the time that the book was published, Strong moved jobs from the 'accustomed warmth' of a largely qualitative research unit, to what he makes sound a far more marginal position in the 'colder but definitely bracing atmosphere of a department filled with epidemiologists and medical statisticians' (Strong 1986: 58). He implies that it was partly as a product of his minority position in this department, that he came to write what is perhaps his most sustained – if demanding – discussion of methodology, included here as Chapter 10.[18]

If those instances illustrate the marginal but well announced, the less immediately obvious remarks on the adequate conduct of qualitative research tend to surface quietly, along the way, in even those pieces which are not explicitly to do with it. The question of counting in qualitative work (cf. Silverman 2000), for instance, threads its way through 'Minor courtesies and macro structures'[19] – in effect, though not in so many words, pointing out the often overlooked manner in which the qualitative and quantitative coincide in presence/absence, one/zero. And time and again, readers will notice Strong's insistence not just on weighing the adequacy of the evidence, but on attending to the extent to which the cases he has marshalled can support generalisation (cf. Payne and Williamson 2005).

---

17 Strong may later have regretted its terse but accurate title, in case his readers missed the methodological implications and noticed only the methods he used, for as he insisted to his students and made plain in a handout for a lecture to them at LSHTM, 10 October 1991: 'The term "methodology" is often used as if it were identical with that of "methods". It is not. Methodology is the *theory of method*; the reasons why we use some methods and not others in particular contexts.' (emphasis in original).

18 Strong invited Klim McPherson to co-author the article, but wrote 'the bulk of it ... though ... heavily influenced by our lengthy discussions' (Strong 1986: 59).

19 Reprinted in this volume as Chapter 3.

Except in very early pieces, Strong rarely sought – in print at least – to locate his own research approach in relation to the changing trends of the times in which he worked.[20] Never having time to contemplate the rift between Strauss and Glaser (Glaser 1992, and see also Melia 1996) it is still worth noting that it was to the latter's discussion of the constant comparative method searching for the deviant case that he remained committed (Glaser 1964). Strong's assumption that reality was socially constructed was long established – clearly evident in his 1968 Essex University MA dissertation, which, in the process, also references Berger and Luckmann's *The Social Construction of Reality* – but a far cry from a post-modern constructionism. Instead, he regarded the very social processes of construction, especially in the allocation of identity, as investigable rather than simply to be asserted, despite the great effort required to do so. And he aligns himself with the insights of ethnomethodology in respect of interview data, not least in declaring time and again that interviews cannot provide adequate representations of behaviour. If encounters and their social order are to be understood, there is no substitute for 'real time' observation, he continued to argue.

At the same time – even if, perhaps representing an internal contradiction that was never resolved – his work assumes that there are truths to be told and that sociologists' accounts are to be more rather than less accurately rendered. In terms of current vocabulary, his sociological stance would most nearly be aligned with Hammersley's 'subtle realism' (1992), Seale's 'fallibilism' (1999) and Murphy and Dingwall's 'realist ethnography' (2003), tempered and enriched by an unremitting search beyond the boundaries of his discipline. This last is a point included on a rare occasion on which he came close to a concluding summary of his position, and which serves as fitting end to this introduction of the twelve essays reprinted here:

> Only when we pay due attention to the facts can we begin to get the kind of theory appropriate to social science. (What that may prove to be is still an empirical question.) And paying attention to the facts about the social world

---

20 Similarly (as students at the LSHTM who attended his lectures in the first half of the 1990s and who still have the dense, demanding, but hugely informative handouts that Strong wrote to accompany them, will know) though occasionally listed as suggested reading, he infrequently paid attention to textbooks. A very rare reference to Strauss and Corbin's (1990) distinction between open, axial and selective coding is immediately qualified by a sharp remark distancing himself from those authors who 'did not invent all this (though they tend to give this impression) – it is simply a codification of others' practice and writing. Their arguments have been included because they spell out what many others leave tacit.' Lecture handout, November 26 1992.

means paying attention to a far wider range of disciplines and data-sources than many sociologists normally consider. It also means, at least in some part, standing close up to your subjects so you can see how they behave – and watching yourself rather closely too; or so I hope. (Strong 1986: 65).

Acknowledgements

I am most grateful to:

- Sara Delamont and Paul Atkinson who originally suggested and encouraged the preparation of this volume;
- the other Series' Editors in making this collection possible and for their thoughtful support and immense patience during its preparation;
- Robert Dingwall and colleagues in IGBiS, University of Nottingham, and Tony Woodiwiss and the Department of Sociology, City University, London, for both moral and practical support;
- Sue Aldworth, Rachel Burr, Tony Coxon, Neil Drury, Matt Freidson, Andrew George, Ed Halsted, Nicky James, Hilly Janes, Diana Leat, David McVicar, David May, Elizabeth Murphy, Virginia Olesen, Rosalind Sharpe, Pam Watson and most especially, Kerry Chester, Dominic Murcott, Karen Murcott, Toby Murcott and Liz Pritchard, for their conversations, companionship and no-nonsense advice during the long period of working on this assignment.

I am indebted to Robert Dingwall, Terry Rees, David Silverman and Rod Watson who kindly made time to read and comment on earlier drafts of this Preface, but I alone am responsible for its deficiencies.

Acknowledgements

For their permission to reprint, the editor and publishers gratefully acknowledge the co-authors, editors and publishers identified below. Every effort has been made to trace the literary executor of the late Alan Davis to obtain permission for the use of copyright material.

A.G. Davis and P.M. Strong (1976) '"Aren't Children Wonderful?": The Allocation of Identity in Developmental Assessment' *in* M. Stacey (ed) *The Sociology of the NHS, Sociological Review Monograph* 22, Keele, Staffs.: University of Keele.

Alan Davis and Philip Strong (1976) 'The management of a therapeutic encounter with young children' *in* M. Wadsworth and D. Robinson (eds) *Studies in Everyday Medical Life* London: Martin Robertson.

P.M. Strong (1979) 'A Methodological Appendix' Chapter 9 *The Ceremonial Order of the Clinic: Doctors, Parents and Medical Bureaucracies*, originally published by Routledge and Kegan Paul, 1979 and republished in 2001 by Ashgate Publishing Company.

P.M. Strong (1979) 'Sociological Imperialism and the Profession of Medicine – A Critical Examination of the Thesis of Medical Imperialism' *Social Science and Medicine* 13A, 199–215 (reprinted with the permission of Elsevier Science).

P.M. Strong and K. McPherson (1981) 'Natural Science and Medicine, Social Science and Medicine: Some Methodological Controversies' (with K. McPherson) *Social Science and Medicine*, 16, 643–657 (reprinted with the permission of Elsevier Science).

P.M. Strong (1983) 'The Rivals: an Essay on the Sociological Trades' *in The Sociology of the Professions: Law, Medicine and Others* (eds) Dingwall R. and Lewis P. London, The Macmillan Press, 59–77 (reproduced with the permission of Palgrave).

P.M. Strong (1984) 'The Academic Encirclement of Medicine?' *Sociology of Health and Illness*, 6, 3, 339–358 (reproduced with the permission of Blackwell Publishing, Oxford).

P.M. Strong (1988) 'Minor Courtesies and Macro Structures' *in* P. Drew and A.J. Wootton (eds) *Erving Goffman: Exploring the Interaction Order* Cambridge: Polity Press.

Philip Strong (1990) 'Epidemic Psychology: A Model' *Sociology of Health and Illness*, 12, 3, 249–259 (reproduced with the permission of Blackwell Publishing, Oxford).

Philip Strong and Jane Robinson (1990) 'NHS Management: history and background' Chapter 2, *The NHS – Under New Management* Milton Keynes: Open University Press (reproduced with the permission of Open University Press).

Phil Strong (1994) 'Two types of Ceremonial Order' in S.J. Lauritzen and L. Sachs (eds) *Health Care Encounters and Culture – Interdisciplinary Perspectives* Botkyrka: Multicultural Centre (reproduced with the permission of the Mångkulturellt centrum Fittja gård, Sweden).

P.M. Strong (1997) 'One Branch of Moral Science: an Early Modern Approach to Public Policy' in G. Miller and R. Dingwall (eds) *Context & Methods in Qualitative Research* London: Sage (reproduced with the permission of Sage Publications).

PART 1
Doctors, Patients and Encounters

PART 4
Doctor, Patients and Encounters

Chapter 1

Aren't Children Wonderful? – A Study of the Allocation of Identity in Development Assessment[1]

Introduction

Freidson has argued that organisations 'create' handicap, for it is their officials who define the parameters of normality and deviance (Freidson 1972). This is not a particularly novel notion as much of the recent literature on deviance has been concerned to examine the activities of agents of social control in defining, creating and sustaining deviant identities (Lemert 1967; Rubington & Weinberg 1968). However, since Freidson's attempt to import this organising perspective into the field of medical sociology, there seems to have been little empirical work which uses such an approach to look at the ways in which doctors create deviance or neutralise the processes leading to the creation of a deviant identity. Further, that work which has been done has concerned itself with the processing of adults (Scott 1970; Goffman 1961a) whereas many handicapping conditions can be 'picked up' at birth or shortly after. The study of the process of official stigmatisation in children is particularly important as there has been increasing concern within the medical professions to identify all handicaps at the earliest possible age. The introduction of early detection systems such as population screening, at-risk registers and the elaboration of medical criteria for intensive follow-up of a target population has meant that young children are increasingly subject to systematic inspection for anticipated or unanticipated deviations from medical versions of childhood normality. There are many versions of clinical normality, usually based on

1 [Editor's note: co-authored with A.G. Davies.] The research on which this paper is based is part of a larger project, entitled 'The Organisational Management of the Young Handicapped', and funded by the S.S.R.C. as part of a programme grant on 'Systems of Medical and Social Care'. Data for the paper were gathered by observation and interview. We would like to thank J. Askman, H. Gibson, G. Horobin, S. Macintyre, A. Murcott and G. Psathas for their helpful comments.

statistically compiled attributes of normal childhood development.[2] The application of these tests of developmental normality to a population of children is an attempt to differentiate 'normal' children from deviant ones and their application at an early age hastens the process of converting primary deviation into secondary deviation with the attendant elaboration of deviant careers for children found to be abnormal (Lemert 1967; Rock 1973).

One important difference between these procedures and those used to uncover other forms of deviance such as delinquency is that handicaps are not assumed by officials to be a form of motivated deviation. Whereas in much judicial work the reconstruction of motivation is a central problem for agents (Emerson 1969), with this type of medical deviance voluntaristic formulations are never invoked. In general, then, deviation is seen as outwith individuals' control (Lorber, 1972). This is not to say that others may not seek to establish such a motivational framework. Indeed, the parents of handicapped children may seek to put the onus for the deviation within the will of the child or even themselves, but such accounts are not honoured. Motivational issues have one other relevance here. One possible effect of such testing is to call into question the motivation and competence of the parents. When a child is compared with an 'ideal type' there is always the possibility that discrepancies between the particular child's development and the ideal type can be explained in terms of the quality of the family. Therefore, there is considerable pressure on parents to have their child accepted as normal and thereby get their own normality confirmed.

Thus, where a child is screened over time there are four problems to which doctors have to address themselves in a routine fashion. Firstly, screening is bound to throw up a number of cases where there is some doubt whether the child is biologically and intellectually capable of becoming a properly constituted adult. The clinical indicators may not be of sufficient magnitude to establish once and for all that the child is handicapped (Davis 1963). Consequently, the doctors are often concerned to delay the pronouncement of handicap for fear that the child may eventually turn out to be normal. In these cases the doctors block the possibility of secondary deviation until there is no doubt that the child is handicapped. Of course, doctors were also concerned about the converse, definitively pronouncing children normal who might later turn out to be abnormal. Secondly, doctors have to pay attention to the indeterminate status that the act of testing confers on the child. They either have to normalise the child's identity immediately or find ways in which the indeterminacy can be maintained until they are certain of normality or abnormality. Thirdly, the doctors

---

2	We are not concerned to adjudicate on which version is correct, rather we argue that all such tests have the implications we outline in this paper.

have in some cases to convert the parents to accepting the correctness of a clinical version of the child's abnormality and to preparing a familial context in which the child's deviation is accepted in a correct manner. Fourthly, the normal stance of the doctor is to deal with presented illness episodes rather than with preventative medicine. But, while for illness episodes the identities of doctor and patient are assumed readily by both interactants, with such medical activities as screening these assumptions are more difficult to sustain, particularly if it turns out that there is little wrong with the child under inspection. In these circumstances it is difficult for the young child to assume the identity of patient and difficult for the parents to present it as such. The doctor therefore has to find a mode of handling the encounter which gives due weight to the child's identity as normal. We argue that this is done through recourse to the normal adult manner in which children are discussed in our culture, rather than through an inappropriate clinical vocabulary.

Some work has been done on how social actors explain or neutralise their deviation (Emerson 1969; Scott & Lyman 1968; Sykes & Matza 1957). Little has been done on how agents themselves go about neutralising doubt about the status of potential deviants. We propose to concentrate on one aspect of this process, the use of neutralising techniques in different medical settings. In particular we shall be concerned to examine the ways in which doctors make recourse to everyday modes of talk about children as a means of neutralising doubts about a child's identity. Since doctors in our culture are typically granted the right and duty to underwrite the identity of young children, their rights to formulate and enforce a particular working consensus were normally validated by the parents in the encounters we observed (Goffman 1961b). We are only concerned with this working consensus in these encounters and thus only with parents' overt worries or the worries doctors treated them as having. There are good reasons why mothers would accept such formulation in public. For a mother to display distance from the normal rhetoric in which children are discussed in our culture would be to formulate themselves as indifferent or peculiar mothers. They may have such doubts or they may find the doctor's remarks gushing and overstated, but they do not seem able to voice such feelings within medical encounters.

Some General Procedures for Formulating Children as Normal

A central means used by doctors to establish a child's normality was to talk about it in the everyday manner appropriate to normally constituted children, to appeal to relevant adult assumptions about what children are like rather than face the task of explaining the clinical version of childhood with which they operated. Besides, even if this were done it might still not convince. Essential normality cannot be demonstrated by a doctor merely ticking off a child's accomplishments on some standardised check-list, although such work is a routine part of assessment, but must be directly addressed and established by the entire manner in which the child is treated. The doctor has to demonstrate a correspondence between the clinical version of normal childhood and the everyday version. To treat the occasion solely in a clinical fashion would not be to establish the child's normality in the everyday world.

Children are treated as a separate class of human actor lacking adult legal and interactional status and requiring in one's interaction with them special interactional skills (Strong & Davis 1976, reprinted as Chapter 2 in this volume). Their nature requires special adult treatment and correspondingly adult maltreatment of children is more heavily sanctioned than other adult crime, e.g. the attitudes and penalties surrounding the battering or sexual molestation of young children (McCaghy 1963). Their special features are treated as requiring special institutional arrangements. Thus, as regards medical treatment there are normally separate children's wards and 'ideally' a separate children's hospital. Perhaps associated with children's lack of competences, adults typically seem to deny the relevance in interaction with children of many of the normal criteria for treating others. Thus, in a study of the intensive care unit of an American hospital which contained both adult and child patients, it was noted:

> It appears that in the minds of the nurses children are not perceived as being black or white, rich or poor, male or female, they are just children. (Coombs & Goldman 1973).

Despite this categorisation of children as a separate class of being, adults generally seem to find their actions readily interpretable and have recourse to the normal model of attributing motives and feelings that they use with fellow-adults. Thus, during the examination of young children the doctors commonly engaged in overt role-taking, imputing a host of intentions and emotions to the child: 'He doesn't seem to like that', 'He's more interested in this', and so on. In doing so they formulated the child as someone whose actions were readily understandable in terms of everyday schemes, i.e. as someone who was essentially normal. At the same time, since they are separate there were other features of their behaviour which were formulated by doctors as routinely uninterpretable, as seemingly odd – 'You never know why they do it' – but nothing to worry about since all babies did it.

The qualities involved in being 'just children' seem somewhat ambiguous. On the one hand children are viewed as potential adults, with the capacity to achieve many things. Thus, the developmental assessment of young children consists in part of their certification as biologically and intellectually capable of *becoming* a properly constituted person. This provides doctors with a routine method of reassurance, for references to a normal future adulthood can be read as a firm statement about a child's present normality. Typical references were:

(1)Doctor: He has the feet of a footballer .... Ha-ha.
(2)Doctor: They say it's the sign of a good athlete .... Ha-ha.
(3)Doctor: (to mother of twins, one male, one female).
Doctor: And does she drink from a cup?
Mother: Aye, she holds it like this.
Doctor: Does he?
Mother: Yes, they both use the baby ones.
Doctor: Oh, yes, I wouldn't expect them to be drinking from a tankard yet.
Mother: No .... Ha-ha.

One variation of this appeal to the future was for the doctor to characterise what the child was doing at present in adult terms, terms which plainly did not literally characterise the present performance. Thus:

(1) A one-year-old child babbled to a doctor who responded – 'That's a nice story you're telling me.'
(2) A six-month-old baby was struggling when the doctor tried to lift her to a sitting position, and the doctor commented – 'Hey, you want to dance! ... Ha-ha'

Although this reference to the future would seem an important way in which one could demonstrate a child's normality, in practice it seemed to be much less used than either of the others, perhaps because of its slight unreality. When it was used it was always in a joking fashion, as if it was somewhat absurd to characterise a day-old baby as a footballer or to picture one-year-old twins drinking from tankards.

Children's essential nature as wonderful

We have noted a variety of features of 'children' to which doctors made appeal, their separate nature, their intelligibility and their potential adulthood. This does not, however, exhaust the list. The feature which doctors' stressed above all was the pleasure which all adults, and they in particular, felt in regarding the bearers of such characteristics, and it is the appeal to this pleasure which forms the main theme of this paper. Children as a class are commonly seen as wonderful. All children it would seem can be described as 'wonderful', 'gorgeous' and a source of 'joy'. In contrast, we feel that to apply such epithets to *all adults* seems a strange claim to make. 'Aren't adults wonderful' seems an odd statement. Even when such claims are made about particular adults, then good grounds must be provided or be available, grounds normally resting on action statements or occasionally on aesthetic criteria. However, this would not seem to be the case for children. Their very existence would seem to constitute sufficient grounds. Of course, being wonderful was not the only quality ascribed to children. It was also recognised that they could and would routinely constitute a source of trouble and anxiety for parents. Both of these features are illustrated in the following excerpt:

Doctor: Apart from her food are there any problems?
Mother: Well, there's her sleeping.
Doctor: Well, what, doesn't she sleep?
Mother: (firmly) ... Well, she does now because she gets something to make her sleep.

Doctor produces her stethoscope, grins and waves it about. She dangles it in front of the child then comments to researcher 'Isn't it marvellous having a baby like this?' ... Researcher smiles, mother smiles at researcher.

Doctor: But it's not always marvellous. What's this about her not sleeping?

We may note, however, that quite often in clinics the problems that children created were glossed by both parents and doctors by the use of hyperbole, thus sustaining the theme that really they were wonderful and things were O.K. Children were commonly described by both doctors and parents as a 'handful', a 'wild thing', a 'terror', or a 'monster'. Such remarks were often addressed to the child itself – 'You're a wild thing, aren't you?' – and said with a smile both to it and to the other adults present calling forth appropriate smiles for them also. Thus, even the trouble they caused was wonderful.

The sources of this wonder seem to lie both in the child's relationship to the adult world and in its own unique qualities. Children seemed to be held to be wonderful for what they were in themselves – they had a special quality of beauty. They also lived in a special world of play and laughter, a world which adults might enter too in a child's company.

Interviewer: People at the children's hospital seem to think that it makes the hospital a happier place having children around.

Doctor: Oh, yes, much better, much better than adult wards. The wards at the infirmary are grim places. There's no comparison ...

Interviewer: Certainly the local authority clinics I've attended seem incredibly cheerful kinds of places.

Doctor: Oh, I think so, because children are spontaneously happy if they get the chance.

But children also seemed to be wonderful for what they were able to achieve despite being so young, for what they would be able to do later on and also for their incomprehension of or non-orientation to the adult world. For example, young babies occasionally urinated during their examination by a doctor. This would be the grossest breach of the rules in most adult encounters but here it was normally treated by parents as extremely funny and doctors too felt obliged to grin.

For a child to be wonderful necessitates that others 'do wonderment'. That is, they have to demonstrate their awe in a public fashion. Such awe would seem to be somewhat patronising since it was normally done with a smile not just to the child but to the other adults as well. Marvelling had other interesting features too; it could legitimately be demanded of any other adult, that is, one had a duty to marvel when called on to do so, parents must be proud and others admiring. Further, admiring could be legitimately initiated by *anyone,* that is, even complete strangers to the child and uninvolved in the examination could initiate such a sequence and expect a response from others, as could the child itself.

We may also note that *all* young children can be treated as wonderful, even the handicapped. It seems that whereas with adults gross physical or mental handicap acts as a 'master status trait' (Hughes 1945), this is not the case with young children. Here handicap tends to be predicated as much of the family as of the child itself – 'It's not a handicapped child, it's a handicapped family.' Blind or deformed babies are formulated primarily not as 'blind' or 'deformed' but as babies. Thus, as noted earlier, child patients are seen as especially rewarding.

> The baby's attractive powers could not be attributed to physical features as its appearance was quite grotesque due to the burned and charred skin from the fire, the large gashes made by the fan blades when the fan exploded, and the surgical incisions down both arms and legs ... (Coombs & Goldman 1973)

The reason for this lies in the fact that all young children are routinely treated as a separate class of social actor. Thus, handicap affects their 'essential nature' in a rather different way from that of adults. Children are treated as separate because if they were treated as equals all would be regarded as handicapped. All new-born babies are blind and helpless. All young children take several years to communicate with any great competence and to develop adult motor skills. Young handicapped children differ from normal children mainly in potential rather than in capacity. Grossly handicapped babies may grow up to be 'monsters' but they are not monsters now. At present they share many of those features which render babies a source of joy and wonder.

However, such arguments apply only to the youngest handicapped children. As they grow up their handicap increases in salience. Whereas once their particular condition may have meant little or no extra effort for their parents compared to that demanded by other babies, now special demands may be made upon them. Further, not only may special treatment be given by the parents but special organisational facilities may be required also, in particular, special schooling. Thus, within a few years the handicapped child may become defined as a special case requiring separate treatment from all the relevant institutions – familial, medical and educational – which define one's being. This process has no set course or time period but varies according to type of handicap and social circumstances. Nevertheless, within a few years of birth handicap becomes a master status trait and wonderment increasingly difficult.

Appeals to the wonderfulness of children were common in clinics and could serve a variety of purposes. On occasion, doctors who were being harassed by parents seemed to praise the child as a means of formulating themselves as good people with good intentions. Both doctors and parents appealed to it to persuade a child to co-operate during physical examination and many doctors seemed to use such appeals on occasion to avoid talking to parents. Thus, a continual stream of praise by the doctor during examination addressed to the child served to exclude parents from the interaction and allow complete concentration on the examination itself. However, the use of the appeal on which we focus here is the way in which it can formulate a child as essentially normal. It can be used in this way because, although as we have argued, one may hold that all children are wonderful, such a statement as regards handicapped children applies only to the present, whereas in developmental assessment it is precisely the future that is at question. The more serious handicapping conditions such as mongolism, deafness, blindness, cerebral palsy, spina bifida, hydrocephalous and general mental retardation threaten a wide range of those competences that are held necessary to a properly constituted person. Sufferers may be unable variously to walk, talk, write, see, hear, establish continence, receive a normal education, or carry out a normal job, and those most severely affected may never be granted adult legal status.

In developmental assessment there were great difficulties in talking about children so affected and a study of the problems involved reveals some of the assumptions about children that we normally take for granted. The clumsiness and incomprehension that may be considered funny in a one-year-old – 'They're just like drunken old men at this stage' – may seem potentially tragic if repeated at 4, and terrifying at 24. With someone whose own understanding is in doubt, it becomes difficult for us to understand them. Whereas in most settings doctors and parents would confidently ascribe motives and feelings to children, with very severely retarded older children it was often not at all clear what they were doing. Since the future of such children was unclear, references to it could not be brought off with any ease. All that might be capable of being praised during the testing was the child's mood or outward appearance and even this was difficult with some. In the last resort, all the doctor might be able to say was that a child 'seemed happy', was 'a good patient' – i.e. he had not caused any fuss; had 'a nice dress', or 'a nicely-healed scar anyway.' Such children could not gaily be called 'monsters' or 'terrors' for these might seem too literal descriptions, nor could they be readily called 'wonderful' since it was not clear that they were such as others could admire or of whom parents felt proud. For a doctor to appeal to 'wonder' during testing could therefore be read as a claim that this 'wonder' was medically warranted. Whereas for him not to make it and to ignore any such appeal by parents was to cast doubt on the normality of the child.

Allocating identity within particular settings

Although we have outlined some general procedures for allocating normal identity to young children, it would be wrong to assume that such procedures are used in the same way in every setting, rather their use depends upon the context and the social actors' purposes at hand. In the four different settings in which we observed developmental assessment being done the extent to which the doctors made use of the different procedures varied. Very differing degrees of doubt about the child were held by both parents and doctors in different contexts and thus doctors made differential use of the procedures for normalisation and stigmatisation. In particular, the greater the apparent parental need for reassurance then, where they felt able to give this, the more doctors cast children as wonderful. Conversely, where they felt unable to provide this reassurance then they normally made no such appeals at all, the *absence* of this normalising procedure thereby constituting part of their general strategy for breaking bad news. Thus, in the local authority clinics where the normality of children was in little doubt, then their wonderfulness was little remarked upon, children were defined as interesting and amusing but as also involving hard work, sore bottoms and dirty nappies. Normalisation here relied mainly on the more routine procedures of heavy overt role-taking. Where, however, this normality was more seriously at issue, as in the maternity hospital and the follow-up clinic, then those found to be normal were routinely marvelled at. In the special neurological clinic, by contrast, where handicap was commonly diagnosed, the emotional atmosphere was heavily neutral and marvelling a rare phenomenon indeed.

The Examination of the Newborn

Babies born in the Maternity Hospital were given a standard inspection by a paediatrician and checked on subsequent ward rounds, those who were problematic on delivery having been removed to a separate nursery. The inspection was done on open wards and though routine was somewhat complicated by the context of its execution. It was a public event with many interested listeners and deviations from the routine could be read as indicating abnormality. Yet the ward round had to be done quickly while for each mother the inspection of her child was seen as an event of great significance. Mothers were assumed to have examined their babies already, to want to hear that their brand-new product was normal and to view the examination with some alarm for what it might uncover. It was therefore a fraught situation for those doing the examinations and staff had many anecdotes about examinations that had 'gone wrong'. In such circumstances doctors[3] made considerable use of the rhetoric of childhood as a way of tacitly dealing with mothers' assumed worries. The 'standard' itself was played down, being variously described as 'a visit to see how baby is' or 'just a check to see that baby is O.K.' Such direct references were rare though and usually, after an initial greeting to the mother, the doctor's main attention was devoted to the child. There was little reason to involve the mother given that the medical notes supplied the necessary clinical details and at this age there was little information that the mother herself could provide.

Throughout the 'standard' the doctors threw off cues to assure mothers that nothing was being found on examination or that if something had been found it was normal. These normalising cues were of various kinds. The baby was approached and greeted with great joviality by the doctors who indicated they were pleased to see them. Babies were treated as a delight

---

3   To preserve the anonymity of the doctors we observed, we have referred to 'doctors' in three of the four settings, though in one, detailed data were available only on one. Further, since most of the doctors involved were female, where particular doctors are mentioned they have been styled 'she', regardless of their actual gender.

to see, a mood sustained throughout the examination. They were routinely greeted as 'Hello, gorgeous' or 'Hello, you look super' or jokingly, e.g. 'Hello ... you're not a fatty, are you, darling?' or 'Hello ... are you going to open your eyes, there's a lot of folk here wanting to say hello to you?' During the examination the joviality was sustained through its punctuation by admiring comments on the child, e.g. 'He's got super toes', 'beautiful leggies', 'he's a splendid chap'. No reference was made to the clinical agenda unless students were present. As the baby reacted doctors would role take with them, imputing reasons, intentions and motives for the babies' actions which rendered the reaction normal – 'You didn't like that, did you?', 'What *are* we doing to you, then?', 'Are you going to come up ?', 'Are you going to show your mother how well you can step out?'. Joking references were also made about babies' characteristics to indicate normality. Large babies were jokingly described, 'I think he's going to be seven feet tall!' and 'He's heavy – he's a *monster* – you (mother) must be tired.' Jokes could also be made about minor worries that mothers managed to raise. In response to a query about spots a doctor replied – 'It's alright – babies are *allowed* to have those! (laughter)'. Final comments echoed the hyperbole of the initial greeting – 'He's marvellous', 'She's a super baby', 'He's in first class condition', 'He's lovely'.

Thus, in seeking to neutralise a potentially difficult situation doctors made use of the terms that any admiring adult would use to render the child normal in the mother's eyes. A clinical rhetoric was strikingly absent. Of course, during the examination some odd features were quite commonly uncovered. Where such features were not visible they were routinely concealed, the rationale being that many would go away quite soon, e.g. heart murmurs, or if they were more serious they could be dealt with later on. However, some odd features were visible to mothers, e.g. bruising, curling feet, birth marks, ear flaps, jaundice and cleft palates, and doctors assumed that mothers would have already noticed these and be worried by them. Great clinical attention was therefore paid to these features, doctors stressing that they were common, almost normal, would rectify themselves or could be rectified by expert medical intervention. They were presented as minor features that in no way impaired the description of the child as a 'super baby'. A child with a cleft palate could still be 'gorgeous'.

Local Authority Population Screening
In City clinics the Health Department ran a screening programme for all children of six and twelve months of age. The parents of those already identified as handicapped tended not to appear so that most attenders could be presumed to be developmentally normal. Screening was done to a standard form in infant welfare clinics. As it was voluntary and as

the doctors concerned could not prescribe or directly refer except to other Health Department facilities or to the G.P., the maintenance of cooperation was a prime concern.

The most striking feature of Local Authority assessment was its consistent demedicalisation. The clinical rationale for the screening was only spelt out when mothers inquired about it and few did. Further, the occasion was not overtly defined by doctors as problematic. Questions were asked about 'problems' during pregnancy, delivery and the neonatal period but these were located in the past. Otherwise, questions were formulated by doctors without any reference to worries but were posed simply in terms of what the child was doing now. No detailed probing went on to establish what the questions or answers meant, and both doctor and mother 'assumed' that the other knew what was being talked about. Given that there was rarely a 'problem' there was rarely a sad story for the mothers to tell. Rather, mothers gave accounts of their child's accomplishments, character and peculiarities of interest and tastes. Such formulations were usually commented on by the doctor in similar tones of interest, admiration or sometimes commiseration as no clinical problem was evident from the description. Only rarely did mothers ask whether their child should be doing something which they were currently not doing, and doctors answered such questions in terms of a normal variation which was usually taken for granted by both parties.

Despite this, normalisation was a central feature of the testing as 'normal' children routinely 'failed' to carry out many of the doctor's tests. Some items could be checked covertly without needing to formulate them (e.g., walking gait, interest in environment) but on some the child was expected to perform items on demand, and many often did not. However, doctors routinely formulated such behaviour as characteristic of all children, proffering a variety of explanations for such 'failure'. The immediate or the home situation, or simply children's nature could all be invoked. Situational explanations included reactions to the doctor, the physical setting or others present; home situations included the ways in which children varied in what they were allowed or expected to do if they were at home; 'nature-based' explanations were in terms of their unpredictability and their very different orientation to the world. All could be proffered by the doctor in a rueful tone of voice to show they understood what children were like, e.g. 'I don't think he likes me today', 'I think she's more interested in that bucket/box/poster/man over there', 'She's not had her sleep yet', 'Children are often not allowed to pick up china cups at home' or 'She just wants to stack everything today', 'He doesn't feel like it today.'

Throughout the demonstration items and physical examination the doctors continually gave off cues that all was going well in the form of a running commentary, e.g. 'That's *good* – up you come ... there ... that's right ... oh! is that so? (child babbles) ... that's alright ... and that ... now let's see you on your tummy ... is that right? (child babbles) ... that's fine ...'

Similarly, as in the Maternity Hospital, the doctors continually engaged in role-taking with the children, imputing reasons, intentions and motives to the child. The amount of role-taking was rather greater than for the new-born, but the descriptions used were less extravagant. Children were treated as ordinary people whose behaviour was routinely interpretable. Further, it was routinely recognised that children could be troublesome. Fulsome and sentimental statements would only undermine their credibility as knowledgeable adults. Children could also be 'a nuisance', 'a mischief', 'a monster', 'a terror', 'a trouble-maker', 'wild boy' but such descriptions were affectionate and perfectly compatible with the child being 'cute', 'fine', with 'lovely eyebrows', 'well shaped feet' that would lead to the child rising to the elevated status of 'a footballer'. Where problems were presented they were calmly treated as minor defects which would soon pass or be remedied by referral. When admiration was engaged in this too was done in a relaxed fashion. Children were nice creatures, wonderful yes, but not all the time.

The Special Nursery Follow-up Clinic

The follow-up clinic saw all children about whom there had been sufficient medical doubt at birth to admit them to the Special Nursery in the Maternity Hospital. Children were routinely seen at ten months and assessed via a short developmental screening lasting no more than ten minutes. As in the previous two settings all the children were routinely constituted as essentially normal despite the fact that among the cases we saw were one child with a suspected storage syndrome, one with suspected hydrocephalus, another with possible epilepsy and several showing some minor delay.

There seem to be several reasons for this:

(a) All the children from the Special Nursery were seen here. Thus, any one child had not been singled out for current medical problems.
(b) The Special Nursery had very wide criteria for admission – and most of these were indicators for treatment not of permanent malfunction. Most children could therefore be presumed to be normal now.
(c) The business of the clinic was follow-up not treatment.

(d) The clinic was not the sole point of medical contact – other services backed it up.

In this clinic there were more grounds for parents doubting the normality of their child than in the previous two settings. Any trouble there rested initially on lay knowledge, here it was already medically warranted by the very fact of the child's admission to the Special Nursery. For such a child to pass as normal therefore such doubts had to be directly addressed. It was insufficient to say the child was 'doing fine', rather the 'problem' had to be shown to be 'over'. The doctor here therefore used elaborate forms of normalisation:

(a) Rather than simply assuming what the doubts were, she deliberately sought them out on a search-and-destroy principle. Typically a session opened with a question – 'Are there any problems?' This was repeated, often two or three times, and each answer dealt with in turn.

(b) She ascribed the expertise necessary to judge a child as normal to anyone and everyone at hand. She stressed her personal expertise more heavily than the other doctors we observed – but also elevated mothers, nurses and researchers to the role of expert so that it became 'obvious' that a child was doing well. At the Maternity Hospital and in the Local Authority clinics mothers were simply mothers.

(c) Although children were tested here at roughly the same age as those of the Local Authority clinics, they were seen for a rather shorter period of time, ten minutes at the most, compared to up to twenty-five minutes. The detailed testing that went on was much abbreviated, and as a consequence the routine normal failure that was produced at Local Authority clinics was avoided. This meant that the doctor did not have to resort to explanations of the kind, 'You know what children are like', an appeal that could not be made here, precisely because doubt had already been cast on what this particular child was like.

(d) To provide a final reassurance she made the strongest of all the appeals we saw to the commonsense adult assumption that children are wonderful. The mood that she enforced in the clinic was one of extreme jollity. Children were sometimes greeted as they entered with – 'You look happy/marvellous' – and were immediately given toys to play with; interruptions to her conversation with the mother were treated not as a nuisance but as a positive pleasure – 'Hey, you seem to be happy?' – a pleasure because it was further proof that the child was active, alert and essentially normal; she seemed almost to dance during her examination of the child using precise dainty movements, often ending with a flourish as she boldly replaced her stethoscope around her neck. Children were presented as happy funny little things who were an infinite source of wonder and delight to us all, people of whom their mothers should be proud while we, their audience, should be happy to be in their presence. Thus, not only could they be 'marvellous' and 'delightful' but when they cried she became rueful Dr. Jones, for normally 'It's a delight to have such a happy little girl in this clinic?'. A good example of her style is seen in this opening scene with a small boy who was a premature baby and had had jaundice and exchange transfusions. The doctor expected him to be doing well.

Doctor: Now, this is Robert, is it? He's looking very well.
  Have you got any worries, are there any problems with him?
Mother: No.
Doctor: Well, he looks just like an advert for Cow and Gate, doesn't he!
Mother: Yes ... (and smiles)

It is important to note, however, that the doctor seemed to reserve the most extreme appeals to wonder for those children in whom she had the greatest confidence. Other normalising strategies were used for children for whom afterwards she might express some doubt, and indeed all children were treated as if they were delightful, but this was not openly stated where she still had doubts – though as the above quotation indicates she seemed to feel that in some cases it was possible to judge a child's normality at a glance.

The Special Neurological Clinic
This was a specialist clinic located in the Children's Hospital and had several medically different features from the other settings:

(a) To get there a child had already to be defined as a problem here and now.
(b) Far more time was available for elaborate testing by the area specialist.
(c) The doctors here were mandated to diagnose and treat handicapped children, and seemed to feel a duty to reveal their diagnosis to the parents. However, the diagnosis and particularly the treatment of many conditions was very difficult.
(d) Children came here for repeat visits, often over many years.
(e) The issue of normality was defined as *open*; there was no working premise of normality. Further, there was no easy assumption of reciprocal understanding and trust between doctor and parent as

elsewhere. Thus, there was no easy elevation of all mothers to expert status. This was a privilege granted only to a few.

Those children who were found to be normal and discharged were normalised in a somewhat different fashion from those elsewhere. There seemed a much greater emphasis on the fact that very elaborate testing had proved that there was nothing to worry about, though doctors treated these concluding sessions in a more light-hearted fashion. With most cases the doctors seemed to attempt to establish an entirely neutral emotional atmosphere unlike the bonhomie of the other settings. In contrast to that deliberate jolliness here was a purely technical mood where they could be doctor/manager and the parents dispassionate observers. Thus, whereas wonder was frequently expressed in other settings, here it almost never occurred, either from the doctors or parents. The rare exceptions to this rule are most instructive.

(a) Firstly, the birth of a handicapped child represents a considerable challenge to the parents and is thus seen as good grounds for suspecting that one might be less than a good parent. (Voysey 1975). On rare occasions appeals to wonder were made to establish parents as proper parents.

   (i) The 19-year old separated mother of a severely spastic 2-year-old girl had failed to attend the clinic several times and had been virtually frog-marched there by a health visitor. She sat there expressionless answering only 'No' or 'Yes' to each question and displaying no involvement with the situation and almost none with her child. Eventually, with some exasperation, the doctor stated – 'She's an awfully nice baby'. The mother did not reply. This particular doctor never made such statements about other babies.

   (ii) The mother of a violent and destructive 8-year-old microcephalic boy had kept the child in the family for several years after he could have gone to a hospital for the mentally retarded, but had now decided she could no longer cope and had told the doctor this. After discussing future arrangements for her boy she broke down and cried and then said, through her tears –
   Mother: He's such a little angel when he's asleep, you should see his face when he's lying on the pillow.
   Doctor: (softly) ... I know, I know.
   Mother then cries again.
   Such a statement and such tears can be read as formulating the mother as a proper mother, one who feels the sort of things one should feel

about one's children – even though she is asking for her child to be placed in a home.

(b) Secondly, since wonder is a means for normalising a child and whereas in other settings it was mainly the doctors who utilised it, here it was rather parents who attempted to use it to this end though only a few parents did this and they met with no success since the doctors here typically ignored it. One minor form of this was where parents attempted to get a child to show off a few tricks. In the more fullblown version of the appeal they would either attempt to get the doctor to 'ooh' and 'aah' over the child or issue panegyrics about it. Thus –

(i) A 2½-year-old hydrocephalic girl who was still not walking and whose intelligence had been queried. The girl saw the researchers and commented – 'a boy'. The parents laughed and smiled at the doctor, and repeated this, doting on her every move. The child in response continually repeated this and other odd words and the parents broke into the doctor's questions several times to point out what she had just said and laugh and make jokes about it. The doctor ignored this mostly, merely nodding and smiling weakly, though later on she made a reply –

Child: Boys.

Mother: She likes boys.

Doctor (comments rather drily): There are no *boys* here.

Mother: Well, she's giving them the benefit of the doubt ... Ha-ha.

(ii) An 18-month-old spina bifida baby –

Doctor: Are there any questions you'd like to ask me about her?

Mother: Well, is there anything else that needs doing?

Doctor: Well, I think that Mr. Smith (orthopaedic surgeon) will tell us as Elizabeth develops.

Mother says that the child has been very good and she can't see why they said she should have died when she was born.

Doctor says that some spina bifida babies are very handicapped, much more so than Elizabeth, and some mothers may wish that their child had not survived.

Mother: Oh, but she's a wonderful child. I really like her. She's fine, she's a wonder, she's making marvellous progress.

Doctor: Yes, but I think you have to remember there are going to be problems.

Mother continues with panegyric –

Doctor closes session by arranging to see mother in 3 months time.

(c) On one sort of occasion, however, this appeal was validated by doctors. Where a parent seemed to accept the fact of a child's handicap, was co-operating with the doctor to provide a 'neutral' source of information and the child was in fact developing, then both could use an everyday mode of discourse to describe the child and its actions. Praise was given during the testing, pleasure shared in the child's achievements and jokes made about its activities in the clinic. However, except for the occasional surprise – such as when a spina bifida baby unexpectedly achieved continence and the doctor not only enthused to the mother but wrote in her notes – 'This is indeed a wonderful thing' – except for this, the expression of such wonderment was moderate and far from the superlatives of the Maternity hospital or the follow-up clinic. Rather, it resembled the pleasant progress of the Local Authority sessions. However, the validation of such a frame by doctors took time, was found with only a minority of mothers and had several special features which were not found in the other settings.

(i) It was premised upon the child's abnormality, not upon its normality, and held only so long as he was considered a special case, as doing well *for what he was.*
(ii) In other settings the parents figured only as characters in particular incidents, here they were heroes making special efforts.
(iii) Given the fact of developmental delay the time perspective was radically altered – the future could not simply be assumed but was a topic whose handling required the greatest care.

Thus, precisely because the appeal rested on a narrowing of focus to this child alone and at this moment in time, it had a fragility not found in other settings. Comparisons with other children had often to be introduced as bench-marks against which to assess a child's progress and such comparisons were unavoidable when a child's schooling was discussed. So that whereas in other settings both doctor and parent typically made rapid shifts with apparent ease between this and a more medical frame, such movements here were hazardous and clumsy, often carried out in too halting or too deliberate a manner.

Conclusion

In summary, the developmental screening of young children casts potential doubt upon all those who undergo it. Doctors therefore require techniques for normalising the population so assessed. A standard medical technique for such normalisation was to rely less on one's medical expertise than on one's adulthood to talk to mothers, demedicalising the encounter by turning oneself into a willing and appreciative audience for the child's 'performance', transforming tests into 'tricks' and 'party-pieces' and leaving the clinical agenda hidden. Mothers were allowed to be proud of their 'handfuls', clinics were appropriate places for displays of children's virtuosity and doctors were legitimate audiences to validate that pride and encourage it. Conversely, the absence of such features and the encounters, medicalisation was used to indicate that a child's normality was still at issue. This simple dichotomy does not, however, cover the wide variation that was observed in the use of the appeal. Children were sometimes cast as wonderful in all four settings but to different extents and in differing ways. These differences seem best related to variations in the setting and in the particular features of the case. It could be argued that since different doctors were involved in each setting the variation noted might be due to the soft- or hard-hearted nature of particular doctors. There are two arguments against such an analysis. In two of the settings several doctors were observed and though each doctor had his own style there did not appear to be wide variation among doctors in a particular setting in their use of an appeal to 'normal childhood'. Secondly, the occurrence and magnitude of the appeal varied not only as between settings but also as between cases in any one setting, even with the same doctor. Thus, in the follow-up clinic, cases about which the doctor still had private doubts were not overtly characterised as wonderful, though normalised in other ways, while in the neurological clinic those children who were discharged were formulated in a very different way from those who were retained. The key features which explain the variation would therefore seem to be the doctors' mandate; the extent to which the doctors perceived parents as having doubts; and the extent to which doctors felt any doubts to be justified.

Chapter 2

The Management of a
Therapeutic Encounter[1]

Introduction

Different forms of medical treatment require different kinds of cooperation and involvement from the patient. Successful occupational and physiotherapy normally demand the patient's active co-operation with the therapist, whereas, for example, surgery may require only initial assent. This chapter contains a brief analysis of some of the interactional problems encountered by therapists in a children's hospital, and the kinds of solutions they routinely devised. It is based on observational work carried out in three different settings: a physiotherapy department, an occupational therapy department and an orthoptic clinic. The physiotherapists' work comprised treatment of ward in-patients, for such things as chest drainage and limb manipulation, and out-patient treatment of long-term handicapping conditions such as cerebral palsy and spina bifida. The occupational therapists also saw cases of cerebral palsy and spina bifida but concentrated more on arm and hand involvement, as opposed to work on legs and hips. They also treated a few mentally retarded children and psychiatric cases, the latter constituting a third of their referrals. Finally, the orthoptist, who unlike the others also handled adult patients, dealt mainly with the treatment of strabismus (squints). Mentally retarded children were a rarity at the orthoptic clinic.

Work with young or subnormal children is of particular interest in studying how patient involvement is rooted in therapy or other medical treatment. For here the normal rationale that is invoked to justify medical action, and to motivate any necessary client participation – the appeal to 'illness', 'scientific medicine' and the 'normal' desire to 'get better' – is not available to the professional since it is not available to the client. Compliance must, therefore, be sought by other means, and it is these

1   [Editor's note: co-authored with A.G. Davies.] This observational work is part of a larger study carried out by the authors and Heather Gibson into the involvement and treatment of young handicapped children, and financed by the Social Science Research Council as part of a programme grant.

that are explored in this chapter. Since it analyses a situation in which the *normal* assumptions about patients do not apply, it may also serve to clarify those assumptions, for they are often taken for granted. The chapter is also about children and the way adults interact with them, both somewhat neglected topics in sociology.

Our analysis draws mainly on the work of Goffman (1961b, 1972) and of the ethnomethodologists such as Garfinkel (1967) and Cicourel (1973). Both have produced languages in which to talk about interaction, and their work may be very crudely summarised as stating that 'successful' interaction (in the technical sense) requires all parties to be able to define the encounter as of a known sort, and of a beneficial sort. The ethnomethodologists have stressed the constant interpretive task that faces individuals. They have both to work out and to demonstrate that which is going on, namely what is said or thought to be going on. They must continually ground the background rules in concrete behaviour, demonstrating to their own and others' satisfaction that they are oriented to the same features. Thus, in the terms of our chapter, being a doctor, a therapist or a patient is not something that you just passively *are,* it is something that you have to *do,* something that has to be managed or pulled off.

Childhood Competence and Incompetence

Everyone in our society is a 'patient' at times and is, therefore, called upon to do patient-work. But as all medical staff know, not everyone can. Young children, those from very different cultures and the insane may lack or fail to exhibit the appropriate cultural competence required of such an identity.

It is an everyday assumption that, because illness is a bad state, people who are 'ill' will wish to get 'better', because to do so is by definition 'better' than being ill. Thus, those who do not appear to want to get better are 'obviously' suffering from abnormal motivation, and lay thought then appeals to 'psychological' disturbances. Parsons (1964) draws on such assumptions in his formulation of the 'sick role'. However, he then uses them to create a harmonious model in which conflict is eliminated. We argue that medical interaction with young children presents special problems. However, we do not mean to imply that, by contrast, interaction with normal adults who are possessed of everyday medical knowledge such as the above is normally a trouble-free enterprise. On this point see for example Horobin and Bloor (1975).

However, very young children or those who are severely handicapped may not know that they are handicapped, may be unaware that potentially better states exist and may, therefore, lack any motivation to get 'better'.

They may hate hospitals and define medical staff as people who do pointlessly nasty or incomprehensible things to them. Of course, it could be that some such children are well aware of these things but were routinely treated by medical staff as if they were not and could not be.

Therapists distinguished between two different classes of children. First there were young children of normal intelligence, who were held to be incapable of understanding a medical schema because of their age. Only at around the age of five to six might it first be used, and even then its use was rare and occurred only under provocation.

Second there were retarded children. For those held to be only moderately affected, an appropriate reduction was made to arrive at their 'real' mental age. For the severe cases the problem was, could they understand anything at all? There were no recognised procedures for this; therapists, like parents, fluctuated in their opinion, and there always seemed to be evidence that could be read in either direction. However, such children were routinely classified with the very young.

In either case therapists had to make their activities meaningful to the child and had to create the same involvement in and commitment to the therapy that they might expect the medical schema to create in adults. They coped by appealing to that background knowledge about children that adults in our culture are expected to share. We shall argue that this knowledge contains a central ambiguity about children's 'essential nature', and this ambiguity is reflected in the way they were handled and talked about by therapists.

On one hand the world of children is often portrayed as an essentially different one from that of adults. Play is commonly held to be a constitutive part of a child's identity. Thus, adults in our society 'know' that even if a child cannot do anything else it can always play; and to understand why this is so we must first comprehend what is meant by play. Babies who lack any social competences whatsoever and are thus in a sense non-persons can still be said, quite properly, to play. As the Opies (1967, 1970) have shown, children in our culture have created their own self-sustaining culture of play with its own membership rules and activities. In such a culture children can learn to play social games as equals. It is open to any child to be a competent member and to demand by right that he be treated fairly and according to the rules.

On the other hand adults routinely treat children as not merely incompetent within the terms of their own adult world but as subordinate to them. The world of childhood in this model is not separate and equal but an inferior early stage from which one progresses to adulthood. Children are defined as 'learners', and since adult life is complex they have a lot to learn. They have to learn what sorts of things there are available to be done in the world, the regulative rules for each of these activities, the sorts of people who do them and their reasons for such actions, and the practical ways of recognising, doing and being each of these things (Mead, 1934).

When they are treating children, 'therapists can, therefore, appeal to either of these models or, as often happens in practice, to both simultaneously. But adults often view play as part of the serious business of learning about life, and one of the tasks of the occupational therapists was to teach mothers not to see their retarded children as 'lazy' and only capable of 'just play', but to view their activities as constructive learning, as an exploration of the world. Seen this way games can be made to serve other purposes besides their own intrinsic rewards. Primary school children may use games to display their various talents, while parents and adults may attempt to intervene in a child's play and guide it in directions which they think most fit. Teaching young children through play is now commonly felt to be the ideal solution to the same educational problems, and in line with this therapists routinely sought to translate their purposes into play – 'It looks like play and it is – but it's play with a purpose.'

For the staff this was a routine solution. New members who often had done most of their training with adults found children's work 'completely different' at first but soon learned to cope, as the practice of this solution to the interpretive problem was a constant topic of conversation and analysis. Therapeutic journals report on the latest transformation attempts, being full of ingenious ideas and elaborate equipment. Professional prestige accrues to those who can most adequately solve the transformation problem. Although we argued earlier that in some sense all children could be held capable of play, in practice therapists were uncertain as to whether severely retarded children could do this. On one occasion a child was described by a therapist as engaging in 'repetitive play' but on another she commented: 'most subnormal children who like playing with water, play with boats or pour water in a funnel. ... Arthur does not play, he just likes to feel the water.' This seemed to mean that some children were incapable of playing any sustained game with another, or even by themselves. If children could not even play, then therapy was of little or no practical use but was done, if at all, merely to comfort the parents.

Finally, although some therapists said that ideally they would like all their patients to see treatment as play, they seemed in practice not to describe it as such to the children. Therapeutic activities were often presented in game-like forms but the terms 'game' and 'play' themselves were reserved for other occasions, for those times when patients were allowed to play their own games, or when they were held to be not carrying out the therapy properly but merely indulging in 'fun and games'. In fact, apart from the orthoptist no one seemed to have a general term to describe the therapeutic activities to the child. Instead, children were invited to 'throw the ball', 'stand on the board', 'pile these blocks', that is, to take part in activities that could be read as games but were not stated openly to be so. This is not surprising. The medical framework of therapeutic terminology is not used, while if 'play' was extended to cover the therapy, therapists would be unable to discriminate for the children between 'messing about' and the serious matters at hand.

Therapeutic Identities

Therapists had difficulty in presenting a therapeutic identity to other medical personnel, to parents, and in particular to the children because of their recourse to 'play' rather than to overt medical treatment in order to accomplish their objectives. Therefore, therapists took considerable trouble to spell out to other medical staff that they were in the business of *treating patients* and not playing with children. They stressed their professional competence in many ways, such as by adopting a highly technical vocabulary with medical superiors and inferiors, while reserving rights to joke about 'playing' for equals and people who 'understood' what therapy is about. These were mainly other therapists.

As well as asserting competence, the therapists also had to acquire the necessary licence to treat the patients. While the medical status of their work was legitimated by the actions of doctors who through referrals created a medical licence to work with the child, the therapist in many ways depended on the co-operation of the parents in creating, sustaining and reinforcing the therapeutic agenda. The therapeutic agenda underlying seemingly trivial activities – such as by getting the child to wear a toy watch on a weak left arm to encourage movement – was explained to parents by showing how the 'work' of the parents complemented that of the therapists, and by dropping their therapeutic identity in favour of a friendly, concerned manner, encouraging parents to feel they could 'really' talk to the therapists in a way that they could not with doctors.

How then did the therapist present herself to the child, and how did she achieve the co-operation of the child? The therapeutic encounter was limited in time and did not have the all-encompassing nature of the family in defining reality for the child. Also, therapy had to begin quickly and was a serious business. The therapist could not rely on direct command alone and had to be judicious in the use of sanctions. She had to find an identity to enable her to involve the child quickly, which required minimal use of sanctions, allowed the child to define the situation as pleasurable, pleased the parents and did not cause trouble with the doctors. It was a game framework that enabled the therapist to solve these problems.

Once established, it allowed other aspects in the relationship to develop over time. Many children eventually showed great affection for their therapist and resented being taken away at the end of the treatment session. Therapists, too, developed attachments to particular children, and these personal ties could be mobilised at a later stage, such as by threatening to withdraw, in order to control the child's misdemeanours. Generally, children seemed to define the treatment situation as pleasurable and perhaps this is not surprising, since in therapy they were the sole focus of the therapists' attention for the one-half to three-quarters of an hour of the treatment. However, despite these attractions, the game framework itself generated a series of interactional problems which the competent therapist had to master in order to bring off a successful treatment session. Before diagnosing the problems, we need to consider the relevant aspects of the medical work in which the therapists engaged.

Therapeutic Agendas

Underlying any treatment session was a 'hidden agenda' (Scheff, 1968) to which the therapist worked and which was often written in the child's record. These agendas required the therapist to move through a repeated set of activities which were designed to bring into action, and in sequence, various muscle groups to enable the child to function as normally as possible. In spina bifida or cerebral palsy, the extent to which normal muscle and limb function can be attained varies. The sequencing of activities was important in that the objective was to take children through developmental stages, adding new ones once the child had achieved some muscle or limb function.

While the underlying rationale, the acquisition of basic motor competences, made sense to the parents and other medical personnel, the mode of its accomplishment with a young child was problematic. The game framework allowed the therapeutic agenda to be hidden under a set of games which therapists played with children. This was particularly important in gaining co-operation, for with young children 'active' movements are required. 'Passive' manipulation of limbs by the therapists are a minimum treatment. However, 'active' movements could not be called out by detailing their therapeutic significance to the child: they had to be brought out by covert means. For example, a very young child who was awaiting heart surgery did not perhaps grasp the therapeutic object in breathing exercises before the operation and refused to co-operate. But blowing 'birdies' made of tissue paper around the bedside called out the necessary breathing activities.

We must now distinguish games therapists play with children, or allow the children to play, and those 'games' that have a hidden therapeutic objective. One advantage of the game framework was that it became possible to move between the two without any overt change in the surface activity. Non-therapeutic games also had their place. They could be used on first contact to create the initial background against which the therapist could identify herself as a playmate, and they filled in the time when the child was awaiting therapy or removal from therapy, or in those cases where there was no serious therapeutic rationale for the child's presence. Once therapeutic 'games' were started the play vocabulary was dropped. Nevertheless, ordinary games had their uses in the actual course of therapy as well, usually either as a reward for good work in 'games' or in situations where the child was flagging in involvement and interest. They were also played when the 'game' framework was in danger of collapse, being inserted into the programme if the therapist feared that discrepant definitions of the situation might become apparent, with a resultant 'scene'. Games also provided the necessary set of rules to be appealed to when 'games' were being played. Games were established as *typical* activities into which hidden therapeutic agendas could be inserted without disruption. They were also played when a sequence of 'games' was difficult to create, the therapist inserting a game into the sequence in order to move through her therapeutic agenda of 'games' in good order.

How did the therapist go about creating 'games'? She had to make them suitable for each child's level of competence and progress. In particular, she had to build upon activities that were already available in the child's vocabulary of games. Mothers were questioned to see if the child was doing anything that might be of therapeutic use. On initial and subsequent contact the therapist watched the child to see what it would and would not do, what it could and could not do. Equipment and toys were given to the child to see what use was made of them.

Having established the child's basic vocabulary of games, the therapist then attempted to enlarge this stock in ways that the child found pleasurable, introducing new items of equipment and getting the child to incorporate them into 'games' with her. If children themselves invented therapeutically valid games then they too might be incorporated. As the sequence developed the therapist modified these games with new regulative rules so that the therapy was better served, but the constitutive rules were left intact; and the child was hopefully still able to see it as a game. Successful therapy demanded that as the child's abilities increased new rules were progressively added to each 'game', so that his or her powers were fully stretched. This tricky task required constant negotiation with the child to build it into the treatment repertoire.

In devising 'games' that called out appropriate responses, the therapists relied partly on recipe knowledge of attractive 'games' that had worked in the past. Thus, blowing paper birds for breathing exercises and inserting a doll in the therapist's tunic top for the child to reach up and kiss were recipes handed on for other cases. Piling bricks as a game could become a 'game' by introducing further sets of rules. For example, piling blocks might first be done with a child's 'good' hand, then with its 'bad' hand in order to build a castle, and then the castle could be kicked over using the 'good' and the 'bad' leg alternately. To start again the child could be encouraged to retrieve the bricks using its 'good' hand, but doing this in a sitting position in which it uses its 'bad' hand to prop itself up.

Applying the Game in Therapy

We now turn to some examples of the game framework in use, and the problems of its implementation. To begin with the child was encouraged to apply a game framework to the therapy through equipment being defined as 'toys' and through the setting being defined as one in which it was legitimate for the child to play. Therapists presented themselves as persons interested in the child to the exclusion of all others around them, as friendly and helpful, as facilitators of pleasant games, as constant sources of praise in success and comfort in distress, and so on. In short, they presented themselves as ideal playmates.

After initial assessment therapists spent some sessions reinforcing this set of definitions, playing games that were like games, since they did not have a strict therapeutic agenda. This came later. During these sessions equipment was explored as a source of 'toys', the therapist talked to the child a lot to establish her interest in him, or allowed the child to define topics of conversation if it was able to do so. At this stage children periodically became aware that their parents were absent or found that they did not like the games or setting, but the therapist was now the only person available to provide comfort, amusement and distraction. Trouble usually ensued when the therapist sought to move on to therapeutic 'games' because the game framework might then be breached in a number of ways. Once the therapist started to manipulate games to conform to her hidden therapeutic agenda, there was always a danger that the reality of the 'game' would break down, to present the child with a new situation which he might not be able to define but might feel threatening. What then were these sources of threat to the 'game'?

The setting itself was a source of problems. For example, while some of the therapeutic props were like toys in shape and design, others were not. Also, the setting was a hospital, in which almost everyone wore a uniform. Other children might be present but were not normally available for games with the child, and he could only play with *his* therapist. Other people were continually walking in and out, and in physiotherapy the child had most of its clothes removed.

As we have argued, one of the major uses of applying a game framework is to motivate the child to engage in the therapeutic activities. Therapists continually monitored the child's motivation to determine whether he was 'really' trying or not. One major factor that might affect this was tiredness, and here again the young child was unable to inform the therapist about this. If the child was not cooperating the reasons for it might be sought in 'tiredness', and the child, therefore, was not worked so hard. If the child did not appear tired then it might lead to sanctioning. Either way, the game framework was liable to break down.

Another difficulty lay in sustaining the exclusiveness of the relationship between therapist and child. Games are usually felt not to be exclusive, and anyone can play. The therapist often had to divert the child's attempts to incorporate other people or objects inappropriate to the therapy.

The rules of the 'games' were a further source of trouble. If in front of game rules both therapist and child are equal, how could the therapist change them without losing credibility as a playmate? If the therapist suddenly appealed to her age and status as a warrant to change the rules, then the child might decide he did not want to play anymore. Indirect tactics were used to prevent conflicts over game rules, like suggesting a new 'game' or incorporating a new object or person to head off a direct confrontation and disruption of the game framework.

Because games for two persons usually involve turn-taking and choosing moves, this also could cause impediments to therapy. Therapists continually tried to construct 'games' in which the child made all the moves and took all the turns. The therapist in her role of playmate had to honour turn-taking some of the time, and if the child demanded she take a turn she had to agree or face a possible row about the rules which might reveal that it was not a game at all. The good therapist was one who was able to develop a set of satisfactory 'games' in which she had minimal involvement as a player and maximum involvement as a facilitator of the child's playing.

Therapeutic activity sometimes produced pain and fright; some tasks could be performed only with great difficulty and uncertainty and there was a corresponding difficulty in getting them defined as fun. When pain and difficulty occurred they were treated in either of two ways. First, they might be treated as incidental to the action and not intimately involved *in* it. Since there was always the chance that the child might withdraw co-operation, the usual strategy was to see how much the child would take before withdrawing and then to divert the child with another 'game' as quickly as possible. The second way was to continue with the treatment while relying throughout on praise and reinforcement to retain involvement. This carried more likelihood of the game breaking down and was used only when the therapist was very sure of the child's relationship with her. Surprise and fear were also problematic and might break the game, and yet involuntary correcting movement of muscles and limbs often can be achieved only if the child is suddenly thrown off balance or startled. This could create problems unless it was defined as a game and therefore safe, but as soon as it was seen as safe by the child it lost its therapeutic value. Consequently, new sources of surprise had to be found by varying the routine or inserting a novel item, or even transferring the child to another therapist.

Games are supposed to be sources of pleasure, and players usually continue playing until they become bored or tired. They may also incorporate new features if both parties consent to a change in the rules. From the therapists' point of view this had disadvantages in that their therapeutic programme required a rapid switching of activities in a set order and no elaboration of the games beyond therapeutic necessity. Children soon developed favourites among the 'games' and wanted to play these all the time and not the others. Since participants have to agree on what game is to be played, the child had rights as a player to choose *his* games. If he chose the wrong ones the therapist had to negotiate the therapy session trying all the while to get the child to play therapeutically improving 'games', while recognising that she had to give way on some demands in order to achieve a balance of satisfactions. To do so she had to obtain the child's acceptance that while some 'games' were not much fun, others were and that you had to honour each other's boring as well as exciting games.

Participants' rewards from the 'games' were also problematic as the two participants had different criteria for allocating rewards. The question then arose whether they were, in fact, playing the same game. For example, if the therapist wanted a child to develop grip and throwing action in a weak left hand she might get the child to throw a ball as far as it could in a certain way and then catch it in return. However, children often mistakenly thought that the game was simply to throw the ball as far as possible, while the therapist would reward only therapeutically correct throwing technique. If such a child hung on to his definition he did not get rewards for success but got sanctions instead. Eventually he might refuse to play any more, forcing the therapist into some accommodation of therapeutic and game-generated rewards.

Sanctions, however, raised problems of authority. If the therapist sanctioned the child she did this by reference either to game-rules or to her position as an adult authority. The former were tried first but in a last resort the therapist withdrew from her identity as playmate and became a serious adult who demanded that the child did as he was told. This was always a last resort as it usually fractured the 'game' framework seriously. Interestingly, in physiotherapy severe sanctioning was usually done by a different therapist. Sometimes the child was threatened with its parents, or the therapist herself might become intractable and refuse to 'play', but insist on the performance of therapy with no escape for the child. After such a confrontation, which the therapist almost invariably won, but at a cost, extra dimensions were added to the 'game' framework. There was now a continual threat that the 'game' framework would be withdrawn entirely, with problematic and unpleasant consequences for the child. Even this appeal might on occasions fail and therapy was then held to be impossible. The two models of childhood which we described earlier contain within them definitions of abnormality. Thus, just as children who would not play were held to be psychiatrically disturbed, so also were children who persistently refused to recognise a properly licensed adult, such as a therapist, as an 'authority'. One six-year-old girl suffering from mild hemiplegia, who was also a day-patient in the child psychiatric unit, persistently disobeyed therapists and was held to be an impossible patient. Werthman (1968) describes the problems created by such children in American schools.

Since sessions were problematic for young children, the sudden withdrawal of a frame that made some sense of what was going on, and the sudden shift in identities, rendered their situation potentially harmful and unpleasant, especially as they were without their parents' protection. Children were often frightened when this happened, and therefore welcomed the offer to carry on in the 'game' framework within the limits imposed by the therapist. Transfer to another therapist, more active cossetting by the therapist or an appeal to the parents were all employed to warm the child back in again, but whatever the costs, at least the seriousness of the enterprise was firmly established.

Workers' Playtime

Since therapy may last for several years, the therapeutic encounter may stabilise as children learn the routines and develop a more intimate relationship with the therapists. Over this period the normal child's comprehension of the adult world is also growing and the therapist can therefore start to use a medical or work framework in addition to the game one. The constant work of therapists with a child suffering from a mild physical handicap may itself create some of the conditions for the relevance of the medical schema. A limb that is not used may be 'forgotten' by its owner who learns to make do in other, often ingenious, ways. By insisting that it be used 'properly' and often exclusively in the 'games', the therapist may create consciousness of the handicap so that it can be dealt with directly. However the game framework is never entirely superseded but is put to rather different uses. Reasons for the routines can be seen in their immediate beneficial effects and in their place in some long-term programme, and so children can be adjured to work hard to achieve 'success'.

Although a game framework was typically used to provide activities with meaning before the transition to a medical model, there were some important exceptions to this rule, and analysis of these suggests that mental age was not the sole criterion used by therapists for the schema's application. Part of the work of the occupational therapists was to educate their patients in the 'activities of daily living'. Thus, they taught physically handicapped children how to eat with a knife, fork and spoon, how to write properly or how to type with a modified typewriter, and how to dress and tie shoelaces. It is harder to turn such activities into games, but this may not be a drawback, in so far as the child is oriented towards the adult world and wishes to attain some of its competences.

The orthoptist's problems in this respect were far more complex. Almost none of his therapeutic routines could be passed off as 'play', but nor could they be seen as estimable adult skills. The clinic was full of technical equipment, and the tasks demanded a very high level of both intellectual competence and motivation to perform a series of complex acts of recognition over a period of fifteen to twenty minutes. This seems to have radically affected the definitional work of the therapist, although since we observed the work of only one orthoptist, this could simply be his particular style. But whatever the causes there were two important differences between the orthoptic and other departments. Unlike the other therapeutic departments we observed, children were exhorted to 'work' from an early age. Unlike other departments, young children were frequently told as soon as they entered the room that of course they could do it because 'You're a big boy now, aren't you'. It seemed that the appeal to a game framework depended not simply on the patient's age but also on the complexity and nature of the task to be performed, and some therapeutic tasks seemed incapable of being successfully transformed into games.

Just as some tasks could not be turned into games, so it was held that some children could not be games-players, so that for them also the game framework was irrelevant. As we have already noted, therapists held that some children were hardly capable of 'play' let alone 'work'. All the therapeutic games demanded active participation from the children and thus a minimum ability to understand and carry out commands. For those who lacked this, therapy in the orthoptic and occupational therapy departments was held to be impossible. The physiotherapists could, however, treat some of these children if they were physically handicapped as well, since part of their work involved 'passive' therapy. Here the child's body was treated as an object to be manipulated by the therapist rather than by the patient. Since such tasks did not require the child's active co-operation there was no need for a games schema to make sense of the activity, and the therapist could use an overtly *clinical* framework.

The game framework therefore could not be applied under all conditions, and even when it seemed appropriate, its use demanded considerable skills from the therapist. We conclude by noting that therapeutic games are not confined solely to young children. With adults there is less of a problem of comprehension of the therapeutic rationale. However, there is a new problem in that they may define such activities as childish and demeaning. Comprehension does not guarantee motivation. Adult paraplegics from all over the world compete in the Paraplegic Olympics in contests such as archery, basketball and swimming, and such games may form a regular part of adult therapy. Similarly, some of the older children we observed found a valuable incentive to effort in therapy in the games and leisure pursuits of the adult world. Some older boys treated the exercises in physiotherapy like gymnastics as occasions for demonstrating their bodily skills and strength. A ten-year-old girl in occupational therapy who had consistently failed to wear a corrective splint or carry out her prescribed home exercises suddenly became most keen when a therapist gave her a specially modified sewing-ring and taught her to use it. Such games or pastimes, however, although perhaps therapeutic, are rather different from those that are played with young children, for the patients are *aware* of their therapeutic value. They do not, therefore, act as a framework to make the therapy meaningful, though of course the forms they take may render it more palatable.

Chapter 3

Minor Courtesies and Macro Structures

Introduction: The Goffmanian Legacy

> It seems to me that the dramaturgical approach may constitute a fifth perspective to be added to the technical, political, structural and cultural perspectives.
>
> (Goffman 1959: 240)

> My concern over the years has been to promote acceptance of this face-to-face domain as an analytically viable one.
>
> (Goffman 1983: 2)

Goffman may have changed his terms but he rarely changed his tune. What began as the 'dramaturgical approach' ended up, much more broadly, as the 'interaction order', but the notion of a distinctive micro-social world remained: a world with its own special forms, rules, processes and problems. In his vision, this fifth perspective was linked to, but analytically separable from, the realms more traditionally studied by social science. To sketch its nature and establish its viability, he devoted 30 years, a thesis, 10 books and collections of essays, and several important but so far ungathered articles.

This legacy is vast, diverse and has much to offer on the key topics with which this paper deals; power and, above all, ceremony. The analysis of etiquette – of that ritual order which links the micro to the macro world, lending weight and stability to each and every encounter – is central to Goffman's writings. Yet most subsequent commentators and researchers have had little to say on ceremony. This paper tries to redress the balance. It contains four things: an exposition of Goffman's view of the ritual order; a description of systematic ethnographic methods for its analysis; an illustration of the use of such methods (via research into a particular class of encounters); and, in the light of this research, an appraisal and critique of Goffman's position.

The absence of much sociological commentary or research on ceremony is not, in fact, unusual; much of his work has received relatively little development from others. Indeed, the great pomp of the funeral has not stilled the loud mutterings of a good many of the mourners. For all the fame that Goffman achieved in disciplines besides sociology, many in his own trade were reluctant to grant him much importance. As he remarked in his final essay on the interaction order, 'My colleagues have not been overwhelmed by the merits of the case' (1983b: 2). Part of this failure is due to the peculiar reluctance by many sociologists to concede any importance to the micro sphere. And some part, no doubt, to Goffman's particular theoretical and empirical frailties. But another part, perhaps the most important part, stems from his distinctive idiosyncrasies, which were large, varied and, though attractive to some, offputting to many. Understanding any part of his work – and, more particularly, grasping the problems faced by all researchers in the fields that he mapped out – demands that these idiosyncrasies be tackled head on. I shall begin, therefore, by citing a rare general statement of his aims and methods; things that Goffman never normally spelt out and which in consequence have been the cause of much confusion:

> I am impatient for a few conceptual distinctions (nothing so ambitious as a theory) that show we are getting some place in uncovering elementary variables that simplify and order, delineating generic classes whose members share lots of properties, not merely a qualifying similarity. To do this I think one has to start with ethnological or scholarly experience in a particular area of behaviour and then exercise the right to dip into any body of literature that helps, and move in any unanticipated but indicated direction. The aim is to follow where a concept (or small set of them) seems to lead. That development, not narrative or drama, is what dictates. Of course nothing gets proven, only delineated, but I believe that in many areas of social conduct that's just where we are right now. A simple classification pondered over, worked over to try to get it to fit, may be all that we can do right now. Casting one's endeavour in the more respectable forms of the mature sciences is often just a rhetoric. In the main I don't believe we're there yet. And I like to think that accepting these limits and working like a one-armed botanist is what a social naturalist unashamedly has to do.
>
> (Goffman: personal communication)

So, contrary to common belief, Goffman viewed himself as a scientist, though one using naturalistic methods and working in an adolescent (possibly neonatal) area. Moreover, as Robin Williams (1986) argues, he saw his scientific task as primarily conceptual, bringing some initial order to a morass of data through the selection and preliminary testing of elementary variables.

In short, he was a theorist, though of a most unusual kind, for data were central to his method of generating concepts (alas, a rarity in the theoretically inclined). On the other hand, this close interest in the empirical did not endear him to most conventional researchers. To them (and to some of his students) his methods seemed wild. As for links to other theorists, these too were often strained; though he discussed data endlessly, he rarely discussed other writers, save only in footnotes. In addition to these sins, he invented a cornucopia of theoretical terms – but changed them in almost every book. Likewise, though he acknowledged the power and priority of wider social realms, he himself worked solely in the micro-social sphere and rarely bothered about making links. Finally, in a solemn, committed and largely graceless profession (as the public image has it), he was a cynic, a wit and a literary stylist; all potent sources of misunderstanding.

What then did he leave us? The answer, obvious enough, is a dazzling array of concepts and some major problems. Since he was primarily a theorist he was not too fussy about the means by which he derived his terms, or the manner in which others might operationalize them. And since he was driven on by his desire to map, however provisionally, the many contours of his presumed newfound domain, he tended to love the view he had just noticed and be bored by autobiographical exegesis. Precisely how he had got there, how one foray linked with another, were usually matters of little interest.[1] Thus the more systematic explorers who plod after him are faced with both a vast terrain and, littered across the landscape, a multitude of exploratory terminologies, most of them intriguing but many apparently abandoned. Some perhaps wrecked, some only partly built, some possibly in good repair, but none possessing any clear set of maker's instructions. What this paper offers is, I hope, an empirical way forward with one bunch of his ideas.

Minor Courtesies and Signs of Deference: Goffman's Theory of Ceremony

> A lot of life is about things so trivial that we do not bother to record them – only sometimes note their absence, as with manners.
>
> (Oscar Wilde, cited in Shattuck 1986: 67)

A central argument in much of Goffman's work is that the ceremonial order of the encounter, the etiquette that can be found on any social occasion, is not some trivial matter, of interest solely to mothers, pedants

---

1   There are two major exceptions to this rule. Some prefaces contain brief but important statements on general theoretical and methodological issues. See, for example, *Relations in Public* (1971), *Interaction Ritual* (1967) and *Frame Analysis* (1974). In the last year or so of his life he also produced two valuable general essays in which he reflected at length on his own work, 'A reply to Denzin and Keller' (1981a) and 'The interaction order' (1983b). All these seem worthy of detailed exegesis.

and social climbers, but has instead a profound importance for the viability of the micro-social order. Later sections of this paper attempt to test this argument, but I shall begin by spelling out Goffman's own theory of these matters in some detail. Consider, for instance, the main components of the ordinary service relationship:

> The interaction that occurs when client and server are together ideally takes a relatively structured form. The server can engage in mechanical handiwork operations ... he can also engage in verbal exchanges with the client. The verbal part itself contains three components: a *technical* part ... a *contractual* part and, finally, a *sociable* part, consisting of a few minor courtesies, civilities, and signs of deference.
>
> (Goffman 1961a: 328–9)

The first quote indicates that on particular occasions particular events, roles and manners are in order. Such elements can be found in any relationship whatsoever; they are not specific to service relationships. Moreover, two of these, so Goffman argues, together generate the distinctive reality of any one encounter. The specification of *this* set of events and *that* set of roles, constitute the *rules of the game* which, when adhered to, produce a separate little world; be it a medical consultation, a boxing-match or whatever:

> A matrix of possible events and a cast of roles through whose enactment the events occur constitute together a field of fateful dramatic action, a place of being, an engine of meaning, a world in itself, different from all other worlds, except the ones generated when the same game is played at other times.
>
> (Goffman 1961b: 26–7)

But there are lots of different games. How is the reality of any particular game (or *play* or *frame* in other Goffmanian metaphors) kept alive in the face of all our other involvements? It is here, so he asserts, that manners achieve their importance:

> The process of mutually sustaining a definition of the situation in face-to-face interaction is socially organized through rules of relevance and irrelevance. These rules for the management of engrossment appear to be an insubstantial element of social life, a matter of courtesy, manners, and etiquette. But it is to these flimsy rules, and not to the unshaking character of the external world, that we owe our unshaking sense of realities.
>
> (Goffman 1961b: 30–1)

Such principles for the management of engrossment, the *rules of relevance and irrelevance,* focus primarily on what should *not* be done. Their main concern is with indelicacy, with what must be avoided or ignored. And studying this is a useful heuristic device for understanding the entire encounter:

> It seems characteristic of encounters, as distinguished from other elements of social organization, that their order pertains largely to what shall be attended and disattended, and through this, to what shall be accepted as the definition of the situation. Instead of beginning by asking what happens when this definition of the situation breaks down, we can begin by asking what perspectives this definition of the situation excludes when it is being satisfactorily sustained.
>
> (Goffman 1961b: 19)

Here then, in the 'elegance and strength of the structure of inattention' (Goffman 1961b: 19) is the source of the sustained reality of the encounter. The powerful focus on just one set of meanings and the systematic exclusion of all others: this is the nub; not breakdown, nor the necessity of constant repair. The little world of the encounter is not a fragile thing.[2] Instead, it is an extraordinarily robust structure, capable of ignoring all kinds of routine trouble. Only in the most exceptional of circumstances is it seriously and overtly threatened. For present purposes in interaction, any features of the setting that do not fit, any alien qualities, emotions or involvements, all these, if they form no part of the current order, are treated, for the time being, as if they did not exist. Little children turn themselves into soldiers, old clothes into uniforms, chairs and tables into forts. So too, adults become lovers, parents, teachers, shoppers and politicians as the occasion fits.

But inattention is not quite everything. Two further quotations provide us with additional considerations. Both deal, according to Goffman, with other aspects of the ritual order which are equally fundamental:

> We have then a kind of interactional modus vivendi. Together the participants contribute to a single over-all definition of the situation which involves not so much a real agreement as to what exists but rather a real agreement as to whose claims concerning what issues will be temporarily honoured. Real agreement will also exist concerning the desirability of avoiding an open conflict of definitions of the situation. I will refer to this level of agreement as a working consensus.
>
> (Goffman 1959: 9–10)

---

2 Gonos (1977) contains an excellent analysis of Goffman's views on structure which brings out this point well. Its only flaw is that it makes Goffman nothing but a structuralist. As I show later, this is only half the picture. See also Strong (1983a) and Goffman's crushing response (1981a) to Denzin and Keller (1981).

To the degree that a performance highlights the common official values of the society in which it occurs, we may look upon it ... as an expressive rejuvenation and reaffirmation of the moral values of the community ... (as) a celebration ... The world in truth is a wedding.

(Goffman 1959: 35–6)

These quotations bring out the Janus-like nature of etiquette in Goffman's theory. One face is Machiavellian; it speaks of performances and actors, of merely overt ceremony, and of the delicate, covert assessment of power and place within the encounter. The other face is Durkheimian; it tells, instead, of the wider social values which ceremony necessarily celebrates – however murky the origins (or consequences) of these rituals may sometimes be.

Put another way, when we encounter others we are forced to put on public dress. That dress is determined by many different factors – power, status, role, the situation, our fellow-participants and even (partly) personal choice. But whatever we end up wearing, and whether we like it or not, our public garments invest that encounter with its own form and meaning, creating for the moment a distinct and palpable little world. Simultaneously (and equally for the moment) they reinforce and reaffirm some wider set of social values, however cynical or unwilling we may sometimes covertly feel: or so Goffman argues.[3]

So in our investigation of ceremony, we must look to both the *overt* and the *covert* sides of the interaction, to what people display publicly and what they say and do only in private. But we must also grasp the celebratory aspect. How may this be done? Several more hints are given by Goffman. *The Presentation of Self in Everyday Life* speaks of the *idealization* (1959: 34–51) that is essential to proper performances; it is in this sense that the world is a wedding. 'On face-work' then argues, first that *all* participants within the interaction are, typically, idealized – this is a *joint* venture: 'The person tends to conduct himself during the encounter so as to maintain both his own face and the face of the other participants' (Goffman 1967: 11). Second, that the *rules of relevance* and *irrelevance* are fundamentally moral rules; rules which have profound significance for the participants' identity and sense of self; rules which also, when taken together, form a coherent and (in part) self-equilibrating whole – we are dealing here with a kind of ritual micro-functionalism:

These rules, when followed, determine the evaluation he (the actor) will make of himself and of his fellow-participants in the encounter, the distribution of

---

3   Goffman is thus a moralist (of a cynical and stoical kind) as well as a sociologist. On his account, public morality is necessarily and unreformably ambiguous and flawed.

his feelings and the kinds of practices he will employ to maintain a specified and obligatory kind of ritual equilibrium. The general capacity to be bound by moral rules may well belong to the individual, but the particular set of rules ... (is) ... established in the ritual organization of social encounters.

(Goffman 1967: 45)

In short, in any type of encounter, so Goffman claims, there exists a distinctive and robust set of moral rules, rules which both knit together into a single, harmonious whole and which also present each participant in an idealized light, a light which in turn celebrates wider social values. That idealization and celebration is a joint task in which everyone has a part to play; but at the same time it is based on a purely temporary agreement. The ritual order is simply an overt display, a performance, which may well conceal great covert differences in opinion and power. Some people may be forced to celebrate against their will. Finally, the moral rules which compose any particular ritual order get their sustained reality from a further set of rules – rules of relevance and irrelevance – which govern precisely which matters the participants may focus on and those which they must gloss over and ignore. The joint idealization of this (often) purely working consensus depends on a shared and systematic inattention to anything that might disrupt the overt order of things.

But if that is the theory it was not one that Goffman himself ever tested. He never studied the minutiae of any particular ceremony, never systematically examined any specific rules of relevance or irrelevance, never rigorously probed the workings of this, or that, ritual equilibrium. For some this is a terrible fault but, as we saw earlier, Goffman was not a researcher in any conventional sense. He was a theorist working in an unexplored area, trying to make some initial sense, as best he could, of a huge and unfamiliar terrain. What he has to offer is, therefore, an array of (merely) plausible ideas – of possible forms, processes, rules, tasks and problems. Of course, Goffman's best may still turn out to be better than most others. But when we get right down and look in detail at a particular bunch of encounters, who knows what we will actually find?

Finding Rules in Ceremony

Goffman's theory of the ceremonial order of encounters could be explored in many ways. The way I chose was to concentrate on just one type of encounter – paediatric consultation – and to explore this via intensive ethnographic methods. But if the focus was small, the instances were both large and varied. I gathered systematic data (via handwritten verbatim notes)[4] on the interaction in 1120 paediatric encounters. One hundred took place in an eastern city of the United States, some fee-paying ('private' in British terminology), some charity, the rest payed for by the Federal Government. The other 1000 consultations all occurred in a Scottish city of similar size and all took place within the National Health Service (NHS).

Aside from the differences in location and financing, these consultations occurred in many different types of clinic and with many different doctors – 40 in all (though focussing principally on just a handful). Such variety was more than matched in the types of case seen: from the rare to the routine, from the retarded to the insane, from the brief to the lengthy (some meetings lasted nearly an hour), from the one-off to the repeat (a few patients were observed up to 13 times in three years), from the chronic to the acute, from the rich to the poor, from the healthy to the doomed, from the hospital to the community clinic. Not all human life was there, but a lot was; enough perhaps for a beginning.

One central methodological problem was posed by the *rule of irrelevance*: how to notice significant absences, how to discover what might have been there but was instead systematically excluded? Consider the Scottish NHS clinics. A central part of their ceremonial order was the portrayal of the doctor as obviously and necessarily competent; a competence that could not be challenged by parents and did not stem from particular intelligence or training, but depended simply on being a doctor. Medical authority was (normally) anonymous, all-powerful and *ex officio*. It did not need to be proved; it was simply taken for granted. Parents, as non-members of the club, were portrayed, by contrast, as both passive and technically ignorant, whatever their other qualities. But getting to see these rules proved hard. Not only was my own medical experience solely within the NHS, but swimming inside the Scottish data (as I was for the first three years of the project) I was aware only of its variety; of how this parent, clinic or doctor differed, so markedly, from that. How then did I get to see the striking uniformities of the NHS clinic and the great diversity of action that was systematically excluded? How does the fish get to notice that it is surrounded by water (since it is there all the time)? Only when it is hooked out on to dry land, when it encounters the *deviant case*.

Here, the dry land came, above all, from the American data. Three thousand miles away in the United States one saw, at least in some clinics,[5]

---

4 These were made together with a co-worker, Alan Davis, who was conducting another study of paediatric clinics (Davis 1982). Handwritten notes are less accurate than machine recording but, for a given volume of resources, enable a larger body of data to be analysed.

5 Most of the non-fee-paying American patients were treated in similar ways to the British NHS patients. The exceptions occurred with one of the doctors in a charity clinic for the poor.

routine happenings that never or almost never occurred in any Scottish clinic; things that were (sometimes) unimaginable in Scotland; things which immediately revealed what was systematically absent from most NHS consultations. Consider, for example, the following Scottish extract. A young, middle-class child who had been seeing a psychiatrist has been referred to a paediatric neurology clinic for the first time. At the end of the half-hour consultation, the paediatrician asks:

Doctor: What was Dr Maxwell (the psychiatrist) planning for her?
Mother: Well, she said that someone would be seeing her. Someone interested in specific speech delay. Is that you?
Doctor: Well, I'm interested in it, but I don't think it could be me.
Mother: And the other person we'd be seeing is a paediatrician with an interest in coordination.
Doctor: That's me. The other one may be a psychologist.

(Strong 1979: 75)

How can we interpret this? Viewed from within the Scottish data, it was simply an oddity: an apparently competent woman sitting through a half-hour consultation without knowing who she was talking to. But, in the light cast by the data on American private consultations, it suddenly took on a new form. It could now be seen as merely an extreme instance of both a general patient passivity and a medical anonymity that were characteristic of almost all NHS consultations. Thus, routine occurrences in private practice revealed systematic absences in that of the NHS. Consider two private American extracts:

Intern: How did you get here?
Mother: Well, he's been seeing a psychiatrist and he diagnosed minimal brain dysfunction and prescribed X. But we also wanted to get Dr Stein's opinion as we felt we ought not just to have a psychiatric opinion.

(Strong 1979: 79–80)

Father: So it's a little too early to do this now?
Doctor: Right. We talk about this problem all the time at the moment and I've had discussions at the (New York) and (Boston) hospitals with the experts in the fields. I've spoken to Drs A, B, and C about it. We're all very interested in it but it's early days yet ... Remember, it's not just me who's telling you this, I've talked to lots of people who know more about this than I do. (He names them again plus some others.) And they all agree that it's too risky at the moment.

(Strong 1979: 78)

In the first extract there is an important similarity to our previous Scottish case. Here too we are dealing with a child who has seen a psychiatrist and is now attending a paediatric neurology clinic for the first time. However, there are important differences. This is the beginning of the consultation (in fact the 'work-up' by an intern) and the American mother (slightly lower in social class) not only knows who she is going to see but has herself chosen this person. Moreover, she makes it plain from the beginning, though politely, that she has seen another specialist and is checking his opinion, just as she might, by implication, check that of Dr Stein.

By contrast, Scottish patients never displayed such open consumerism. Though they had nominal rights to seek a second opinion, in practice few patients dared. Moreover, whereas both private patients and doctors regularly commented on other doctors' views, this almost never happened in NHS clinics. Contrast, however, the second extract above. Here the doctor backs up his own opinion with a long list of other doctors' names and opinions. What is for sale here are highly specific skills and contacts. Private medicine is necessarily individualized; colleagues are also competitors; patients can and do go elsewhere. So doctors must display both their own skills and opinions and pass judgement on those of others. American doctors saw private patients not in the ordinary clinic but in their own room in the hospital, a room whose walls were covered with certificates from medical school. NHS patients were seen in anonymous public rooms; rooms which matched the impersonal, *ex officio* style of the expertise on offer.

Vivid deviant cases, like the data from American private practice, thus allowed the formulation of very general rules of relevance and irrelevance. Once my eyes were opened, I could then start looking much more systematically, both for fresh instances of the same phenomena and for other related kinds of activity and passivity. But. this too requires a method. What kind of system can be used in this search? Ethnographic techniques have had a bad press from some students of the micro social; sloppy, subjective, impressionistic: these are common terms of abuse. Of course, some ethnographies do indeed have these characteristics, but such a description ignores the careful analytic techniques that have been developed. Two, in particular, stand out: the methods of, respectively, *constant comparison* (Glaser 1964) and *analytic induction* (Robinson 1951; Cressey 1971; Bloor 1978). I used both.

Constant comparison is a means for systematically elaborating detailed hypotheses about a complex, general phenomenon. It is also ideally suited to the analysis of very large bodies of data. For in this method, coding takes place only when one discovers variations from, exceptions to, or particularly dramatic instances of the rule in question. Each datum is used as a check on the validity of the hypotheses and classifications that have been developed up till that point. If the datum fits readily with what has gone before, no note is made; if it does not then either a new hypothesis is required, or an old version will need some suitable amendment. Consider further NHS extracts:

Doctor: We do like to see you just once in a while. I think I'm a charlatan really because there's nothing much we can do, but we just like to keep an eye on things to see if there is anything we can do.

(Strong 1979: 87)

Mother: Dr Brown (London) said that this hospital (Scotland) hadn't ruled out a hereditary cause.
Doctor: ... I'm sure Dr McAllister (Scotland) couldn't have said that ... Quite frankly the report from London is a puzzle to us. What they say under the heading 'diagnosis', where they say they don't know, differs from the bottom where they say it's genetic ...
Mother: ... At the (London) hospital, Dr Brown seemed right out on a limb. He seemed definite, but no one else paid much attention to him.

(Strong 1979: 211)

Such instances illustrate the analytic power of the search for deviant cases; both turn out to be exceptions that help prove the rule. For example, behaviour of the first type was quite common with children suffering from severe, chronic conditions. But for a doctor to say such things was not to discount medical expertise, merely to describe its limitations from an expert point of view. It was medical staff, not parents who typically set bounds to medical competence. Likewise, the second extract (which breaks the rules of medical anonymity and consensus, and thus resembles a private rather than an NHS consultation) reveals the one chink in medical anonymity within the Scottish clinic. This particular mother was one of only two Scottish mothers in the study to request a second opinion from another hospital doctor. Getting that opinion (a difficult thing to do within the NHS)[6] transformed subsequent consultations at her local hospital; medical opinion was no longer collective but individual (and contradictory).

Constant comparison therefore broadens and deepens the initial set of hypotheses by its sharp focus on deviant cases. However, the method has a major flaw. While it is good at elaborating hypotheses, it is inappropriate to test them on the same body of data as that from which they have been

---

6   Every NHS patient has the right to a second opinion; in practice this rarely happens – they are never normally informed of such rights. Those who do make a fuss run some small (but felt) risk of being blackballed.

generated. Enter analytic induction. Here the researcher is urged to collect only a small, initial body of data; to derive from it some initial hypotheses; to collect a further body of data; to test and modify the hypotheses on this fresh evidence; and to continue this sequence of data-gathering and hypothesis-testing until no further body of data produces any significant modification to the developed hypotheses. My data were collected all in one go. So, instead, I simply divided them; the first half being used to generate detailed hypotheses (via constant comparison) about the ritual order of the paediatric clinics; the second half to test those same hypotheses. How, then, did Goffman's theory of encounter etiquette stand up?

A Re-ordered Ritual

Further work may add detail to his analysis of ceremony,[7] but this initial examination strongly suggests that Goffman has got much of the broad outline right. Much, but not all: some qualifications must be made, two with important consequences for the links between the interaction order and those macro worlds which sociologists more conventionally treat. I shall begin, however, with the many key points on which he does seem to be correct. There was, indeed, a minute attention to a ritual etiquette in all these consultations. Each participant was offered a heavily idealized public character (whatever their private qualities) and the combined set of ceremonial identities formed a harmonious and smoothly interlocking whole. But to grasp this fully, it is important to complete my rough sketch of consultation etiquette. There were two equally central dimensions to this particular ceremonial order; the first, described in the prior section of this chapter, deals with the technical medical competence of server and client; the second, as described below, concerns their moral character.

Take, for example, the character proffered to mothers. As every Scottish doctor was (overtly) competent, so every Scottish mother was normally treated as loving, honest, reliable and intelligent; not, of course, capable of passing judgement on medicine, but certainly fulfilling every maternal duty to her child. Consider the following extracts; the first from a routine consultation in a hospital clinic; the second from a local authority well-baby clinic, where the baby, at six months, is grossly fat (twice the expected weight) and from a family who have been notorious amongst health and social-service staff for three generations:

---

7   These details concern the components out of which frames are constructed (rights, duties, qualities, etc.). It seems likely these are limited in number. Strong (1979: 188–9) hazards preliminary guesses.

Doctor: Is there anybody in the house with you?
Mother: Well, my husband.

(Strong 1979: 46)

Doctor: And you feed him on Farex?
Mother In the morning and evening.
Doctor: And porridge?
Mother: Aye.
Doctor: Does he get anything else for elevenses?
Mother: Just biscuits ...
Doctor: How much does he get a lunchtime?
Mother: Oh just mince and tatties ...
Doctor: And what does he get for his tea?
Mother: Oh a boiled egg or a scrambled egg.
Doctor: And this is as well as milk?
Mother: Aye ...
Doctor: If I were you, I'd miss out the Farex and the porridge at breakfast and the biscuit as well. It's best to do this now because if children get fat now then they tend to be fatter later on in life. He's supposed to be twice his birthweight now and he's a good bit more than that, isn't he? This is very important. He's putting on a bit too much weight.

(Strong 1979: 46–7)

The first extract illustrates that all medical inquiry, however apparently trivial, routinely involves the production of potentially discrediting information; every consultation necessarily touches on the patient or parent's moral character. It also shows how, in the Scottish clinics at least, medical questioning was typically conducted with some delicacy; thereby preserving for every mother that pristine image of the ideal mother. This was most obvious where there was grave doubt about a mother's competence and character. In the second extract, the mother had ignored all previous medical advice about feeding her baby but the doctor's tone is still polite and friendly; she makes no mention of the mother's delinquency; her questions are posed in a neutral fashion; her advice is phrased simply as what she herself would do. Overtly the mother is treated as a good woman who simply needs to be informed of the best way to proceed.

In short, in the Scottish clinics, every doctor was an expert and every mother was good. Whatever their actual morality or expertise, consultation etiquette routinely cloaked them in these special and complementary identities. The sustained reality of their encounter was thus made possible not just by a special set of roles and events, but also by the rigorous exclusion of anything that might spoil such ideals. Rules of irrelevance enabled a prolonged mutual engrossment in the action almost regardless of circumstance – consultations were formal, polite and mostly free of emotion. Moreover, just as it sustained the internal action, so such ritual simultaneously celebrated key external, societal values; doctors were wise and mothers were motherly. But there are, none the less, three qualifications to be made to Goffman.

(1) *The unmentioned ideal:* The rule of irrelevance could go rather further than Goffman implies. For it could rest on the routine omission of any mention of the very things that were being idealized. For example, in the Scottish clinics, medical expertise was never praised, it was just taken for granted. Likewise, mothers were never normally praised for their motherliness. A ritual is thus involved but one of some delicacy. This is (quite often) one of those religions where the name of God cannot be mentioned. Compare, however, the standard treatment of Scottish mothers with the following cases (also Scottish):

Doctor: You have children of your own?
Foster mother: Yes, one – and I've had nine foster children.
Doctor: Ah well, your opinion is worth its weight in gold.

(Strong 1979: 179)

Doctor: What was the weight at birth then?
Father: Seven and a half pounds.
Doctor: Gosh, you've got a good memory! I expect mothers but not fathers to remember. It's seven and a half pounds, you think.

(Strong 1979: 63)

Foster mothers (in very short supply) and fathers (who rarely came but were being encouraged to do so) could get lavish praise, but with mothers this was unnecessary. Mothers' competence was just not an issue, it was simply taken for granted. Moreover, overt praise might even be a sign that a character was seriously in doubt. (Note the way the doctor ends his response to the father with 'you think' – a qualification never made for mothers.)

(2) *Ceremonial orders:* The second and third qualifications involve key aspects of Goffman's theory of etiquette which, though important, I have left for discussion until now. The first concerns the crucial issue of the *plurality* of ritual orders. Is the same set of events and roles, the same

activity system (Goffman 1961b: 8) framed in just one standard fashion, all variations being simply variations on a theme, or must we speak of etiquettes instead of etiquette; of distinctive ceremonial orders, each with their own motif?

Goffman's own position is hard to judge. I have found no clear statement of his general views on the matter. However, his analysis of service encounters does imply that, here at least, there is only one basic, ritual order; that there is an 'ideal model' (Goffman 1961a: 326–9) which shapes the etiquette of every service encounter. There is thus a suspicion that, for all its sophistication, his own model of the ceremonial world still carries some of the unitary assumptions favoured in traditional role analysis – the implicit belief that each and every role relationship has just one socially specified form, thus allowing us to talk of the 'doctor's role', the 'patient's role' and so forth. But this is uncertain.

What he definitely says – at great length and in several different versions – is that within any one order, there can be many reasons for variation. Particular circumstances may not readily fit with the ideal roles (1961c); participants are often allowed a degree of 'distance' (1961b) from the roles they are given to portray; the original frame may serve as a base from which all kinds of transformations or keyings (jokes, rehearsals, etc.) may occur during the encounter (1974); and, finally, though a slightly different point, any one 'strip of action' (1974) may contain a series of different activities, each of which has a different frame.

All this can readily be granted; my discussion of the paediatric research has already shown some of the many variations that can occur within a single order. However, what that research also revealed was that amongst these consultations there were at least three basic ritual orders. The 'ideal model' which Goffman sketched of the server–client relationship was certainly among these but it was not the only one. Indeed, his assumption of just one ideal form looks rather parochial: ethnocentric, ahistorical and middle class.

The most common type of ceremonial order in my particular data set has already been described at some length. What I eventually termed the *bureaucratic format* was standard in every Scottish NHS consultation, and was also used with most non-fee-paying American patients. But there was in addition, as we have also seen, a *private* mode in routine use for the fee-paying patients (this is the model that Goffman describes as the ideal). And, as well as these – and not so far discussed – there was what might be called a *charity* mode, used for the very poor by one American doctor. The charity format is of some interest both for itself and for the other modes.

Consider the following extract:

Doctor: Are there any other problems?
Mother: Well he chews cigarette ends ... (she laughs) ... It's very difficult
 to stop him.
Doctor: Why are you laughing? Do you think it's funny?
Mother: No, I don't think it's funny.
Doctor: Well, why did you laugh then? Do you always laugh at this?[8]

             (Strong 1979: 44)

The private mode was like the bureaucratic mode in that mothers' character was idealized. But in the charity format the principle was reversed; the initial rule here being that every mother was now stupid, lazy, incompetent and unloving, unless she could prove otherwise. Thus, this particular ritual order contained, as one of its central ingredients, the overt and detailed investigation of the moral character of a key participant. Such investigation (which I term *character work*) is a very different kind of moral work to the cosmetic face work of the two ritual orders discussed so far. In these others, doctors glossed over the vast array of potentially discrediting material that medical inquiry necessarily revealed. In the charity format, by contrast, the doctor publicly seized on every shred of such evidence.

 This discovery of radically different expressive orders, co-existing within the same type of encounter, is not, from a common sense point of view, particularly surprising. Indeed, within the medical arena, it merely confirms the long-held view that doctors and patients behave in very different ways according to their relative status and the commercial basis of the transaction.[9] However, it seems to be an important break from Goffman's own discussion of the ritual order. For once we admit the possibility that the same activity may be ritually framed in very different ways, then we also give space for a mechanism through which systematic variations in the balance of power between participants may, in turn, have systematic effects upon the ritual order of their encounters.

---

 8 The field notes on this particular doctor were not (unlike the rest) written verbatim at the time, but reconstructed immediately afterwards in the clinic's lavatory.

 9 'To put it rather unofficially ... to put it rather crudely, in an (NHS) out-patient session, the patient listens to the doctor, whereas in a private practice, the consultant listens to the patient' (Sir Thomas Holmes Sellors, a consultant giving evidence to the Pilkington Commission on doctors' pay in 1958, cited in Ferris 1967: 34).

(3) *The micro and the macro worlds:* At various odd points in Goffman's work, but particularly in 'Fun and games' (1961b) and in 'The interaction order' (1983b), a quick sketch is attempted of the relations between the micro and the macro. Here is a typical comment:

> An encounter provides a world for its participants but the character and stability of this world is intimately related to its selective relationship to the wider one. The naturalistic study of encounters, then, is more closely tied to studies of social structure on one hand, and more separate from them, than one might at first imagine.
>
> (Goffman 1961b: 80)

Goffman makes several other points too on micro–macro relations: that external effects are a mixed bag (and in some encounters as much weight may be given to noise as to social class); that some powerful external features are excluded from the ritual order while others take a rather different shape; that we can therefore speak of a *membrane* (1961c: 65–6) which surrounds the little world of the encounter, and of *transformation rules* which determine whether, and in what manner, the outside world may officially intrude; and, finally, that his own work had little relevance to the macro world (or to its students):[10]

> I make no claim to be talking about the core matters of sociology – social organization and social structure. These matters have been and can continue to be quite nicely studied without reference to frame at all ... I personally hold society to be first in every way and any individuals current involvements to be second ...
>
> (Goffman 1974: 13)

This last quotation displays several important things about Goffman's views on the macro-social world: that he held it to be more important; that he wasn't himself that interested in it (his insistence on talking solely about the micro was not confined solely to *Frame Analysis*); and, finally, that he didn't think core sociology needed to bother itself with the interaction order. On the basis of my paediatric research, I want to agree with the first, discuss the second and challenge the third of these propositions.

Let's begin with the second: the notion that, to put it most strongly, Goffman respected the power of macro phenomena but was (sociologically) bored by them. 'Fun in games', the first paper in *Encounters* (1961b) analyses the links between the micro and the macro worlds, emphasizing

---

10 Attempts such as Collins (1981) to enlist him in the cause of micro imperialism and assert the priority of the micro over the macro realm were firmly squashed (Goffman 1983).

both the power of the ties and the importance of the separation. But, in practice, almost all his examples are of ways in which the encounter is systematically detached from the outer world and, though he introduces the notion of transformation rules, he gives no serious instances of such rules. Twenty years later, in 'The interaction order' (1983b), the story is much the same. Though he emphasizes, once again, the priority of the macro, what he wants primarily to focus on is the separation, not the tie. Interactional practices, so he stresses, are only *loosely coupled* to the wider social structure, at least in our society. There is never a one-to-one relationship.

Why did he touch on but then ignore the crucial macro dimension? The answer, I think, lies in Goffman's particular interest in ceremony. What he loved to look at, above all else, was not the ceremony itself but the complex relationship between the individual and the ritual,[11] an interest which my paper has scarcely touched upon. Thus, while the macro is recognized, it doesn't particularly concern him. One can certainly produce, as Rogers (1980) has most valuably done, a reconstruction of what Goffman's theories imply about power, hierarchy and status, but these are not topics which he himself systematically explored. Nonetheless, the fact that he did not, does not mean we cannot. Indeed, it only makes sense to stress loose-coupling, if we also recognize the phenomenon of *tight-coupling* too; that particular power is liable to breed particular ceremony.

Like all social-science generalizations, this is only a rule of thumb, not a universal law. There will always be exceptions. Not every encounter will be tightly coupled to the external world. Likewise, even where there are tight links, not every detail of the ritual order will be so linked, and there will certainly never be a one-to-one specification such that members of a particular status will invariably be addressed in a distinctive fashion; the modern world is not like that (Goffman 1983: 11–12). Moreover, the average encounter will also have a penumbra of ritual practices which are rarely, never or only loosely coupled to the wider social structure. However, what does need stressing is that such a penumbra will often surround a solid core, a central ceremony which stems from and is tightly linked to the outer world.

What's the evidence for this? I can only offer the findings from my own research which dealt solely with server–client relations – and indeed with

---

11 As with frame, Goffman's model of the individual is Janus-faced. On the one hand, people are either puppets, mere devices for creating and sustaining ceremony, or else victims, trapped helplessly within frames unable to escape. On the other hand, and more optimistically, they are also subtle manipulators of frame, endlessly either using the ritual order to achieve their own ends, or else, cunningly slipping away, creating margins of freedom for their own interests and identity.

Table 1 Four types of consultation etiquette

Ritual style	Distribution of power	Type of moral work	Medical authority
Aristocratic[a]	V. high patient V. low doctor	Face work + character work by patient on Dr	Individual
Private	Medium patient Medium doctor	Face work	Individual
Bureaucratic	Low patient High doctor	Face work	*Ex officio*
Charity	V. low patient V. high doctor	Face work + character work by Dr on patient	*Ex officio*

[a]The aristocratic mode is not to be found in any of the consultations in my study. However, something like it may well have been true in the past. See, for example, Jewson's (1974) account of the problems faced by some 18th-century doctors when their patient was an aristocratic amateur scholar who dabbled in medical theory.

one limited form of that. Nonetheless, an intriguing relationship (Table 1) did emerge between the different ceremonial orders and particular balances of power; a relationship which *a priori* seems true not just of paediatric clinics but of many other kinds of customer service, and one which can also be illustrated from a wide variety of other research.[12]

Such a model needs a good deal of further empirical testing and, besides, even if correct, it is only one of the many, many links which bind the micro to the macro worlds, all of which need detailed exploration.[13] However, if such a programme of research were ever to be undertaken, it might no longer be possible to claim that the core matters of sociology

---

12 Three of these relationships are based principally on my own research. However, Silverman (1981, 1984) has subsequently found further evidence to support the analysis of the private and bureaucratic formats, while Dingwall, Eekelaar and Murray (1983) have shown that the latter relationship exists in client relationships with social workers as well as with doctors. There is also supporting evidence for the bureaucratic and charity frames from other contemporary research which, though not using this vocabulary, may still be interpreted in these terms (see Strong 1979: 198–201). Historical versions of the charity mode may be discerned in Ferris (1967: 200), Turner (1958: 102–3) and (an intriguing variant) in Bulgakov (1975) – see Strong 1983b.

13 A very tentative description of another such link is described in Strong and Dingwall (1983) and Dingwall and Strong (1985).

could be nicely studied without any reference to the interaction order. But of course, so far at least, we are a very long way off that.

Note

I would like to thank Robert Dingwall, Paul Drew, Anne Murcott and Tony Wootton for their extensive comments on earlier drafts of this paper.

Chapter 4

Two Types of Ceremonial Order

Introduction

However tiny our focus on health encounters may be, all human life is there; or a good deal of it. Meetings between staff and patients involve both culture and biology, history as much as psychology, the economy as well as medicine. The work described in this paper is, therefore, both modest and ambitious. Modest because it can only touch on a small fraction of the complexity of health care encounters; ambitious because unless we can, in effect, see the world in a grain of sand, we will not get very far in understanding that grain.[1]

The paper offers two very different perspectives on health care encounters. The first is a close-up of paediatric consultation; so close up that we are actually inside particular encounters, peering at the minutiae of the way doctors and patients talk with one another, inspecting the powers and the overt etiquette of the occasion. The second very different view resembles a rather confusing TV documentary, shot from a helicopter, in which a whole city or country is filmed rapidly from far above. The subject is a public debate over AIDS in 1987. This part of the paper examines an extraordinary mix of claims and fears about what was happening across the UK – and remedies as to how it could be put right; all of them the product of a parliamentary inquiry into the crisis.

Public debate about the threat of an epidemic may seem a long way from the minutiae of routine paediatric consultation. Both, however, have more in common than might initially be expected. Talk in both circumstances seems to involve a special, social ritual – the systematic

1   For helping me see some of the things in this paper, I must thank Anne Murcott, Virginia Berridge and the participants at the Botkyrka conference, in particular Viveka Adelswärd, Karin Aronsson, Sonja Olin Lauritzen, Ingrid Lundberg, Lisbeth Sachs, Roger Säljö and Charles Westin. Similar thanks are also due to the generous funders of the two projects described here: the (then) Social Science Research Council and the Medical Research Council for the paediatric project; the Nuffield Provincial Hospitals' Trust for the AIDS project. This latter study is part of a larger, ongoing programme of research into the Social History of AIDS in the UK.

invocation of an idealized world. A model society is conjured up with its own self-sustaining, moral and technical division of labour, identity and authority. Whatever people want to say must be said through the grid imposed by the functionalist, rhetorical etiquette. Yet, precisely because that grid is always there, it is rarely, if ever, seen. This paper is about that grid: why it is there, ways in which to make invisible, the similarities and differences between its various forms; the way it seems to link both the micro and the macro worlds in which we live.

This is, however, an exploratory work. No certain answers can be given to any of the questions posed. Nor is it known how far that ritual extends – whether, for example, it covers each and every form of social interaction, or just these two. The nature of the ritual grid has been relatively little explored and the AIDS work is still not completed. For all this, it seems plausible to suppose that it may be a much more general phenomenon. Paying close comparative attention to the functionalist social rhetoric invoked in such apparently disparate matters may help us understand its mysteries a little better and, thus, know more about its possible consequences for the actual world in which we live.

The two empirical parts of the paper, therefore, possess a common conceptual core. The core stems primarily from the model of encounters and ritual developed by Erving Goffman. The paper begins with an account of his work; outlines methods for systematically applying his model to interactional data; extends it to capture links between the micro and the macro worlds; then considers the two case-studies: the paediatric consultations and the AIDS public debate and what they reveal about the functionalist etiquette through which we seem to live a key part of our social lives.

Functionalism as Etiquette and Rhetoric: Goffman's Model of the Encounter

Descriptions of Goffman's complex and overlapping arguments can be found in a variety of secondary works (Ditton 1980, Collins 1985, Drew & Wootton 1988, Turner 1988, Burns 1992, Strong 1983a, Strong 1988). My own reading is this. Although, at heart, a Durkheimian, what obsessed Goffman was the collective psychology, not of the wider group or the whole society but of the miniature world of focused, face-to-face interaction. Such encounters, as he called these small-scale worlds, take many forms: from conversations to court proceedings, from boxing-matches to seminars. Despite this huge diversity, they share a few things in common. Each encounter is a kind of game which, like all games, depends for its existence on some prior legislation. Obeying these rules transforms the raw material of everyday life into distinct, ordered and meaningful occasions. Little children turn themselves into soldiers; old clothes into uniforms; chairs and tables into forts. Adults, likewise, become lovers, parents, citizens and shoppers, as the occasion fits.[2]

Goffman makes several suggestions as to how this can come to generate an all-enveloping force and reality for its participants. The rules for any encounter are typically embodied in unspoken agreement about an apparently trivial matter, good manners. Manners are fundamental to the allocation and constitution of proper action and identity.[3] What is to be done, who gets to do it, how they do it and when: all these things are prescribed by the etiquette appropriate to particular occasions.

Each encounter is, thus, a separate little society with its own tacit ceremonial order; its special vocabulary for the public description of actors, actions, circumstances, morals and motives. This order prescribes an idealized version of each of the participants and the events in which they engage. The particular rules of relevance and irrelevance which shape each occasion portray the enclosed interaction as a single, harmonious system in which each contributes to the greater good; all the players are suited to and know their parts. Incompatible behaviours, facts and identities are overtly ignored or glossed over; at least on most occasions.

As such, but only in a very special sense, Goffman is a kind of functionalist; a temporary, bounded micro-functionalist of appearances. He writes of self-equilibrating systems, but these are to be found solely at the level of face-to-face interaction, and not in society as a whole. Moreover, this micro-functionalism deals only with surfaces. Overt harmony is typically maintained but only through systematic avoidance, disregard and, when necessary, cosmetic repair-work. There is no invisible hand. Instead, all the participants must play a part in mutually sustaining the fictions of these little worlds if life is to be breathed into the microcosms in which we actually live. His micro-functionalism is, thus, a matter of routine etiquette, of ceremonial duty; not something which everyone necessarily believes or internally acts upon. We live, so Goffman seems to argue, not

---

2 Goffman was not, however, a reductionist. At the beginning of *The Presentation of Self in Everyday Life,* where he first outlined his model in some detail, he took care to emphasize that this was merely one perspective among the many that were needed and he focused on it simply because it had been seriously neglected in the past (Goffman, 1959).

3 In everyday social life, etiquette and ontology are inseparable.

in an actually functionalist society but in a world of functionalist social rhetoric.[4]

One key task, therefore, for the cultural analyst[5] is to examine the way this rhetoric works in particular types of encounter; to show, in detail, the constraints and opportunities it creates for the participants and the things they wish to do or to avoid. Such an examination requires us to go well beyond the etiquette itself. Unlike other functionalist models of society, harmony here rests on a hidden and shifting balance of power and interest; interaction is Janus-faced. Goffman's model is, thus Hobbesian as well as Durkheimian. The overt argument is purely temporary "working consensus". What we do or say on other occasions and with other people may be very different.[6]

Finally, because of the potential discrepancy between what is open and what is hidden, between what is claimed and the mundane circumstances of our lives, between our real and overt interests, between our behaviour now and with other people in other encounters, tension surrounds certain events, topics and situations. A handful of particularly awkward encounters requires huge amounts of repair-work if the interaction is to be

---

4   I am not aware of Goffman himself having used this vocabulary – perhaps because he was at pains to distinguish himself from the Parsonian model that then dominated North American sociology. However, I think he does use a functionalist approach – though only in the most unusual sense in which I characterize it here.

5   To study encounters, to examine etiquette, face-work, framing and ceremonial order, is to grasp a central part of culture in its immediate, lived form. Wuthnow puts the argument like this: "It was once commonplace for theorists and researchers in the social sciences to speak of culture as if it consisted of deep norms and values, beliefs and orientations, predispositions and assumptions – all with an implicit stability and orderliness to which speech and action merely gave expression. Now, an increasing number of scholars question the fixity, even the reality of these unobservables. Increasingly speech and action themselves have risen to prominence, losing the superficiality of their earlier reflective character and becoming the constitutive features of social reality itself." (Wuthnow 1992).

6   Goffman's position has an interesting resemblance to the Scottish Enlightenment view of human nature: "Ferguson's man in civil society is animated by what Adam Smith calls both 'social' and 'unsocial' passions, with 'selfish' passions in a 'sort of middle place between them'. He has a 'mixed disposition to friendship or enmity' and 'dissension', 'war' and 'amity', 'affection' and 'fear'. Most of all he is, like Humean man, 'partial', in that he is bound to others by localized bonds of both cohesive and divisive partisanships which mutually nourish each other: the 'dis-interested passions' of love and hatred go together, the divisive hatred of enemies promoting the cohesive love of friends." (Burchell, 1991: 135) Goffman's dramaturgic point is obviously different from any of those mentioned by the Scottish students of human nature but seems wholly complementary.

sustained; all involve routine maintenance; only a few will be an occasion for sustained "spontaneity".

Encounters, Quasi-encounters and Micro–macro Relationships

The work described in this paper derives from the model of encounter etiquette described above but breaks with it in two respects. It extends the range of events to which encounter analysis can be applied, and it moves beyond Goffman's highly limited version of the relationship between the micro world of the encounter and the macro worlds which surround it.

Consider the range of encounter first. Public debate, as its name suggests, is made up both of encounters and of what may be termed *quasi-encounters* with many of the distinctive properties of more smaller-scale interaction. Moreover, not only is public debate partially constituted through encounters but a good deal of its subject matter concerns the nature, structure and etiquette of other encounters – what they are and what they ought to be. The good society is invoked and the good forms of interaction which supposedly create that society are held up for scrutiny, perhaps even reform, or in some fashion specified. Likewise, the actual forms are revealed – or concealed – depending on the purposes of the debaters. In short, we cannot understand the distinctive nature of public debate unless we examine it with a micro as well as a macro focus. Goffman's model may, therefore, be extended to cover a much wider range of phenomena than he himself covered.

The break with Goffman's analysis of micro–macro relationships is a more complex affair. Goffman argued that a kind of membrane surrounds and separates each encounter, a membrane with its own transformation rules which determine whether and in what manner external matters may officially intrude. Some powerful external features may be officially excluded from the ritual order of an encounter, while those that do get inside must dress to suit local custom and circumstance (as much overt weight may be given, say, to noise as to social class). Thus, the micro-social world is not a transparent, socially neutral medium through which macro forces operate unchecked and unimpaired but resides in its own partially independent realm.

At the same time, despite this partial independence of the micro realm, Goffman considered that macro-social matters were, in the end, much more important in shaping human affairs. As he took care to note: "I personally consider society to be first in every way and any individual's current involvements to be second ..." (Goffman 1974: 13). Some of his followers have proclaimed a form of micro-imperialism.[7] Goffman did not.

Goffman's broad claims on both these matters strike me as essentially correct. However, though he stresses the primacy of the macro level, whenever he analyses the links between the macro and the micro worlds, his account is always biased towards micro-social features. Though he invents for example the idea of transformation rules – local principles through which macro matters are modified in particular interaction contexts – he neglects to give any detailed instances of these. Though he stresses the priority of the macro over the micro what he actually focuses on is the separation not the tie between the two. Above all he claimed that, "the core matters of sociology – social organization and social structure – ... have been and can continue to be quite nicely studied without reference to frame at all".

This bias presents difficulties for those who wish to build on the foundations which Goffman laid. Any coherent social theory needs both a micro and a macro arm. However, if Goffman's model of ceremonial order and its functionalist rhetoric is basically right, then it should be possible to specify some of the ways in which encounters are systematically linked with the macro-social arena and the effects such links have, both on individual encounters and on the external social world. This paper suggests one way in which this connection might begin to be made.

Methods

Goffman's typical way of working was to collect a huge range of examples chosen from many different walks of life, then generalize from these.[8] His corpus of data was, therefore, vast but not systematically specified. Such a technique, while essential for the initial exploration and delineation of a field, needs serious modification by the plodders who work at the narrower task of local excavation. However, plodding presents its own

---

7   See Collins 1975. Some earlier versions of conversation analysis also, to my mind at least, contained elements of micro-imperialism.

8   Goffman could in fact work very closely with a particular corpus. *Gender Advertisements,* (1976) is a wonderful example of what he could do. However, this was not his standard method of procedure.

special problems. Systematic, empirical advance in applying his ideas has typically been slow.[9]

What sort of methods are most appropriate to a systematic analysis of ritual form? The approach described here has several components.[10] The first involves the construction of an appropriate corpus of data. Face-to-face interaction creates coherent little worlds, each with systematic properties which can be detected through methodical study. Single specimens can be recorded at one go by a single witness or tape-recorder. Samples of different specimens may be readily gathered. The basis of the consultation analysis is, therefore, provided by an observational study, using semi-verbatim written recordings of paediatric consultations, one thousand or so in a Scottish city, around one hundred more in an American city. Subsequent development of this analysis has been grounded in other systematic studies as well as more fugitive ethnographic materials.

Constructing an appropriate corpus for public debate presents a much harder task. Individual items of debate have their own coherence and may be analysed rigorously. But the world of public debate is made up of an unknown number of such items, constituted in many different ways and each related to one another in an opaque, often unknowable fashion. For the whole study I have chosen a small cross-section of the debate over AIDS, limiting my analysis to the four months of a parliamentary inquiry in 1987 and, within that period, to the inquiry itself (Social Services Committee 1987) to the national press and to television programmes. Only the parliamentary committee data are used in this paper, and a small portion of them at that. They do seem to contain clear regularities. But they are instances from a single type of data and from (relatively) straightforward encounters. How far such regularities will extend across the other areas of AIDS debate in this period remains to be seen.

The second crucial method is to find conceptually interesting comparison groups (Garfinkel 1956). In the work described here, there are three main

---

9   The major exception has been conversation analysis, a much more formal approach created by some of his students, which has brought considerable progress, if on a more limited front than the one Goffman himself tried to explore. Schegloff (1988), reviews the subsequent battle between Goffman and his ex-students.

10   The type of plodding described here currently lacks a name. I tend to favour 'ethnographic micro-sociology', though Robert Dingwall has suggested 'ethnomethodological ethnography' to me. Both phrases are awkward, perhaps because the school is a hybrid, born in the 1970s of two distinct intellectual movements; ethnographic micro-sociology trying to learn from the new precision of the conversation analysts while retaining the interest in content, as well as form, of the older ethnographic tradition. Goffman was methodologically an ethnographer but conceptually helped inspire the conversation analysts.

contrasts of this kind: between different modes of Scottish and American etiquette in paediatric clinics; between different styles of self-presentation by the various interest groups who appeared as witnesses in the parliamentary inquiry into AIDS;[11] finally and most importantly, between the encounter forms and dimensions identified in both the consultation and public debate data.

The importance of such comparison may be illustrated by an example from the paediatric study. In the Scottish clinics, which I studied first, all I could see was variety. Observing a radically different health care system in the United States changed all that. When I returned to the Scottish data, the main thing that now struck me was the extraordinary similarity of one bit of Scottish material with another. The American comparison revealed a fundamental sameness in the etiquette of Scottish clinics that I had never noticed previously – and could not have seen until my eyes were opened by new sights abroad. Since we cannot normally see the ritual grids which we use to frame everyday social life, only dramatic contrasts can restore our vision.

Startling comparisons are, by themselves, insufficient to generate systematic analysis. To aid this, I have used the method of constant comparison (Glaser 1964) for the detailed study of each corpus. This is a general method for elaborating hypotheses about a complex phenomenon; a special form of coding which focuses much less on the counting of instances and much more on the generation of valid categories. It is, then, a taxonomic, not a survey method. Once basic analytic categories have been developed by the researcher, coding only takes place when one discovers variations from, exceptions to, or particularly dramatic instances of, a particular phenomenon. Each datum is therefore used as a check on the validity of the ideas and classifications that have gone before. The overall taxonomy is constantly modified as both the analysis and the

---

11 These data contain a cross-section of official statements – both memoranda and verbal evidence – from the key institutions, occupations and pressure groups then involved with AIDS in the UK. Here, in almost parodic form, is a cross-section of what might be characterized, from a Goffmanesque perspective, as professional and organizational self-presentation: nurses being nurses, policemen being policemen, lawyers being lawyers, insurers being insurers and so forth. Only a fragment of this comparative study is visible in this particular paper. (A more detailed example is contained in P. Strong, "What do professional ethicists do? A sociological study of parliamentary witness on AIDS", a paper given at the International Symposium on Ethical Issues in Social and Biomedical Research in Community Settings, Brunel, The University of West London, 13–14 April, 1992.

writing proceed. Indeed, it is not until the end of the first full draft that a stable classification begins to emerge.

Such a method involves a good deal more than coding. Detailed analytic notes have been made on any and every item that drew my attention. At the same time, the data that sparked the ideas were also written out in full. This writing out is fundamental to the analysis. Only through this – or some equivalent – can any detailed awareness of the intricacies of the material start to become possible.[12]

In some versions of constant comparison, the data are worked through several times, each trawl focusing on a different topic. This allows a more precise focus and captures more instances of a particular phenomenon. Here, however, I have, with some modifications, tried to analyse the entire corpus from beginning to end in just one, very slow, go. Such a procedure is less rigorous in some senses but is more suited to very large data bases. It also creates the possibility of a much broader perspective – though to do this means holding a much larger number of potential categories in one's head at any one time. However, since the later stages of the analysis produce a much more sophisticated set of ideas, it is often necessary to go back and re-analyse some of the early material. Since major re-thinking of key parts of the analysis usually takes place during writing, this too may require a return to the original data.

Constant comparison is an excellent method for creating and elaborating hypotheses. It is, however, rather poor at actually testing them. Analytic induction tries to cure this (Robinson 1951, Cressey 1971, Bloor 1978). In it, the researcher is urged to gather a small corpus of data to begin with; to analyse this, derive hypotheses from it, then test them on a further small corpus; proceeding in this crab-like fashion until no further body of data produces any modifications to the elaborated hypotheses. In the paediatric research, I used a simplified version of this ideal, dividing the 1100 consultations into two halves, analysing one half, writing the first draft on this basis, then testing the consequent hypotheses on the second half; a process which produced no major change but added both refinement and speed to the analysis. In the AIDS research, I am using a different version: analysing some data, writing a paper, analysing some more data, then writing a further paper, and so on. This is more complex but, so far, much more loosely specified; looser because I am still at the hypothesis generating stage and the papers range across very broad areas of inquiry.

---

12 This is an ethnographic parallel to the massively detailed transcription of tape-recordings pioneered by the conversation analysts; a technique that serves the same analytic purpose though at a much finer level of detail.

Only now I am beginning to focus down and use the precision that analytic induction requires.

Finally, one key theme runs through the use of comparison, constant comparison and analytic induction; the importance of the deviant case. Too often, the unusual or the odd is removed from the analytic corpus. "It only happened once" is the standard plea. But in comparative analysis deviant cases should be treasured. These are the exceptions that can help find and prove the rule (Strong 1979a). Besides, many of the key rules which govern encounters pass unspoken.[13] Noticing them is, therefore, extraordinarily difficult. Their spelling out occurs mainly when deviations from them have occurred and even then most aberrations are simply glossed over without comment. Moreover, some rules are so deeply embedded that even the participants themselves have no access to them. Finding deviant cases is, therefore, central to the task of locating such rules. And, once we have found what seems to be a general rule, the best way to test it is to examine what happens in extreme circumstances; is it bent and, if so, how? So once again, a search for deviant cases is in order. The paediatric data were thoroughly analysed in this fashion. As yet, the AIDS data have only been partially investigated.

The Ritual Structure of Health Care Encounters

One of the clearest pictures of the sorts of ritual order through which interaction seems to be framed can be found in the area of health care encounters. This section describes the findings of a large comparative study of the etiquette of paediatric consultation conducted in the 1970s and summarises the work of subsequent research which has tended to confirm these initial ideas.

The initial study revealed several distinctive forms of ceremonial order (elsewhere referred to in terms of role formats[14]) each linked to, though not wholly determined by, a particular balance of power. What made the ceremonial orders distinctive was the way each format uniquely combined two key variables: the amount and type of *technical authority* claimed by the participants; and the overt types of *moral work* that actors engaged in with respect to the other participants. A few striking examples can be given here to illustrate the general rules that seemed to be involved. Take

---

13 "A lot of life is about things so trivial that we do not bother to record them – only sometimes note their absence, as with manners." Oscar Wilde, cited in R. Shattuck, 1986, "Catching up with the avant-garde," *New York Review of Books,* 18 December, 66–74.

14 For discussion of terminology, see P. Strong, 1979a: 8–13.

authority first. The first extract comes from a Scottish National Health Service (NHS) clinic, the second and third are from American fee-for-service consultations. All the parents are middle-class but there are radical differences between the Scottish and American consultations in parental status and authority within the interaction:

(1) A Scottish NHS clinic
Doctor: What was Dr Maxwell (a psychiatrist) planning for her?
Mother: Well she said that someone would be seeing her. Someone interested in specific speech delay. Is that you?
Doctor: Well, I'm interested in it, but I don't think it could be me.
Mother: And the other person we'd be seeing is a paediatrician with an interest in coordination.
Doctor: That's me. The other one may be a psychologist (Strong 1979a: 75).

(2) First American fee-for-service consultation
Intern: How did you get here?
Mother: Well he's been seeing a psychiatrist and he diagnosed minimal brain dysfunction and prescribed X. But we also wanted to get Dr Stein's opinion as we felt we ought not just to have a psychiatrist's opinion.

(3) Second American fee-for-service consultation
Father: So it's a little early to do this right now?
Doctor: Right. We talk about this problem all the time at the moment and I've had discussions at (New York) and (Boston) hospitals with the experts in the field. I've spoken to Drs A, B and C about it. We're all very interested in it but it's early days yet ... Remember, it's not just me that's telling you this. I've talked to lots of people who know more about this than I do. (He names them again and adds more names.) And they all agree that it's too risky at the moment (Strong 1975a: 75).

These three quotations have been chosen because they dramatically illustrate one key difference between the bureaucratic form of ceremonial order characteristic of most NHS and some American consultations and the private or fee-for-service mode. Of course, not every encounter was as striking as this, but these examples do highlight key aspects of the systematic differences between the different role formats (Strong 1975a: 226–34[15]). Though some other interaction was less dramatic, the general

---

15 Demonstrating the truth of general propositions is a difficult business in qualitative work since, even where detailed analysis has been done, there is,

lessons still hold true. In bureaucratic consultations, medical staff were granted massive but anonymous medical expertise. Their authority was collective and *ex officio*. It went with the job and was, at least nominally, shared by everyone who was a doctor. Parents, however, were typically passive and granted little overt technical authority. In private consultations, by contrast, parents were customers with a choice and a presumed measure of expertise to go with that choice.

Thus, the middle-class Scottish mother had sat through a half hour consultation without knowing whether she was seeing a paediatrician or a specialist in speech delay – and had not liked to ask until the very end. The private patients, however, knew the name of the doctor they were seeing, could indicate if they were checking up on an earlier diagnosis and could clearly hint that they might also check on the opinion of the doctor they were now seeing. Moreover, in the private mode, not only might parents choose named individual physicians but doctors felt obliged to name their colleagues in similar fashion. Whereas the Scottish consultants merely referred to general discussions with unnamed experts elsewhere, the doctor in the second fee-for-service consultation felt obliged to mention specific individuals to whom he had talked (individuals whom the father might potentially consult). Thus, the doctor's authority was individual not collegial. His judgement in this particular case was warranted, not just by his being a doctor but by having talked with named experts. What was for sale here were individual skills and contacts. Colleagues were also competitors; patients could and did go elsewhere. So doctors had to display both their own skills and pass judgements on those of others. American doctors saw private patients not in the ordinary clinic but in their own room in the hospital, a room whose walls were covered with certificates from the medical schools they had attended. NHS patients, like non-fee-paying American patients, were seen in anonymous public rooms; rooms which matched the impersonal, *ex officio* style of the expertise in offer.

If technical authority was one major domain of variation in consultation etiquette, the other was the type and direction of the moral work that could legitimately be conducted therein. Consider three further extracts: each, again, chosen for its illustrative power. Whereas the first set of extracts concerned middle-class parents, all these deal with the very poor. The first and second example involve a doctor in a charity clinic in an American city; the third is from a local authority well-baby clinic in Scotland. Once again there are major differences in the forms of etiquette but, this time,

---

typically, sufficient space only for illustrative material to be used. Strong (1979: 226–34) describes the different ways I tried to demonstrate the existence of particular rules.

what is at stake is not the technical authority of doctor or mother, but the mother's moral status:[16]

(1) An American charity clinic
Doctor: What do you wash her diapers in?
Mother: Ivory Snow
Doctor: Why do you use Ivory Snow?
Mother: Well its supposed to make the diapers softer than other washing powders.
Doctor: How do you know Ivory Snow makes diapers softer?
Mother: (shrugs awkwardly) Well umm ... (mumbles in embarrassed fashion about advertisements)
Doctor: You don't want to believe everything you see in the adverts. It's a business. That's their business. Your business is your baby.
(2) An American charity clinic
Doctor: Are there any other problems?
Mother: Well he chews cigarette ends ... (she laughs) ... It's very difficult to stop him.
Doctor: Why are you laughing? Do you think it's funny?
Mother: No, I don't think it's funny.
Doctor: Well, why did you laugh then? Do you always laugh at this?[17]

(3) A Scottish well-baby clinic
Doctor: And you feed him on Farex?
Mother: In the morning and evening
Doctor: And porridge?
Mother: Aye.
Doctor: Does he get anything for elevenses?
Mother: Just biscuits ...
Doctor: How much does he get at lunchtime?
Mother: Oh, just mince (meat) and tatties (potatoes) ...
Doctor: And what does he get for his tea?
Mother: Oh, a boiled egg and a scrambled egg.
Doctor: And this is as well as milk?
Mother: Aye ...

---

16 In fact the doctor's moral status was also at issue, although that is not illustrated here. The American doctor, cited below, who strongly attacked the mothers she saw was implicitly criticized by one of the nurses who stepped in to defend one of the mothers.

17 Strong, P. 1979: 44. Unlike the other data in the study, all the data on this particular doctor was written up, not at the time, but in breaks in the clinic's lavatory. It is therefore much more reconstructed than the other material.

Doctor: If I were you, I'd miss out the Farex and the porridge at break-fast and the biscuit as well. It's best to do this now because if children get fat now they tend to be fatter later on in life. He's supposed to be twice his birthweight now (6 months) and he's a good bit more than that isn't he? (The baby, in fact, looks like a Michelin man). This is very important. He's putting on a bit too much weight.

All these three extracts illustrate one cardinal feature of encounters, one central aspect of their functionalist rhetoric – the idealization of the overt character of the participants. In the last extract, the baby is almost ludicrously overweight and the mother comes from a notorious family, known to health visitors for their incompetence for at least three generations. Yet the overt rule in the Scottish clinics was that every mother was a good mother, loving, honest, reliable, intelligent and caring, whatever she had actually done. Medical questioning which might potentially undermine this pristine image had to be conducted with some care. Here the doctor makes no mention of the mother's failure to follow nursing and medical advice, poses all her questions in a neutral fashion and phrases her advice as simply what she would do herself. Overtly the mother is a good mother who merely needs to be informed of the best way to proceed. By contrast, the doctor in the American clinic (in which the other doctors, however, behaved like their Scottish counterparts) used what might be termed a *charity* mode. This one doctor idealized mothers in the opposite direction. Those who were forced to attend a charity clinic had already proved their incompetence as mothers.[18] Thus, every mother in the clinic was, *a priori*, stupid, lazy, incompetent and unloving; unless she could prove otherwise (only one mother out of eleven did so to this particular clinician's satisfaction).

These different forms of idealization reflect the two broad types of moral work to be found in all forms of interaction. Given the idealization of the actors in every encounter's ceremonial order, constant attention needs to be paid to the minor blemishes which routinely threaten this ideal. Such *face-work*, as Goffman first noted (1955) and Aronsson (1994) has shown in great detail in medical consultation, is a central feature of all interaction work in which we must all share if the encounter is to proceed in a harmonious fashion. In the Scottish clinic, the baby's weight and the mother's incompetence together threatened the mother's overtly excellent

---

18 Two further short exchanges illustrate this point:

  a) Dr: "Have you got a job?" Mother: "No." Doctor: "Why not?"

  b) Dr: "Where do you live?" Mother: "Don't worry. I live in a real nice part of town."

Table 1. Four types of service etiquette*

Style	Power	Moral work	Authority
aristocratic	very high client very low server	face work + character work by client	individual
private	medium client medium server	face work	individual
bureaucratic	low client high server	face work	*ex officio*
charity	very low client very high server	face work + character work by server	*ex officio*

* Viveka Adelswärd points out that modern usage of alternative medicine has both private and aristocratic elements. Some of its clients, like the eighteenth-century aristocrats described by Jewson (1974, *op. cit*), are amateurs of alternative medicine.

character. The doctor had, therefore, to engage in constant, careful face-work in order to preserve it.

By contrast, although the mothers in the American charity clinic presented themselves as good mothers (and were defended as such by the nurses present in the clinic), that particular form of idealization was not permitted by the doctor in charge of the consultation. For her, a much more radical form of moral work was in order. *Character-work*, a term inspired by Garfinkel's note on degradation ceremonies (1956), aims not only to maintain or repair the presented ideal image but to reveal a radically different nature from that which is on display. Character-work is therefore the routine business of police interrogations and courtrooms – and is occasionally to be found in certain sorts of medical consultation. It too idealizes, but first it overturns a presented character then presents another, whether ideally bad or ideally good.

This section, then, has swiftly and crudely summarised two of the principal findings about the ceremonial order of the paediatric consultations in my study. However, the implications seem to go well beyond paediatrics. An initial review of research in a range of other staff–client relationships (Roth 1975, Stimson & Webb 1975, Byrne & Long 1976, Macintyre 1977, Stimson 1977, Jeffrey 1979) suggested that the three distinct types of ceremonial order which I have identified (bureaucratic, charity, and private) might be found in many other forms of medical relationships beyond paediatrics. And, subsequent to the paediatric study, there has

72 _Sociology and Medicine_

been a variety of work in medical and non-medical settings which draws explicitly on its own findings and provides rather better empirical warrant for such generalization. Indeed, the evidence suggests an ambitious model of four potential types of service etiquette that characterise different forms of provider-client relationships (see Table 1); a model which seems to apply to nursing and social work as well as medicine and may possibly apply to other forms of service relationship. (For further evidence which might support such a model, see Jewson 1974, Dingwall et al. 1983, Strong 1980, Strong 1983b, Silverman 1987, Lauritsen 1991, Thorogood 1992.)

Each of these four types is, in turn, determined by macro-social variables such as power, status, income and structural opportunity. As part and parcel of its own etiquette, each has its own division of technical and moral labour. Each type of etiquette also contains its own mode of functionalist rhetoric. In the modern private form, the individualized skill of the doctor is matched by the consumerist skills of the patients,[19] in the bureaucratic form, the ignorance of the patient is rendered safe by the certain skills possessed by every medical practitioner; in the charity form, maternal delinquency is rooted out and punished by a doctor come to judgement. The predominant etiquette in such encounters revolves around different modes of providing and receiving a service. All manner of things may be done in interaction but they must normally be done through a particular type of etiquette and the constraints and opportunities each type imposes.

Authority and Morality in Public Debate

Let us now turn to a very different set of encounters. This part of the paper moves from the sequestered locale of the medical consultation to a public forum, the Social Services Committee of the House of Commons. Health care encounters and types of etiquette are each still at issue, but here they are interlaced with one another in a more complex, even recursive, fashion than is the case with practitioner–client encounters. Nonetheless, the Goffmanesque analysis developed to elaborate the encounters between doctors and patients can be extended to unravel interaction in the public arena in question. Indeed its virtue lies in permitting access to the nub of the complexity. As will be seen, an analysis of the types of etiquette in the

---

19 Mother: "We liked him (Dr Levy) particularly because he was critical of schools and said, 'Don't believe what they say.' That's what got us here." Doctor: "True. It's very important work the Learning Disability Group does in building up consumer appreciation. There's gotta be a dialogue. It's the only way." (Strong 1979: 79)

public forum reveals the same major dimensions that were identified in the paediatric consultations. Once developed, the analysis readily exposes the nicety that a key part of the substance of the public forum encounter itself turns to concern types of etiquette.

Extending the analysis set out in the previous section depends on recognising that types of service etiquette are particular instances of the more general feature of all encounters, namely, their ceremonial order. Obviously, not all encounters entail a service, but dimensions detectable in service etiquette can be shown to occur in encounters which revolve around other rationales for interaction. The etiquette of the Social Services Committee of the House of Commons is highly distinctive. Its ceremonial order is, in principle, very formal, and on the surface, entrenched in an upper-class definition of good manners with a somewhat outdated air. At the same time, both dimensions evident in the service etiquette of paediatric encounters are found in the ceremonial order of the public forum devoted to enquiring into problems associated with AIDS.

Consider the first key dimension of encounter etiquette, that of technical authority. What sort of expertise, and in what areas, is to be overtly granted to the participants? This too turns out to be a central item in public debate. Consider two extracts from the minutes of evidence of the parliamentary inquiry into AIDS. The main witness is a senior Government Minister, Mr Kenneth Baker, then the Secretary of State at the Department of Education and Science. He, together with two doctors, Drs Cope and Pickles, is being questioned by the members of parliament (MPs) who sit on the committee:

(1)
Mr Powley (MP): Can I then ask will the MRC [Medical Research Council] (get) the full sum of £10 million a year which (it) is estimated would be needed to fund the AIDS research programme once it is running?
Mr Baker: ... I am responsible for the funding of the MRC, and I may call on Dr Cope in a moment (a doctor from the staff of MRC) ... before Christmas I announced an extra £1 million a year to fund general research on AIDS. That was a request from the MRC. When we agreed that ... we were told by the Chairman of the MRC, Sir James Gowans, that he would like to come forward with a further proposal ... He did

come forward and we accepted it completely. That proposal involved an extra £14½ million ... we accepted (it) in its totality.

Dr Cope: I do not think I need to add anything.

Mr Winterton (MP): How autonomous will the MRC be in the decisions on the directed research?

Mr Baker: ... The position is that the MRC are the experts upon this and we have taken their advice ... The MRC grant from my Department is normally given without direction as to how it should be spent; we are here in the hands of the professionals and the experts are very, very considerable ones, of course. There is the Laboratory for Molecular Biology at Cambridge which has been established for 40 years and there will be many other laboratories around the country engaged in this. However the Council will be constrained to spend extra money allocated for AIDS research on AIDS research. We will monitor it to ensure that it goes on AIDS research and not on other things. ...

(2)

Sir David Prince (MP): Secretary of State, from the evidence we have had so far, it is certainly clear to me that as a society we know less and less about the sexual practices of our fellow citizens ... When we have had professors of sociology in front of us they do admit there are great gaps in our knowledge of how we behave. It seems to me that this alone is a matter for rather more work to be done, in social research and through the ESRC [the Economic and Social Research Council funded by his Ministry] than appears from what you have said and the brief reference in your paper.

Mr Baker: ... it would appear from the evidence I have seen or the news that I have gathered, largely from the centres that deal with sexually transmitted diseases, that there has been a change of behavioural pattern, certainly among homosexuals ... You raise a much broader question of the general sexual behaviour of the whole of the population, and certainly that is more difficult to measure. I think that the groups most at risk of AIDS seem to be getting the message about it. That is the feeling one has. But when, in fact, you watch these programmes on television with young people the attitude of most young people – of the ones I have seen – is "Well, it is all very interesting we know all about the preventative measures but actually it is not going to happen to us ..." Could Dr Pickles say something on behavioural pattern? [Dr Pickles is the head of the AIDS Unit at the Department of Health and Social Services who has accompanied the Minister.]

Dr Pickles: This is actually a very, very difficult area as you can imagine. There is a fundamental problem in validating any research findings here because people may not clearly tell you what they do in private ... I think as a result of AIDS people have discovered they do not actually know what male homosexuals have been doing to each others over the years; they do not know the extent of homosexuality. This is really very important to us for planning purposes, in trying to calculate how the disease is going to be spreading, because we do not know how often people change sexual partners or how early they start ... At the conference that the Secretary of State for Social Services held about a fortnight ago, this was one of the conclusions, that we needed more information on sexual practices ... there is already some research that has been done; some research projects funded by the MRC. There has also been some good work done by the Central Office of Information over the last year where they have quizzed hundreds or rather thousands of people about their sexual practices (Social Services Committee 1987: 334).

Government Ministers have to appear credible as makers of state policy. In other words, if they are to be able to claim the right to determine how society – or some part of it – should operate, they first have to demonstrate that they possess relevant, specialized knowledge of how the society actually works and the British actually behave. A good deal of public debate, therefore, focuses, not just on what ought to happen in particular types of encounter, but on the equally problematic issue of what is actually happening and, in particular, how one knows about this. Thus, just as doctors display their technical expertise in one fashion or another, so too must Ministers – and they must do so in situations where that expertise is regularly and publicly challenged.

Baker does this with some skill. He first demonstrates that he knows about the changing incidence of sexually transmitted disease amongst male homosexuals as reported by clinics; the key indicator of substantial change in these particular sexual encounters. He also turns to an accompanying civil servant to show what other research has been undertaken and is envisaged. Ministers are not required to demonstrate that they themselves possess all the relevant expertise; merely that they have seriously consulted those who do know. Dr Pickles obliges. Next, consider Baker's remarks about television. These are particularly interesting in what they reveal of everyday assumptions about the nature of expertise in the social realm and how such expertise may be demonstrated. Research has obvious credibility in the eyes of academics – such as those who may read this article. The role of television is less obvious.

Television is treated by Baker as a part of collective personal experience which provides tolerably good documentary evidence to all who watch it –

and can, therefore, serve as a reasonable basis for authoritative comment. Consider his remark, "But when, in fact you watch these programmes on television". The references to "You" and to "these programmes" suggests that he is trying to point to a generally available experience; one that any of us can be typically assumed to have had, or might have had. These programmes are there for us to watch and we can watch them if we want. And, if we do watch them, the assumption seems to be that we will all draw much the same conclusions. Although the experience of the television documentary is indirect, it is treated here as a reasonable equivalent to direct experience – and such experience is thereby treated as sufficient and satisfactory knowledge. We can still hear and see what people do and say, even if we do so through another medium than direct interaction. We are still in an important sense sufficiently there; so much that we can incorporate it into our own personal experience and treat it as equivalent. Baker is careful to say that his own television watching may have been selective. But, this is no more than the aside anyone might add when recounting things based on their own, direct experience of a topic. The phenomena are still real and still experienced. Thus, there seems to be nothing shameful in ministers revealing that some of their opinions are based on television viewing. Or, more accurately, Baker does not think so and does not expect his audience to do so.

There will obviously be limits to this. It would have been odd, I suspect, if Baker had prefaced his earlier discussion of natural science funding by an account of what he had seen on *Horizon* (a major BBC science documentary series). Instead, he spoke at length about the expert nature of the advice he had received.[20] Likewise, Chancellors of the Exchequer do not say they got it all from *Money Box* (a BBC Radio 4 financial advice programme) if they wish to stay in office. Again reference to the Treasury and economic theory is advisable. However, when it comes to young peoples' attitudes, television appears to be treated as a way of establishing authority. Not the only way, of course – Baker uses others too – but a perfectly reasonable source when put alongside others. In this part of the encounter, then, protagonists are engaged in displaying and checking on the various warrants for their skill, expertise and knowledge

---

20 "The position is that the MRC (Medical Research Council) are the experts upon this and we have taken their advice, in effect ... The MRC grant from my Department is normally given without direction as to how it should be spent; we are here in the hands of the professionals and the experts are very, very, considerable ones, of course." Social Services Committee 1987: 332)

of the phenomena under discussion, in a fashion directly parallel to the requirement to parade technical authority in the paediatric consultation.

Now move on to examine the second key dimension of encounter etiquette, that of moral work. Consider the following extract from evidence to the parliamentary inquiry into AIDS. Mrs Renee Short MP, the chair of the Social Services Committee of the House of Commons, began this particular day's session with some questions to Mr W. Sutherland, the Chief Constable of Lothian and the Borders (a police district which includes Edinburgh, then as now the main centre of drug-related AIDS in the UK). The subject was the form of moral work and range of overt moral identities most appropriate to injecting illegal drug users and those public officials who had to deal with them:

Short: You are mostly involved with the sharing needles problem?
Sutherland: Yes, I suppose you could say we are mostly involved with the
    problem of drug abusers.
Short: Your reputation has gone before you. You are tough on drug users
    and abusers?
Sutherland: I would hope that would be true. I think it is important that we
    should be (Social Services Committee 1987: 217).

The meeting between Mrs Short and Mr Sutherland was, of course, an encounter in its own right with its own distinctive ceremonial order, its own special parliamentary etiquette. But this was an encounter of a most peculiar kind. At one level, it could be analysed solely in the terms which apply to any face-to-face interaction. Yet, at another level, it was a public event and part of a public debate about matters that not only involved the whole society but dealt centrally with the ceremonial orders appropriate to managing the grave problem at hand. This particular dialogue involved elected representatives and public officials, was held in a public place, was witnessed by reporters from the mass media. Its verbal content was transcribed and officially published within a few days of its occurrence by the elected parliament of the British people. Almost everyone in the society was both a potential witness of their dialogue and a potential participant in the wider moral forum of which their encounter was only one small part. Thus, these hearings had the power, potentially at least, to reformulate millions of other occasions, both official and private. Public debate can reshape the rules, identities and opportunities through which society is endlessly constituted and reconstituted.

The actual subject of this particular debate is already familiar from the analysis of the varied etiquettes that may be used in medical consultation. The dialogue between Mrs Short and Mr Sutherland reflects two very different approaches to AIDS, two very different styles for conducting encounters with heroin addicts. Is the real problem one of sharing needles or of drug abuse? Should one speak of drug abusers or talk instead of drug use? And is a tough response something of which one should be proud or ashamed? While both talk of a "problem", the way they talk about it suggests strongly that they disagree on its nature, on the sort of people who are involved and on the proper role of the authorities. In Goffmanesque language, they disagree fundamentally on the moral etiquette appropriate to official encounters with injecting drug users. One party recommends punitive or charity format and favours character-work. Stigmatization, in this view, is the proper moral and societally functional response. The other favours the more tolerant approach of the bureaucratic frame. For them, face-work is the proper societal response. Injecting drug users, like erring mothers, are still to be treated as part of the wider community; every junkie is a good junkie just as every mother is a good mother, no matter what she has done.

Finally, in public debate, as in the paediatric clinics, we can catch glimpses of an implicit functionalist rhetoric. Ministers portray themselves as wise and their wisdom is demonstrated by the authority of those they have consulted. Policemen portray themselves as tough and their toughness is vindicated by the degraded nature of those they police.

Concluding Observations

Thus, like medical consultation, the debates surrounding AIDS were shaped by competing ceremonial orders. There were, however, some important differences in the way this was done. *First level ceremonial orders,* such as those described in the paediatric clinic study, form a central part of an encounter's structure and are tied to particular actors, events and a particular temporality. The *second level ceremonial orders* to be found in the AIDS debate float free of particular people, time and space.[21] Second-level modes of etiquette come in blueprint form; they are models held up in debate as to what might or should be done in interaction, available for potential use in a vast number of possible future encounters. Such orders come in rather different forms from their encounter-based counterparts and play rather different roles. Nonetheless, they still have many properties in common. There is evidence of the same idealized vocabulary of motives,

---

21 The fact that ceremonial orders can exist quite apart from encounters is implied in *Asylums* (Goffman 1961a) and explicitly made in *Frame Analysis* (Goffman 1974) and Strong (1979a:183–94). However, all these treatments still focus essentially on embedded encounters and none draw out the implications considered here for macro analysis.

actions and roles; the same systematic transformation of mundane events into these idealized forms; the same sustained disregard for matters which do not readily fit; the same overt functionalism which conceals a working consensus covertly shaped by powerful interests.

Where, then, do the differences lie? Since second-level ceremonial orders are blueprints, they can be presented in a much wider variety of forms – in speech, writing, print, radio and television. Unlike their first-level working counterparts, they are not so immediately tied to the distinctive medium of interpersonal interaction. Not only can they appear in a much wider range of media but their scope is also far more extensive. As very general types of instruction, they can potentially guide a great variety of actual interactions; indeed, they may attempt to specify basic ceremonial orders for whole sectors of a society. At the same time, since they are sets of instructions, rather than embodied practices, they are typically far more explicit. The etiquette which is embedded within the first-level encounters is normally tacit or implied, rarely directly stated. But second-level ceremonial orders are always deliberately spelt out for others to consider, copy, modify or reject. Moreover, since they are still only blueprints, they are also, in one most important sense, inert.[22] The working etiquette embedded as a first level within encounters is constantly subject to the unforeseen twists and turns of actual interaction. By contrast, the formal sets of rules found in second-level ceremonial orders are static rather than dynamic and unable to specify all the circumstances of their application.[23]

Finally, given the much more explicit nature of second-level ceremonial orders, all these features can take on a highly dramatic public form. In *The Presentation of Self in Everyday Life* (1959) Goffman took a theatrical analogy and systematically applied it to mundane interaction. My point here is that we need to think the other way too. All the world can, indeed, be valuably seen as a stage but in public action and interaction

22 Morris, J. Paradox in the discourse of science, in Wuthnow, 1992: 94, gives a useful summary of the differences between the spoken and the written word.

23 This is a standard point in micro-sociology. Garfinkel (1967) is the classic source. Jonathan Grimshaw from Body Positive gave a vivid example to the Social Services Committee: "If you take the case of a young man now who may have read the Government's health education information, he decides to start using condoms. Now he has read the information; it has made him take some action, but at a party, for example, he meets a girl and they go to bed and he gets out the condom. The girl turns round and says, 'What are you doing that for? I'm on the pill.' Now how does he deal with that situation?" (SSC: 25/2/1987:105). Over time, however, the blueprints found in detached ceremonial orders can still evolve, sometimes quite rapidly, to meet the demands of new situations and events. AIDS has been a classic example of such rapid evolution in the public sphere.

this dramaturgical quality is considerably heightened. Politicians are made up before they appear on television and are now partly selected for their ability to appear at ease in front of the camera. Many of the media in which second-level ceremonial orders are manifested have a far greater dramatic form. Tape and film are normally edited so that they focus solely on highlights. Written prose is polished and repolished so that it bears little resemblance to the everyday burblings found in most face-to-face encounters.[24]

This heightened dramatic quality is further enhanced by the public nature of the action. The public arena is evaluated according to public criteria. In theory, at least, everyone who appears within it must give a satisfactory report of their actions. Institutions such as the parliamentary committee that investigated AIDS use a semi-judicial vocabulary; they "examine witnesses" and publish minutes of "evidence". Public debate and inquiry, therefore, has its own distinctive rhetoric, the language of "accounts"; a special sort of vocabulary in which everyone is continuously obliged to demonstrate that they are acting in proper ways and from appropriate motives.

To sum up: what has been presented here extends an analysis of ceremonial orders in the small-scale intimacy of service encounters to the dramatically different arena of public debate about a major threat to public health and public order. In the process a further layer is exposed; the first-level ceremonial order co-exists in the public arena with a second-level whose substance is, itself, the question of apposite ceremonial orders. In any one encounter – of which an exchange during the conduct of the Social Service Committee's deliberations is an example every bit as much as is a paediatric consultation – the participants usually manage to sustain an overt consensus on tasks and identities as an integral part of the first-level ceremonial order. In the case of public debate, the addition of the second-level ceremonial order enshrines the maintenance of a single mode of etiquette across a myriad of different distant encounters.[25] So doing is a task of quite extraordinary difficulty. That it may sometimes be achieved, that it may even be thought possible to achieve, is, in turn, a quite extraordinary fact about ourselves and about human society.

---

24 The parliamentary minutes of evidence are, of course, an example of the latter but the selective use made of them by most media means that what we typically see of them resembles the former.

25 Quite how this is achieved is a topic pursued in P. Strong, 1992, "Constructing a national moral order", paper presented at the British Sociological Association Medical Study Croup and European Society of Medical Sociology joint conference "Health in Europe: diversity, integration and change" Edinburgh University, 18–21 September, 1992.

PART 2
Professional Place, Occupational Boundary

Chapter 5

Sociological Imperialism and the Profession of Medicine – A Critical Examination of the Thesis of Medical Imperialism

The thesis of "medical imperialism"', that is of the increasing and illegitimate medicalization of the social world, is one of the most influential recent developments in the sociologies of deviance and medicine. Part of its attraction lies in its generality. Most researchers are concerned with problems that are far smaller in scale and yet they still have a need for some overall picture into which they can fit both their own research findings and the wider thoughts that occur to them in their daily lives and in their general reading. This polemical essay, which is a reflection upon the nature of the critique and a discussion of the conditions for successful medicalization, has itself grown out of these more mundane concerns. The difficulties encountered in trying to reconcile the data from my own fieldwork with some of the more extreme claims made by those who write of medical imperialism has led me to believe that this thesis, although containing much that is of value, is nevertheless, in certain respects, both exaggerated and self-serving.

The argument will take the following form: after briefly reviewing the modern analysis of professional imperialism particularly that of medicine, I shall apply the same method to sociology and argue that, as a fellow-profession within bourgeois society, it too has imperial ambitions and opportunities. A sociological critique of medicine, however radical, cannot be disinterested for, whatever its intentions, it also serves to advance the sociologists' own cause. Thus, ambition may lead sociology to distort the nature of medical imperialism and exaggerate its threat; to overlook the limits to medical expansion that currently exist within our society and, finally, to neglect the potential danger posed by its own imperialism and that of its allies.

Never Trust an Expert – The Sociological Critique

Although distrust of doctors seems to be a fairly widespread phenomenon, *vide* G.B. Shaw, its clearest and most systematic articulation has been largely an American product. The libertarianism of American social thought when coupled with the anti-intellectual tradition noted by Hofstadter (1963)[1] (to which it is of course related) has led some American sociologists into a sustained attack upon the power and privileges of experts. The critique of medical imperialism is thus merely one part of a general debunking of professional pretensions. The basic assumptions of this wider thesis may be stated thus:

(1) That there is an increasing tendency to assign the handling of social problems to full-time professions and professionals, the latter often working in ever-larger bureaucracies, i.e. there are more professions, more professionals, and more bureaucracies;

(2) That individual professions seek a monopoly of certain kinds of service provision or problem solution – barring activity both by other types of professional and by the laity;

(3) That professions do not simply supply a service that is predefined by their clientele but tend to control the nature of that service and the criteria by which good and bad work is to be judged:

> Not merely do the practitioners, by virtue of gaining admission to the charmed circle of colleagues, individually exercise the licence to do things others do not, but collectively they presume to tell society what is good and right for the individual and for society at large in some aspect of life. Indeed, they set the very terms in which people may think about this aspect of life Hughes (1968).

(4) That the aspect of life which professions seek to control is not restricted to their original remit; rather, it is in the nature of professions to seek to expand their empire, to redefine others' problems in their own terms and to discover wholly new ones for which they alone can provide solutions:

> All viable professions contain tendencies to transcend the limits of traditionally ascribed and assumed competence ... the growth of professions consists only in part of the expansion of inherent principle and in larger part of *ad hoc* responses to changing conditions (Bittner 1968: 424).

---

1 Hawthorn (1976) notes this anti-intellectual tradition but sees it as a blight upon American sociology, failing to see that it had its own highly valuable intellectual consequences.

(5) That the "needs" which professions service or the "problems" which they solve are capable of indefinite expansion. Traditionally human needs have been seen in absolutist not relative terms and have been tied to some supposedly fixed "biological" standard. The general realization that needs or problems were not given but were a product, in one vital sense, of human definition, has come from a growing awareness that poverty did not disappear with increased wealth, nor was illness conquered by the creation of a national health service and that the very agencies which dealt with problems played a central role in their discovery and growth.[2]

(6) That given the relative nature of need and the highly flexible nature of professions, any one profession is capable of potentially limitless expansion and can indeed encompass the whole of human life. Bittner has argued that historically, first religion and then law have achieved this position in the thought and structure of Western societies. Here for instance is his description of the place of law in American society of the late 18th century:

> Legal terms and ideas became autonomously meaningful and were perceived to have a general relevance for life that could be grasped directly without presuming an outside interpretative background. In fact, they moved into the position of being the background for thinking about collective life, and their availability exerted a strong pressure towards finding in the law the grounds for virtually every form of human enterprise and a solution for virtually all human problems (Bittner 1968: 425).

(7) That there is a tendency to perceive the aetiology of social problems in terms of the individual characteristics of those who are deemed to have the problem.[3] This individualism obscures three fundamental processes: the causal contribution of social process in the aetiology of the problem; the "natural history" of the problem – how it came to be

---

2   Note that this relativist approach to social problems faces one major analytical difficulty. It is typically used to unmask "spurious" claims by professionals, the argument being that far from clients "really" having need *X*, this is instead a professional product and one which serves the professionals' interests rather than the clients'. However, to criticize professions for ignoring or distorting their clients' needs, is to talk in absolutist terms once again and entails all the old difficulties which beset the search for fixed criteria of human need. Since neither extreme relativism or extreme absolutism are tenable, many writers hover vaguely in the middle with only the more religious or more Marxist coming out wholeheartedly for real needs.

3   This is itself only a reflection of that individualism so central to Western thought that it is embedded deep within its own sociology. See Helmer (1970).

seen as such[4]; and the definitional work by which particular individuals are identified as having a problem and selected for particular types of treatment.[5] The neglect of these three processes renders the role of both the state and the professions transparent and thus serves to depoliticise social problems.

(8) That given this individualization of social problems, coupled with the modern emphasis on science, the professions which are typically called upon to deal with these matters are those with a scientific interest in the properties of individuals, i.e. psychologists, psychiatrists, biologists, doctors. Moreover, even where they themselves do not directly handle clients, their doctrines inform those professions which do, e.g. the influence of psychiatry upon social work. In consequence, the feature which is most distinctive about the handling of contemporary social problems is their formulation in predominantly "medical" terms using this in its widest sense. This particular theme is a comparatively recent addition to the analysis. In the earlier form, psychiatry was the new imperial power while the rest of medicine was viewed as a rather more neutral enterprise, but later writers have seen psychiatry as merely one part of a far wider medical empire:

> Although many have noted aspects of this process (medicalization) by confining their concern to the field of psychiatry those criticisms have been misplaced. For psychiatry has by no means distorted the mandate of medicine but indeed, though perhaps faster than other medical specialisms, is following instead some of the basic claims and directions of that profession (Zola 1972: 487).[6]

(9) That even those matters which appear to be strictly medical problems best treated by the medically qualified, that is, lesions within the body of the individual, are in fact often the product of social forces. Disease is predominantly a matter of life-style, social structure, working conditions, and nutrition, and the effective prevention of disease must therefore involve major social change rather than the ineffectual meddling at the individual level which has become institutionalized as the only proper way of dealing with illness.[7]

---

4   See Fuller and Myers (1940) and Becker (1963). Recent examples of the natural history approach in medicine include Szasz (1970); Pfohl (1977); Conrad (1975).

5   See Rubington and Weinburg (1968) for a selection of articles on the official construction of individual problems.

6   See also the slight variations on this in his: 'In the name of health and illness' (Zola 1975) and 'Healthism and disabling medicalisation' (Zola 1977).

7   Writers such as Renaud (1975) and Navarro (1977), have here drawn upon and extended the work of McKeown (1976).

(10) That clients have become addicted to the products which professionals have to sell and in the throes of their delirium now demand that the professional empire be expanded; once hooked the addict craves ever bigger and stronger doses of his drug. Thus, Illich represents the British National Health Service as a product not just of ambitious doctors but of deluded patients also (Illich 1975, 1977).

Variations and Objections

Such then are the propositions that form the analysis of medical imperialism.[8] Of course, in summarising the argument thus I have necessarily done some violence to the positions held by individual writers. A variety of movements have contributed to the general thesis and their contributions bear the stamp of their different origins.[9] Moreover, although the proponents of the thesis share a rough consensus about the shape of medical imperialism there is no such agreement about the nature of the society in which this expansion occurs. In consequence, writers differ as to the ultimate cause and significance of the phenomenon. To take just one example: Navarro (1977), while essentially concurring with Illich's (1975, 1977) description of the process of medical expansion, argues that medicine, far from being an independent power, is under the ultimate control of a capitalist ruling class. He therefore sees the creation and manipulation of consumer addiction to a misdirected medicine as merely one instance of a general consumer addiction which is propagated by that class.

It should also be noted that although the thesis of medical imperialism is now commonplace in medical sociology, not every sociologist sees it as a major threat. Krause (1977) for example treats it as a relatively minor phenomenon. However, with the exception of the Ehrenreichs, no one has

---

8   Zola has criticised the use of this phrase on the grounds that it "leads us to think of the issue in terms of misguided human efforts or motives", rather than in any broader structural context. However, the metaphor of imperialism seems to me to capture rather well the expansionary potential inherent within professions and the political threat this presents to others. When we talk of cultural, military or economic imperialism most of us are not simply referring to motives.

9   In the early stages of its sociological development the predominant influence was the work of Hughes and his students – though Korn (1964) is a good critique from a libertarian, non-Chicago position. Important later contributions have been made by the anti-psychiatry movement, by the recent Marxist renaissance and by the echoes within sociology of the revolt of certain client groups, such as blacks, homosexuals and, in particular, women.

so far systematically examined the limits to medical expansion. Thus the excesses of the doctrine have so far gone relatively unchallenged.

Before I proceed to mount my own attack I must first point out that I shall examine merely one portion of the thesis. My principal concern is with what doctors actually control and do. I am less concerned with the para-medical professions and I shall give no detailed consideration to any wider ramifications of the argument – such as the extent to which medicine informs our daily talk and serves as a background to our everyday social life. These matters, although important, are none the less peripheral to the main body of the thesis. If it can be established, as I think it can, that the medical profession is at present focussed on largely organic concerns, then the rest of the argument looks distinctly dubious. If it were true, in any important sense, that we saw everything now in medical terms, we might reasonably expect there to be a dramatic expansion by medical professionals to cater for this new vision, whereas in reality such evidence is hard to find and most doctors seem only too keen to stick to the well-worn paths of biology.

This is not to say that the thesis is without foundation. Some developments in medicine are profoundly disturbing and worthy of much further investigation, publicity and action. However I feel that in certain important respects the *general* danger from medicine has been exaggerated. Before I proceed to any analysis of this exaggeration, however, I wish first to examine the reasons for its occurrence, for this in its turn may reveal other dangers that have been hitherto neglected.

Professional Pessimism

One explanation of sociologists' fears about trends in medicine and related disciplines has been given by Halmos, whose own work on the rise of the "personal service" professions runs directly counter to the pessimism of most other analysts (Halmos 1966, 1970).[10] Although he notes the rapid growth of such occupations and the self-serving nature of at least part

---

10 These works, are in many ways both akin to and yet the reverse of that of Illich. Halmos too was fundamentally concerned with the enormous growth of the "personal service" professions and he too thought this an inevitable product of the increasing material surplus provided by industrialisation. Like Illich, he saw such expansion as, in many respects, the distinguishing characteristic of all industrial societies and regarded the professional sector as one from which their leadership was increasingly drawn. Finally, he too wrote in an eloquent and almost religious manner. However, whereas Illich is deeply troubled by these developments, Halmos, for all their faults, saw them as a significant step forward in human civilisation.

of their ideology, he sees their development as a significant advance for humanity and is not so fearful of the uses to which their expertise may be put. His explanation of other writers' gloom lies in the detachment and ideological position of the sociological profession. On his analysis it is their job to be sceptical and they do not feel they have done it properly unless they have been so. There is of course great value in such a stance, for through it sociologists may avoid at least some of the contemporary delusions and deceits and warn others of the danger which they see. But such an attitude can readily harden into a doctrinaire cynicism:

> The sociologist expresses objections against conceptions of progressive improvements in life, because thoughts and imaginings of this kind convey to him a reprehensible complacency, which he feels he must combat with all his might. Unless the sociologist does his daily toilet of scepticism, he feels he is unlikely to advance his discipline (Halmos 1973: 292).

Thus:

> There is an almost invariable tendency to link analysis with devaluation and to take discovery as if it were always disclosure ... the grey mood and the unflattering anticipations are occupational afflictions of the searching sociological mind (Halmos 1973: 296).

Moreover, as he puts it, scepticism has considerable dramatic rewards. In writing in this fashion sociologists both formulate themselves as members of some insightful and incorruptible elite and, at the same time, gain considerable pleasure by the exposure and thus potential overthrow of those whom they dislike:

> If revenge is sweet, sociological truth is gratifying if it can be hurled against the heads of oppressors, of the unjust or of the deceivers. The truth of Marxism, for example, is dramatically enhanced by the discomfiture and shame of those who will have to let go of ill-gotten advantages because of a wider acceptance of this truth (Halmos 1973: 298).

There is much truth in these arguments; a truth that is enhanced by the ahistorical nature of most sociology. Lacking any great knowledge of the past and motivated, not unworthily, by hopes for a better future, many radical critics commonly assess such advances as have been made, not in their own terms but by the rigorous humanitarian, democratic or socialist criteria that would apply in an ideal society. Much of the analytical and moral power of sociology is derived from this stance but, as Halmos indicates, it may also lead to exaggerated fear and devaluation of present trends.

However, although professional scepticism may account for a good deal of the distortion that creeps into our analysis, there are other factors which are surely also present. One of these is the fact that sociologists, as well as being students of medicine, are not infrequently its patients as well. Given the natural importance to them of their own health and the somewhat bureaucratic and impersonal nature of those medical services which are, these days, available to the professional middle-class, many harbour distinctly personal grudges against medicine.[11] Such feelings are likely to be amplified where particular sociologists are members of subordinate groups within our society or have chosen to act as their representative.

Another more subtle influence is the impact of sociologists' own professional status. They are not simply detached commentators on medicine but rivals to it. The more sociological explanations prevail, then the more sociologists' status will increase and that of other professions diminish. Such an analysis smacks of the same scepticism that Halmos identifies as a weakness in sociology, but since it is also one of its strengths the argument may well prove worth pursuing.

Sociology – A Rival Empire

To grasp the way in which sociology can represent a rival to medicine we must, for the moment, stand back a little from medical sociology and view the discipline as a whole.

There have been many recent attempts to sketch the situation of modern sociology, for the last decade has seen a great rise in sociological self-consciousness and numerous writers have attempted to portray the history, social position, and ideological functions of the discipline, mostly from a highly critical perspective. The most famous of these critiques is that of Gouldner (1970).[12] On his interpretation, academic sociology is a child of the Welfare State, both a product and a servant of modern interventionist capitalism for whom it performs various investigatory and legitimating functions. Thus its most typical research product is a mindless empiricism, an atheoretical managerial sociology which answers whatever questions the administrators think fit to ask.

That much sociology is of this nature cannot be disputed. However it is misleading to portray our subordination as a purely passive affair. In Gouldner's version the servant of capitalism is a rather old-fashioned

---

11 The collection by Davis and Horobin of personal accounts of their illnesses by medical sociologists (1977).

12 See also two more Marxist critiques by Shaw (1972) and Nicolaus (1972).

retainer, happy in his daily round of duties, proud of his performance, and deferential to his superiors. On my analysis he (or these days, she as well) is more ambitious, less contented and more idealistic; keen to get on in the world, but at the same time worried about the plight of many of those he studies and somewhat cynical about the immediate possibility of action. As such he hopes that better days will come and that capitalism will change; thus altering, by a happy coincidence, both his own status and that of the oppressed.

My reasoning here is based upon an application of the thesis of professional imperialism to sociology itself – viewed in this wider context the Gouldner thesis must, for all its virtues, be seen as a special case. For what it does not explain is its own success; as we shall see, even in an area as outrageously managerial in inclination as medical sociology, variations of Gouldnerism are now a commonplace in every journal and the popularity of this critique can I think only be explained in terms of shifting professional opportunity.

Up till now, for all their recent self-consciousness, most sociologists have been remarkably unreflexive about the thesis of professional imperialism. This is less true of the Hughes tradition for Hughes (1958) himself has satirised the professional ambitions of social science and Roth has been a fierce and cynical opponent of attempts to professionalise sociology (e.g. 1969). Nevertheless, despite such exceptions it is striking how sociologists have not only failed to analyse their own imperial ambitions but those of the universities as a whole. Thus, there is no equivalent analysis of "academic imperialism" within the sociology of education to parallel that of medical imperialism – and this despite the enormous expansion of universities since the War; the massive increase in research budgets; university control over the content of the secondary curriculum; the increasing penetration of government by academics (both as members of parliament and as civil service advisors); and the use of university degrees as necessary qualification for entrance to an ever widening range of jobs – a process that in Britain is now encompassing professions such as accountancy and the law which traditionally had their own external methods of training. This is not to say that these matters have gone altogether unnoticed, merely that they have not made the same impact on sociologists or provoked the same response as their equivalents in medicine. Instead, as Lewis (1973) points out, most sociological studies of universities have been self-congratulatory.

One possible excuse for the omission, though a flimsy one, is that there can be no straightforward application of the thesis of professional imperialism to sociology, for it, like many other disciplines, is not a practising profession. It has no individual clients and has mostly resisted the various attempts to surround it with the trappings of fully professionalised occupations – a code of ethics, restricted membership and so on.[13] In this narrow sense, then, sociology is not a profession – something on which many sociologists congratulate themselves. But to hold on these grounds that the thesis of professional imperialism cannot therefore be applied seems unnecessarily finicky, for sociology does possess most of the crucial traits by which we normally identity professional occupations. It is centred around an academic body of knowledge, it is continually concerned with the practical application of that knowledge – even if that application is rarely carried out by sociologists, it certainly has clients, though these tend to be organizations, not individuals – and it is marked by a continuing and often agonized concern for how best to serve humanity.[14]

Having established, at least in a broad sense, that sociology may reasonably be seen as a profession. I can now apply the analysis of professional imperialism and show how this perspective enables us to grasp the appeal of both managerial *and* radical perspectives to the practising sociologist.

In doing this I want to point initially to two of the central conditions of production of sociology within modern bourgeois society. First, there is the relatively great intellectual freedom which its practitioners enjoy compared to their colleagues elsewhere; a freedom which allows sociologists, if they so wish, to be highly critical of the society in which they live. At the same time, and this is my second point, such comments are not wholly disinterested for sociologists, like every other profession in our society, are in the market-place – in this case an ideological and technical marketplace. Given the relatively open trade in ideas, every profession is free to compete with every other to provide formulations and solutions for contemporary social issues. "Discovering" social problems and, more especially, casting them in such terms that one has exclusive rights to them, is the basic strategy of every bourgeois profession and the

---

13 A major attempt was however made to professionalise American sociology in this manner in the period around 1960 – this being due to pressure from an already professionalised discipline, psychology, which was refusing to grant academic recognition to sociologists who taught social psychology in psychology departments, being itself under pressure from medicine. Every issue of the *American Sociological Review* for 1960 carried articles on the subject. The issue is nicely discussed in Goode 1960. More recently, there has been a call in Britain for a more fully professionalised discipline, this too seemingly due to external pressure – this time, the political pressure exerted on teachers in polytechnics see Rustin 1976.

14 Hawthorn (1976) brings out well the intensely moral concerns of the classical theorists in sociology.

highest professional rewards accrue to the early explorers. (Most often, of course, the initial discovery is made outside the discipline and it latches on to it as best and as fast as it can.)

Thus sociology has an imperial ambition and potential which is no less than those of the other professions whose pretensions it unmasks. It too attempts to move into new fields – medicine itself is an excellent example. And it too makes claims to encompass almost the whole of human thought and activity. In criticising the imperialism of other professions, sociologists also advance their own empire and do so under exactly the same banner as other professions – the service of humanity; a creed which provides the only public rationale for its existence. Moreover it is precisely because most forms of radical sociology have a greater imperial potential than any other type of theory that they have such great professional charm. By emphasising the social and thus political nature of those vast areas of life that are normally reified, they break down the conventional barriers which serve to exclude the professional sociologist and so make the whole of human existence our preserve.[15]

This is not to say however that a radical position is always professionally advantageous. The conditions under which this holds true need careful specification and for this we must turn to the third factor which constrains the production of bourgeois sociology – its sales appeal. Although a member of the professional elite within our society, sociology has a relatively small influence compared to some of its competitors. In so far as our culture is oriented to individual explanations of social problems, sociological analyses are less eagerly purchased and since it has no individual clients, sociology has less certainty of practice. Its only potential clients are groups; whether they be the powerful – as with governments and the large bureaucracies – or else less powerful groups in revolt or potential revolt against the prevailing social order – trade unions, "patients", "women", and so on.

The relationship of sociology to both these kinds of groups is highly ambiguous and is the major source of political tension within the discipline. On the one hand, an alliance with the powerful is the safer route to secure its own power, but on the other hand, in so far as the powerful prefer individual explanations, such an alliance rewards sociology with only a small piece of the action and ultimately benefits its rivals more than

---

15 In this respect Lenin and Mao-Tse-Tung are role models for the ultimate imperial aspirations of the profession, for they were social theorists who had a whole society at their disposal. Mao, in particular, had almost laboratory conditions for his research: a society largely cut off from the outside world and sufficient political control to test one hypothesis after another, some of them in radical contradiction to each other.

itself. Moreover, as Johnson (1972) has argued, professions with just a few powerful clients are in a far weaker position than those whose clientele are numerous and consist of individuals not organizations.

Alliance with the less powerful has similar contradictions. On the one hand there are important intellectual affinities; those groups among the less powerful which are in revolt against the established order commonly possess some form of social as opposed to individually-based theory. In this respect any advances they make may further the sociological cause. Moreover there is often considerable sympathy among sociologists at the position of the underdog and concern that these injustices be righted. On the other hand not only are such groups powerless but they are not normally organized in any way that enables sociology to ally with them. "Workers" or "patients'" typically remain as classes that are merely "in" themselves, as constructs or possibilities. In this alienated condition they remain even less susceptible to the lure of sociological theory than the powerful. At the same time, in so far as they do achieve some organization, they not only dramatically increase their bargaining power *vis-à-vis* the discipline but simultaneously develop their own theories and become suspicious of the alliance offered them – for their struggle is not the same, even if parts of their approach may overlap in places.

Finally, sociology is in any case compromised. Not only does it belong to an elite class but its structural position within capitalist society prevents the profession as a whole from ever fully committing itself to the less powerful, for such an alliance would seriously threaten its only tangible source of rewards in this world. In consequence, *as a profession*, sociology may be said to play a double game, seeking the support of the less powerful on occasion but in turn using this alliance to foster its other alliance with those in power.[16] In this latter relationship its tactics vary according to three main factors: the extent to which it has successfully penetrated a field; the degree to which any one area is in crisis – and thus its inhabitants and masters are seeking alternative solutions; and finally, the type of theory, research and advice which it has available.

This last factor is probably of less importance than the other two since, given a demand, a large amount of relevant sociology can be fairly rapidly produced. This potential is a result of the great variety of theoretical and methodological positions to be found within the discipline and is itself a product of the intellectual freedom which it is granted. There is always likely to be some doctrine which has a relevance to current social concerns

---

16 Talking of the profession in this manner is of course to reify it, but committing this sin seems better than to accuse individual sociologists of acting in some manipulative fashion – which is not of course my intention.

and, although most lines of work are only in small-scale production, all are capable of a rapid expansion of output given the appropriate demand.[17]

Despite this intellectual flexibility, the profession is of course still tied to the powerful. Nevertheless its great ability to modify its arguments, when coupled with a real concern for the injustices of this world, means that it is well capable of pursuing very different lines at different points in time, each of which may also serve to expand its empire. According to the times, it can threaten capitalists either with consumers or with workers and in both cases offer its services as interpreter, mediator, and ultimately perhaps, planner.

In summary, Gouldner and his fellow-critics do have a point, but their analysis is only partial, failing as it does to explain its own popularity. This failure derives in part from too narrow a vision. By focussing only upon sociology they exaggerate both the extent to which it has benefited from the Welfare State and the role which it plays in its maintenance. It is of course true that sociology has grown with enormous rapidity since the end of the Second World War. In comparison with the impoverished past it has riches indeed. But relative to some of the other professions – and this is the comparison which counts – it has received very little. Moreover, by concentrating solely on the services which it renders to the bourgeois social order, radical critics of sociology make it seem – though this may be far from their intention – as if capitalism was in some way dependent upon the profession's support; as if the legitimation or information that it provided played an important role in its continuing success. But the ordinary practitioner is grateful for whatever he or she can get, envious of other discipline's success and haunted by the fear that if sociology were shut down tomorrow very few people would notice any difference.[18] In such a position sociologists are only marginal members of the elite and have a direct interest in fairly radical political change.[19]

---

17 This expansion is, however, constrained by the primary employment of sociologists as teachers. This and a variety of other factors produces a strong bias towards the production of library rather than field work.

18 Phillips (1973) points out that one of the most surprising features of politically radical critiques of sociology is the assumption that sociologists possess some special body of tested knowledge which is of great use in suppressing the lowly. This is a highly professional delusion for radicals to have for, as Phillips shows, sociology has been singularly unproductive of firmly established propositions. The inadequacy of much professional knowledge is one of the crucial limitations on professional expansion, as I discuss later on in my analysis of medicine.

19 Indeed, it can be argued that the professional class as a whole (viewed in its widest sense) have considerable radical potential. Gouldner himself, in a footnote, makes a point that runs counter to the main body of his text, arguing that one of the crucial tensions in modern capitalist society is that between the

Medical Sociology and Sociological Imperialism

Given this analysis of the position of sociology we can now consider
the specific situation of medical sociology. It is clear that in the past its
role was largely of the managerial or administrative kind that Gouldner
condemns. However, times have changed. The worm has turned – or at
least is thinking about turning.

The sudden attack of self-consciousness that gripped general sociology
in the late 1960s has its parallel, if at a slightly later date, within medical
sociology. Here too there have been histories written of the origins and
growth of the discipline (Draper and Smart, 1974, Illsley 1975, Olesen
1975), assaults made upon mindless empiricism (Johnson 1975), detailed
investigation of the extent to which a purely managerial sociology has
in fact conquered the field (Gold 1977), and, throughout all this, sharp
attacks upon the political dangers of such acquiescence. Here for example
is a summary by Susser of one of the best of such works:

> The history of social science in general is perhaps exemplified in the parochial
> history of the evolution of social science in relation to health policy in Britain,
> a subject dealt with by Peter Draper and Tony Smart in this issue of the *Journal*.
> In a first phase, social science struggled for a place, any kind of place, in the
> health field. In a second phase, social science gained a place in the health field,
> and was perceived as useful in health policy by those who had the power to
> frame policy. At this stage of its evolution, social science proved threatening
> to many individual clinicians, but was no longer seen as threatening by the
> administration at the center of political power. Administrators perceived the
> utility of social science in its capacity to function within the *status quo* while
> illuminating special problems. In a third phase, social science can be said to
> have been co-opted by those at the administrative center of power in forming
> health policy. Draper and Smart's concern is with the increase of the political
> power of the administrative center as a consequence of this process (Susser
> 1974: 408).

With the justice of such accounts I have no quarrel. At the same time,
sociologists and their fellow social scientists within medicine have a duty

---

professional sector of the welfare state and the propertied sector which begrudges
its cost (Gouldner, 1970: 87). Touraine notes that it is precisely this professional
group (and his definition is even wider than mine for he includes students, media
workers, all types of research worker, planners and teachers) which provided the
key support and ideological form of the May 1968 "revolution" in France and he
asserts that the "professionals" now constitute a group rather like the aristocracy of
labour in an earlier epoch. If this analysis is correct, the loyalty of professionals to
the *status quo,* and particularly that of more marginal sections, such as sociologists,
is somewhat provisional (see Hobsbawm, 1977).

to be rather more self-conscious about their social position than they are at present. The danger of an unreflexive radicalism is that only the past is excoriated. In condemning the mistakes of their ancestors or former selves, sociologists may easily imagine that at least they are free now and ignore the way in which such a posture may, at a particular point, serve their own professional ends.

This may be illustrated by examining the rest of Susser's argument which I have just quoted (This formed an introduction to a special issue of the *International Journal of Health Services* which sought to review the position of sociology in medicine.) He begins, appropriately enough, with an imperialist metaphor:

> The incursion of sociology into health has by now become a permanent occupation of territory. The moment seems appropriate for a review of the conduct of the occupying troops (Susser 1974: 407).

However it soon becomes apparent that this is merely an elegant turn of phrase rather than any insight into the nature of sociological imperialism for, after a brief review of the history of medical sociology, he outlines the next step in the profession's long-term strategy to win more territory, while simultaneously denying any such ambition and indeed abusing previous sociologists for their pretensions to power.

> One may hope that in a fourth phase (i.e. after Draper and Smart's three earlier subordinate phases) some of the questions social science has previously addressed will be reformulated in terms of power and control and in terms of the effects of policies on people as patients and workers. For this reason, this issue has aimed for a tone of radical critique rather than of bland discussion. The propaganda for social science that at an earlier time was almost essential to permit growth has been avoided. ... Authors were invited to go as far as they dared in stating their personal positions, and in criticising established positions either in social science or in the health field. The authors have made a brave response, so much so that this special issue might be perceived by some as part of a new movement of "disestablishmentarianism" (Susser 1974: 408).

Oddly however, the authors who then take part in this disestablishment are none other than the European medical sociology establishment, i.e. Sokolowska, Pflanz, Frankenburg, Jeffreys and Illsley; the professors who mediate between government, medicine and sociology. However reasonable their analysis and however radical their intentions, they are also serving the cause of sociology – in this instance by upping the ante. So far, they proclaim to governments, we have co-operated but now, having got established (we hope) we want a little more attention given to the social and political nature of medicine, an area in which, it so happens, we are ourselves expert.

Thus the article by Draper and Smart (1974) that is cited so approvingly by Susser consists first of a detailed critique of the limitations of other social science approaches to the NHS – in particular, economics, psychoanalytic organizations theory and epidemiology – and secondly, of a proposed remedy. After noting the limited contributions so far made by sociology they argue that the latter discipline has a far wider relevance and can be used to do many of the things for which other social sciences have been used and will, in fact, do them far better. As well as calling for the rights of the people to be recognised, they also call for a massive increase in the research budget devoted to sociology.

This strikes me as a good idea too, but what I want to note for the present is this emphasis on the limited access so far granted to sociology, for this is a theme that runs throughout these commentaries. Medical sociology may have expanded rapidly but it is still subservient. Its adherents often work in medical faculties, isolated from their colleagues and forced to do hack work of little sociological value. The call for a properly theoretical approach, made 20 years ago by Straus (1957), must still be made today for, as Illsley (1975) and Pflanz (1975) note, sociologists are still largely excluded from the ultimate formulation of the problems which they investigate.

Put very crudely, these servants of the Welfare State are none too happy about their position, they have got some but they want more. And in demanding this they have useful allies for there are other disciplines, which may be lumped together and broadly termed "public health", which share something of the same intellectual approach to medicine but also feel excluded from the action. There are of course important differences between them, not only in their substantive area but in their historical trajectory. Medical sociology is a youthful aspirant, on its way up and eager to rise higher still; public health is a much older discipline, formerly powerful but now sunk into penury. Nevertheless they have sufficient in common to render an alliance worthwhile (be it somewhat sticky on occasion for what are their aspirations towards each other?) and we may find in public health a similar process of radicalization, involving once again historical review (Susser 1975), the condemnation of mindless empiricism (Powles 1973), and the production of radical social and political theories about medicine (McKeown 1976, Powles 1973, Navarro 1977).[20]

---

20 I should add that the distinction between medical sociology and "public health" is not as clear as I pretend it is. Some writers span both fields, others move from one to the other, and on occasion writers from different fields join together. Draper and Smart make a common plea for more sociology but one is a doctor and the other a sociologist.

One final note; a mutual exclusion from the goodies is not enough to explain this joint radicalization, particularly of two disciplines that have been subservient for so long. Why have the worms turned? It may be remembered that I picked out two principal determinants of professional strategy within any one field – the degree to which the area had been successfully penetrated and the extent to which it was in crisis and thus its inhabitants and masters were seeking alternative solutions. Both of these conditions are satisfied in the present case. As to the first, public health may be low in status but it has long been established as a part of medicine; while sociology, though a newcomer, is now of an age, an experience, and an established importance – however slight – which justifies the risk of rebellion, particularly when it can call upon public health as an ally. Coupled to this, the time is ripe for something new, for it is clear that both medicine and the wider bourgeois social order are currently under some strain, though the seriousness of these crises is a matter of some dispute. Nevertheless they offer fertile ground for professional expansion. If the old interpretations no longer work, maybe new and more critical analyses have something to offer and radicals typically pitch their sale in such terms. Here for instance is the opening statement in a recent article by Navarro:

> According to the means of communication in contemporary capitalist societies, our Western system of power is in a state of crisis. Editorial after editorial appears in the prominent press under variations of the title "What has gone wrong?" And in the quest for answers to this disquieting question, there has emerged an increasing awareness that most of the accepted explanations in the Western system of thought on the nature of our societies are either erroneous or seriously insufficient. Consequently, a rekindling of old theories as well as a presentation of new ones is appearing in the realm of a debate that provides alternate explanations of our realities. And in this search for alternatives, concerns about the distribution of political power, the legitimacy of our political systems and the nature of the State are very much in the centre of the debate. *This work is an attempt to contribute to this debate.* (My emphasis.) (Navarro 1977: 183)

To conclude this section; like any other profession, medical sociology and its allies are in the market for ideas and, in so far as we explain the growth of medicine by reference to its self-interest, then we are surely bound to consider our own analyses in the same light. The thesis of professional imperialism cuts two ways.

The Intellectual Products of Naive Imperialism

To grasp that cynicism is an occupational disease among sociologists and that bourgeois sociology has imperial ambitions like any other profession is not to render their productions invalid. Nor do I think that criticism of sociology's past inadequacies is merely hypocritical. However, unless social scientists understand themselves and their position within society, they are unlikely fully to grasp the social role of those whom they investigate, particularly when the latter have a position which is very similar to their own.

The principal danger which naivety poses is that of exaggeration; a danger which is increased to the extent that political sympathies march in line with professional enthusiasm. Of course it is not the case that exaggeration is a necessary consequence of any lack of self-awareness, but the less social scientists are aware of their direct interest in discovering nasty things about doctors, the more eagerly they are likely to seize upon these and ignore other, and perhaps contradictory, evidence. The mental set common to many young sociologists has been described by Jefferys as comprising "a barely veiled hostility to, and indeed contempt for, the medical profession" (1974).[21] Until one becomes more aware of this attitude and of its origins, it can only exercise a malign influence upon sociology.

Six kinds of distortion seem prevalent:

(1) First, there is a tendency to attack medicine with the benefit of hindsight.[22] Historical treatments of medical attempts at colonisation that failed and which now seem ridiculous are growing in number; (examples of this include masturbation and "neurasthenia" (Englehardt 1974, Haller 1971). Such work is interesting in itself but clearly provides no basis from which to generalise to the whole of medicine. To do this we need accounts of other areas that were successfully medicalised and on the justice of which there is general agreement. If we have no such comparative material then attempts at analysing the growth of medicine will resemble a history of physical anthropology which based its whole argument on the Piltdown forgery.

---

21 Although Jefferys correctly identifies the feelings expressed by many medical sociologists towards medicine, her explanation is spoilt by the omission of any analysis of our professional rivalry. The factors which she notes, our low status and low pay, as well as the incomprehension with which our work is received, only generate hostility in sociologists because of our professional ambition.

22 This point was made by Andrew Weir.

(2) Secondly, many of the critiques of medical imperialism lack any historical or anthropological awareness. Sociologists are prone to accuse doctors of having suddenly invaded an area in ignorance of the fact that this area has long been medicalised, if in a different and often far less satisfactory fashion, both in our own culture and in that of many other types of society. For example, Macintyre (1977a) has shown how many critics of modern gynaecological practice appeal to some entirely mythical golden age in which childbirth was a purely "natural" affair. They warrant their judgement by appeal to the supposed practices of other cultures, but oddly enough provide no references. If one in fact examines the literature on childbirth in these pastoral idylls, as Macintyre has done, a somewhat barbarous picture emerges. Indeed, the plea of working women fifty years ago was for far more proper medicine to save them from the horrors that childbirth then entailed (Davies 1978). The movement for "natural" childbirth only arose when medical advances had largely freed women from these fears. It is thus a product of "medical imperialism" and entirely dependent upon it. To say this is not to deny the force of some criticisms of current medical practice but merely to note that there is a need for care. The use of an appeal to some golden age has a long history in Western polemic (Macintyre 1967) but it is surely most odd for sociologists, and radical ones at that, to subscribe to a belief in the "naturalness" of certain states or processes.

(3) The third kind of distortion also occurs in areas which are currently under dispute. There is here a strong tendency for sociologists to perceive the dispute as one *between* sociology and medicine itself. But it is naive to envisage the members of the various disciplines and sub-disciplines which make up the medical empire as all of one mind. They do not hunt as a pack, but, like every other profession, are riven by differences of interest, expertise and ideology. Indeed, this fission has probably gone to greater lengths within medicine than in any other profession, so that it is now split into an extraordinary variety of different types of specialities (Butler and Strauss 1961). Moreover, even within the same sub-discipline it cannot be assumed that all will think alike. Expansion into new areas is commonly undertaken by small groups of missionaries, full of zeal but spurned by their colleagues. The task of converting their brethren is often formidable and much that may pass for success proves delusive on a closer inspection. Those who are searching for evidence of medical sin, however, ignore the failure and seize eagerly upon the apparent gains.

Take for example alcoholism, an area which some have alleged
has recently been captured by medicine (Conrad 1975) or is about
to be (Zola 1977). At first glance there is much to be said for this
proposition. As Orford and Edwards recount (Orford and Edwards
1977) whereas in Britain the Ministry of Health at first denied the
existence or relevance of alcoholism to the NHS, it had been converted
by the 1960s to a policy of creating specialised alcoholism in-patient
units. A similar transformation has occurred in the United States:

> The American Medical Association, American Psychiatric Association,
> American Public Health Association, American Psychological Association,
> National Association of Social Workers, World Health Organisation
> and the National College of Physicians have now each and all officially
> pronounced alcoholism a disease (Gutlow in Robinson 1976).

Indeed, in recent times even the Pentagon has declared alcoholism
to be a disease (Zola 1977). Similarly, if one examines the research
literature on alcoholism, the bio-medical approach is both dominant and
increasing its predominance (Moll and Narin 1977). Most impressive
of all, recent survey research in these countries has shown that a
majority of both the public (Ries 1977) and of medical professionals
(Rathod 1967, Jones and Helrich 1977) now characterise alcoholism
as in some way a disease. In this respect times have clearly changed
for earlier studies reported rather different findings (Parr 1957).

Some caution is however necessary, for another central and repeated
finding of alcohol research is that although doctors may have been
persuaded that there is a lot of alcoholism about, and they may also
have come to see it at least partly in disease terms, very few of them
think that it is a disease about which they themselves could or should
do very much. By and large, they are content to leave it to the small
band of missionaries, as the following complaint from one of the latter
makes clear:

> Their (physicians) attitudes in general denote a feeling of hostility to the
> alcoholic, one that, simply put, states that they do not wish to be bothered
> with him, that treatment is futile. This might be expressed in the words of
> one internist friend who said at breakfast at the hospital one morning – "I
> never treat alcoholics; I send them to you". This feeling we find true in
> every branch of medicine. It is seen in the surgeons, the orthopaedists, the
> gynaecologists, the internists, the general practitioners and it is also seen
> in the psychiatrists and psychoanalysts (Kendis 1967: 307).

In other words the profession is often divided and sociologists cannot
rely solely on evidence from one segment of it.

(4) The fourth distortion that is common among medical sociologists is a
tendency to under-estimate the technical success of modern medicine.

In so doing they both give reign to their natural scepticism and at the same time, in so far as they advance their own social theories of health, further the claims of their own discipline. Thus it is that sociologists and others seize eagerly on work such as that of McKeown (1976) which seeks to show that high-technology medicine has contributed far less than might be imagined to advances in our health and that these have often come instead from better environmental conditions – from better food, housing, and so on.

While there is undoubtedly great value in McKeown's historical and epidemiological perspective and it provides a necessary corrective to many of the more extravagant claims made for modern scientific medicine, there are grounds for arguing that he has under-estimated the value of the latter. In particular, his critics (Lever 1977, Beeson *et al.* 1977) have noted the following points: it does not follow from his arguments that modern medicine could *not* have reduced mortality rates in the past, if it had been available; nor that it may not be the best method for use with much of the disease as is left. Aside from this, some of his evidence, for example that of death certificates, is unreliable, while he has tended to minimise the effect of age related mortality. He has also ignored morbidity and it is here that many claim that modern medicine has made enormous strides. Finally the belief that modern science has gone about as far as it can go was also held by some 19th century writers and may turn out to be equally wrong. To say all this is not to deny the fundamental contribution to health made by good environmental conditions, nor the great value of McKeown's own work, it is merely to argue that there may still be something to be said on the other side.

(5) A fifth distortion is the misrepresentation of the extent to which a modern capitalist state can control medical imperialism, and this seems to derive not so much from a sociological as from an American imperialism. Some American writers tend to conflate capitalism with American capitalism (Waitzkin and Waterman 1974), disregarding the fact that America is in many respects a most atypical capitalist society. The relatively feeble attempts of the American state to control the medical empire are thus transformed into proof, either that no capitalist state can control medicine, or that none wishes to do so. Both may be true of the United States but things look rather different elsewhere for capitalism comes in many guises and, although there is an important sense in which one can talk of a general style of Welfare State capitalism, the extent of working-class power and thus the extent to which control is exercised over medicine, does vary significantly. In the United States the vague attempts to produce

Welfare State medicine have merely served the financial interests of private medicine:

> Few, if any, countries spend a higher proportion of their national income on health care than the United States – 8.6% of its gross national product in 1976, proportionately about half as much again as Britain. ... Not only has the proportion of GNP devoted to health care increased sharply over the past decade but the acceleration is continuing. On present trends, a study by the Congressional Budget Office has suggested, health expenditure might exceed 10% of the GNP by the early 1980s; but evidence of any corresponding gains in the effectiveness of health care systems is hard to find.
>
> ...[This] ... is, at least partly, a symptom of the perverse incentives in the American system of health care, one which has increasingly become publicly financed but whose expenditure is almost entirely out of public control. Central and local government now finances over two-fifths of the nation's health bill through schemes such as Medicare and Medicaid. It also subsidises private insurance schemes through generous tax exemptions. In making such commitments, however, the government has stepped on to an escalator whose progress it cannot check (*BMJ* 1978).

By contrast, although the NHS budget has grown significantly in real terms since its foundation, the evidence does not suggest that medicine is having everything its own way. Not only is the budget relatively small by international standards but in England, though not in Scotland, the health share of the state's social support budget (i.e. health, education, social security, social services, and assisted housing) has actually been declining (Beeson *et al.* 1977). Again, this is not to defend the amount that is currently spent by the NHS nor the way in which it is spent – some areas are chronically under-financed, while others receive massive funding for matters of relatively little worth – it is merely to note that in at least one type of capitalist society *some* control of the financial size of the medical empire does seem possible.

(6) Finally, it may be argued that the notion of patient addiction to medicine is considerably overstated. The belief that patients are so afflicted is not a new one, as witness Osler's elegant remark, "a desire to take medicine is perhaps the great feature which distinguishes man from animals", a comment which has a certain justice. Moreover, there are clear individual cases of patients who become heavily addicted to disease and good historical examples of whole groups who have suffered from this complaint – as the Ehrenreichs point out, it is hard to tell where the role of woman ended and that of patient began in the 19th century upper classes (Ehrenreich and Ehrenreich 1975).

Less extreme situations are however rather more ambiguous. On the one hand, it is clear that a good deal of modern medicine is merely palliative, that the consumption of drugs is rising faster than GNP (Rabin and Bush 1974) in many countries, and that there is a most worrying increase in the use of psychotropic drugs, egged on by massive advertising campaigns by drug companies. On the other hand, there are a number of things which suggest that patients often place rather less reliance upon medicine than many doctors or medical sociologists tend to assume. Individually, none of the following arguments are conclusive–some indeed are rather weak – but taken together they suggest that the concept of a *general* patient addiction, if not altogether baseless, cannot be held in any extreme form. There is an undoubted element of addiction in the doctor–patient relationship but there are a good many other things as well.

Take first the rather limited number of occasions on which patients actually consult their general practitioner – a figure which, in Britain at least, seems to vary by age and sex between an average of two and a half and four and a half visits a year (with the higher figures all concerning children, childbirth and the elderly) (O.P.C.S. 1978). Such visits are scarcely high in comparison with the number of events about which one might wish to consult a doctor *if* medicine had invaded our daily lives as thoroughly as some writers would have it.

Even if one thinks that such relatively infrequent visits still count as addiction, it must also be established that most people are true believers in doctors' miraculous powers and secondly, that our consumption of medical goods and services is in fact largely irrelevant to our better health. At least some of the evidence for this latter proposition may be seriously challenged as I noted earlier, in which case this consumption becomes highly rational, while it can readily be shown that in some matters the customers are somewhat sceptical of medicine. Thus, it is hard to read the critical statements made by patients in the group interviews in Stimson and Webb's study and still believe that these were complete dupes of medical imperialism (Stimson and Webb 1975).

Moreover not only are patients often critical of the services they do get but, as the attendance rates imply, there is good evidence that they treat the majority of their problems as matters for their own solution rather than that of the doctors: not only is a large amount of organic illness never taken to the doctor (Pearse and Crocker 1949) but most personal matters receive no mention at all (see the accounts of medical practice in Stimson and Webb 1975, Byrne and Long 1976, Strong 1979). That this latter point is so is scarcely surprising, given doctors' lack of time and inability to do much about them. In solving their daily problems, and this of course is to assume that something is defined as problematic, people rely on all kinds of sources, and medical advice is only one of these. It has value to us, no doubt, and it may on some occasions prove extremely valuable, but it is only one of a variety of possible solutions that we may try, even as regards organic illness. Moreover it should not be assumed, as Tudor Hart notes, that people see medicine as the only source of positive health:

> "Treatment by surgery and drugs", says Professor McKeown, "is widely regarded as the basis of health ..." How widely? ... Certainly there are many who do believe; there are some people who will believe anything ... but ... for generations the people have known that good food, housing, education, and working hours and conditions were more important to their health than anything they could get from doctors. ... The positive elements in McKeown's thesis are commonplace to anyone with the least experience of the British or American labour movements (Tudor Hart 1977: 389).

Looked at another way, the thing to be explained here may not be the patients' addiction so much as the strength of the belief among doctors and medical sociologists that patients are so addicted. Thomas, in a recent study which compared the effects of treatment and no treatment in those cases in his practice in which no definite diagnosis could be made, records the following:

> At the start of this investigation I was concerned about the reaction of patients to no treatment. These fears proved groundless. No one outwardly objected; a few patients expressed surprise; and most seemed to accept that if no disease had been found it was reasonable to give no treatment. ... I also thought that no treatment would be more effective in those patients who had chosen to see me often in the past, or who had had a long stay in the practice, and that patients having received no treatment at one consultation would choose to see another doctor at the next consultation. Both these assumptions were proved wrong. It would seem that patients tolerate no treatment better than doctors think they will. Surveys have shown that 43–52% of patients expect to be given a prescription at a consultation, whereas most doctors think the figures would be 80% or more (Thomas 1978).

That doctors perhaps over-rate the importance of medicine to their patients should not surprise us. We all like to dramatise our importance in this world and a little measure of self-delusion is surely necessary to engage in any professional work. It clearly is in medical sociology; indeed in one sense the victims of medical imperialism are not so much the patients as those who practise or study it, for they are all professional valetudinarians, only too prone to belief in the centrality of medical matters. Since medicine is important to them all the time, they tend to assume that this must be so of others. This assumption seriously flaws many patient interview studies, particularly of a more structured kind. By focussing on what patients make of medical services, they fail to set their comments in the wider context of patients' lives and thus often ascribe to them an unwarranted importance, whether for good or for ill.

The mistake here is to elevate good health into an ultimate social value, as if it were an end in itself, whereas for most people it is merely a means to other things. Consulting a doctor is, in Wenglinsky's terminology, merely an "errand" – if an important one – something rather troublesome that one has to do from time to time in order to get on with the more interesting parts of life (Wenglinsky 1973, Strong 1977). Moreover, since nowadays most people are, for whatever reasons, relatively healthy most of the time, at least until we grow old, those who service our errands are simply not that important to us. All in all, when coupled with patients' scepticism about some of the services which they request and the actual success of others, this state of affairs bears little resemblance to the craving feared by some.

Professional Limits to Medical Imperialism

In discussing the various ways in which sociologists have exaggerated the threat of medical imperialism, I have touched upon several factors which serve to limit this threat. In this next section I shall consider the way in which these constraints are in fact embedded in the very position of medicine within modern bourgeois society. Four factors in all deserve some mention:

(1) *Financial constraints*

Without financial rewards there is, as the Ehrenreichs point out, no basis for medical imperialism (Ehrenreich and Ehrenreich 1975). Thus in the 19th century the urban poor were largely deprived of medical services[23] for there was no way in which any significant number of doctors could make a living through treating them. In this sense the coming of the welfare state has provided the financial basis for both a major expansion of medicine

---

23 For a description of the extraordinary conditions in the only medical services available to the urban poor, see Loudon 1978; and Bridges 1878. Bridges timed his work and calculated that staff saw one patient every minute, assuming, that is, that they worked twelve hours a day.

and a considerable upgrading of doctors' income and status.[24] These
benefits to medicine have derived from the fact that state intervention has,
in Johnson's terms, only comprised a partial mediation; that is, although
the state has decreed who shall get the service, it has left the manner in
which that service is given largely up to the profession, thus financing
medical expansion while leaving the professionals with a large amount of
control.

However it would be mistaken to deduce from this that the coming of the
welfare state necessarily means a blank cheque for the medical profession.
As we have already seen, there are significant differences between types
of welfare state in the extent to which medical services are free to expand.
Whereas there are strong incentives within the American system for
individual practitioners or institutions to corral profitable categories of
patient, regardless of the medical worth of such action, there are many
fewer such rewards in the United Kingdom and thus, for example, British
hospital doctors who garner large numbers of fresh patients without first
gaining extra resources from a higher level authority, merely increase their
work load.

Moreover, although the American introduction of federal programmes
for the poor and elderly has undoubtedly led to an exploitation of such
resources by some doctors, the very fact of government intervention,
however inept, has itself politicised medicine and led to demands for more
systematic financial control, while the insurance companies themselves
have taken a major interest in the development of procedures for limiting
the discretion of individual medical practitioners – procedures which are
far more, developed than in Britain even if they have not so far noticeably
contained costs (*BMJ* 1978).

It may be objected to this that since, if we follow Navarro's argument
(1977) the modern capitalist ruling class has a direct interest in medical
expansion, a formal subordination of medicine to the state will not in fact
act as much of a check. Not only does the British case suggest otherwise,
though clearly it has still provided room for a good deal of expansion, but to
argue any other way is to presume that the capitalists' purse is bottomless.
Since it is not, there is a growing emphasis on cost-effectiveness. Again
it is of course true that the effectiveness of large areas of medical practice
has never been properly assessed. Nevertheless the demand for such
evaluation is increasing and will continue to do so (Cochrane 1972).

This principle is already clearly at work in some of the areas which are
supposed, by some, to be under threat of medicalisation and is in fact one

---

24 Ehrenreich (1977) for the U.S.; for the U.K. see the comparison of the
status of the modern doctor with that described by Shaw G.B., as recounted in
Frankenburg (1974).

of the principal barriers to any major expansion there. Zola, having noted the growing interest of some doctors in alcoholism and the elderly, argues that such activity raises the possibility of millions more people being cast under the medical net (Zola 1972). Such fears are clearly delusory where there is relatively tight state control. These areas have almost the lowest prestige in the whole of medicine and have, at least in the United Kingdom, been starved of funds. For all the Ministry of Health's stated policy of creating alcoholism treatment units there were by 1975 only 434 beds in these.[25] Similarly, Macintyre's (1977b) review of British government policy statements concerning the elderly indicates that financial economy and the burden to the taxpayer which care for the elderly represents have been the predominant, if not the only, themes. In both of these cases a principal reason for inaction has been the lack of any adequate medical technology. There is no successful cure for alcoholism and there is little that can be done to prevent ageing. Money spent in these areas has a relatively small return. Health administrators are only too well aware of the fact that there are millions of potential "patients" out there and this of course acts as a major deterrent to their medicalisation.[26] In summary, although the modern capitalist state may increasingly finance professional expansion, the very fact that it does so gives it both the motivation and the leverage to see that its money is well spent – even though it has yet to use the levers to their full extent.

(2) *Medical success and medical pragmatism*

> In professional as in other lines of work, there grows up both inside and outside, some conception of what the essential work of the occupation is, or should be. In any occupation people perform a variety of tasks, some of them approaching more closely the ideal or symbolic work of the profession than others. Some tasks are considered nuisances and impositions or even dirty work – physically, socially or morally beneath the dignity of the profession (Hughes 1958: 121–22).

---

25 Orford and Edwards, *op. cit.* Moreover, this number seems unlikely to increase much if attention is paid to Orford and Edwards' devastating evaluative study of intensive group therapy. For a frightened response, see Kissin B. 1977.

26 It may be that the low status of these areas and others like them, such as mental illness and mental retardation, is really a product of the low social valuation placed on them. The argument could be made that since they are so stigmatised, the criterion of cost effectiveness will be applied more vigorously here than elsewhere and such fields will therefore be starved of both the resources and the personnel needed to produce improvements in medical technique; the whole process being self-fulfilling. This argument does not of course destroy the point that these areas are unlikely to be the subject of major expansion as things stand at present.

It is clear in modern medicine that the more prestigious, the most "essential" work of the profession, is that which revolves around those fundamentally biological matters which are at one and the same time both technically complex and susceptible to practical intervention. Medicine is an applied science, a fundamentally pragmatic discipline. Doctors like to succeed, which makes them prefer to work in areas where success is readily available. The great achievements of high-technology medicine dominate medical training and shape the prestige hierarchy. This not only encourages doctors to concentrate their efforts here but makes administrative parsimony in other less successful areas such as geriatrics or mental illness a most reasonable policy in the eyes of the profession as a whole. Health administrators' power in such cases thus derives not just from their ultimate financial control but from their appeal to central parts of medical ideology – a concern with biology and a concern with effectiveness.

Taking effectiveness first, I must again be careful not to overstate my case. There is no denying that current procedures of quality control are relatively weak (Wolman 1976) or that doctors often delude themselves about the efficacy of medical intervention. Cochrane provides a withering review of large areas of current practice which have never been subject to proper evaluation or in which negative results have been blithely ignored (1972). As he shows there are many social barriers to effective assessment: it is difficult, on ethical grounds, to use random controlled trials to evaluate long-established treatment; there is a tendency to think that any treatment at the margin is better than none; evaluative studies place limits on clinical freedom; and the long and successful tradition of pure science in medicine renders doctors less interested in applied work such as evaluation – there is great prestige to be had from innovation, but much less from seeing if any of it actually works.[27]

Nevertheless, despite all this one must not overstate the medical capacity for self-deception – medicine is an applied science and effectiveness is still a central part of medical ideology, even if it has to fight to make itself heard on occasion. The struggle to professionalise medicine and to secure a monopoly of practice was not simply undertaken to raise doctors' incomes; it was also a major battle to raise standards. Likewise it must not be forgotten that the basic technique for evaluating the worth of medical treatment – the random controlled trial – is, as Cochrane notes, a very recent innovation (Cochrane 1972). Operations research, from which it derived, was a war-time invention and its first medical application followed quickly afterwards in 1952. Cochrane himself complains about

---

27 See for example the morass of innovative, but often poorly evaluated, and somewhat dubious surgical procedures reviewed in Bengmark (1975).

the struggle it has had for acceptance in some quarters and, although there is some justice in this complaint, two further points should also be noted.

First, he himself tends to under-estimate the enormous methodological difficulties involved in the rigorous evaluation of human action – he seems to have little understanding of what he terms "phenomenology" and, oddly enough, like some others use "positivism", sees it as a term of abuse. Secondly, when looked at from another viewpoint, his book is striking evidence of the rapidity with which medical researchers, particularly those in the United Kingdom, have in fact applied the new method, for here are a whole mass of studies which employ this complex and time-consuming technique – studies which the critics of medicine use to demonstrate its ineffectiveness but which may also legitimately be seen as proof of the lively concern that many doctors show for the ultimate value of their procedures.[28]

At the same time, this sceptical and pragmatic attitude – even if it is only imperfectly institutionalised – nevertheless reinforces that other essential concern of the profession, the emphasis upon biology. One of the central themes in the thesis of medical imperialism is that doctors, as well as expanding within the organic realm, are beginning to encroach upon the social sphere – a movement which is doubly threatening, since if sociologists cannot claim this for themselves what have they got? Once again there are certainly worrying developments here (Conrad 1975, Stimson 1977), but there are good grounds for arguing that this threat is not all it might be and there are some signs of movement in the opposite direction also.

Thus, for example, not only is it the case that there are major doubts about the efficacy of psychotherapy or chemotherapy in many types of "mental" problem but there is good evidence that many doctors are, in consequence, unhappy in dealing with this area. In my own research, general practitioners were highly sceptical of the value of medical intervention in alcoholism and saw it as largely a social problem (Strong 1978), similarly the paediatricians whom I observed (Strong 1979), although they encountered all manner of things which had a possible psychiatric relevance, steered well clear of such matters except in extreme circumstances. This is not to say that such intervention is routinely avoided by all doctors. In general practice there is a massive prescription of psychotropic drugs but at the same time there is a growing scepticism among doctors as to their use. Moreover not only may most doctor define "psychiatric" matters as irrelevant or even dirty work but there is evidence that psychiatrists themselves regard much of their own practice in this light and share the same preference for the strictly biological that is typical of their colleagues. Thus McDonald and Patel's

---

28 Cochrane himself notes this in a postscript, 1972: p.87.

study of the attitude towards different conditions shown by the psychiatric staff of eight Glasgow hospitals concluded:

> Psychiatrists had significantly more favourable attitudes towards the organic group of illnesses than the rest of the illnesses, and this despite a training which necessarily puts more emphasis on the emotional and social aspects of illness. (MacDonald and Patel 1975)

It is therefore not surprising that many of the strongest critics of psychiatry have been psychiatrists themselves. The massive and growing emphasis on social factors in psychiatry during the last two decades has led to major reforms of psychiatric institutions and to strong attempts at *demedicalisation* by some psychiatrists[29]; a trend which has reached a current peak in the work of Scott and his colleagues at Napsbury Hospital (Yorkshire Television 1978).[30] Here psychiatrists and social workers, accepting the arguments that psychiatric referral is often contingent and due to family crisis, and that hospitalisation may only make things worse, work together to avoid admission – in so far as this is possible – and to make families face up to the social reasons that may lie behind referral. By such means, Scott emphasises, psychiatrists can rid themselves of irrelevant work and concentrate on the more serious cases and those where professional skills are most in order:

> We were literally the bins of the community ... we had very little control over admissions until we got this crisis service going ... the diagnosis of mental illness is a lay diagnosis – woe betide us if we disagreed (Yorkshire Television 1978).

In other words, in a situation where professionals of very low status are presented with vast numbers of patients with whom they can do little, demedicalisation, not imperialism, is the strategy which serves their interests best – and also, perhaps, those of their patients.

(3) *Restrictions on entry*

One further limit to medical expansion is that set by the professional organization. Like other occupations, medicine has tried to limit the numbers entering the profession, for "dilution" is a major threat to

---

29 The consequences of long-term stay in mental hospitals has been perhaps the most famous example of iatrogenesis, yet the very realisation of its effects has led to major attempts at reform. It is absurd to portray doctors as actually welcoming iatrogenesis or as doing nothing about it once it is revealed.

30 For an account of an earlier period at Napsbury, see Bott (1976).

professional status and income. However, although this policy has had a striking success, particularly in the United States where, relative to that of other groups, doctors' income has risen considerably, it undoubtedly sets limits to professional expansion for it severely constrains the conditions of production available to the average medical practitioner. The normal doctor sees a large number of patients with only a short period of time available for each and is obliged to treat them in a highly bureaucratic and controlled fashion in which almost all personal elements are stripped from the encounter (Stimson and Webb 1975, Strong 1979).[31] Such restrictions can only reinforce the fundamentally biological emphasis in medical ideology. All many doctors have is the patient's body; they lack most information about the patient's life outside the consulting-room or hospital and they have almost no effective means of acting on these "external" matters.

One qualification should, however, be made to this argument. As several writers have noted (Ehrenreich and Ehrenreich 1975, Zola and Miller 1973) one of the most remarkable professional achievements of modern medicine is the way in which doctors have managed to expand their empire, while at the same time severely restricting the production of new doctors. This has been achieved by the expansion of the "paramedical" professions which have been delegated some of the doctors' old tasks and yet still remain firmly under medical control. This strategy has undoubtedly been highly successful and has permitted a rapid growth of medical work without at the same time threatening the doctor's status. Indeed, by creating large, subservient groups it has in many ways reinforced it.

However, there are at least two factors which set limits to this procedure for expanding the medical empire. First, given the prestige of organic medicine, doctors have increasingly concentrated on the more technical and more biological tasks and handed over other matters to their subordinates. Thus, the acquisition of cheap help has merely reinforced this central part of medical ideology. Secondly, although doctors still retain considerable control over their juniors, the possibility of maintaining this in the long-run, at least in any very strong form, looks doubtful. The subordinate groups have reacted first by defensive rule-setting, (Rushing 1964) and secondly, by a distinct shift in their ideology towards the social sciences.[32]

If this were all, the process of the internal dissolution of the medical empire, though steady, would be extremely slow and would have definite limits. Most of the subordinate occupations still owe their ultimate

---

31 Private patients get a more personal treatment, as Strong shows, but the numbers who receive this are relatively few in number.

32 The contrast between the reaction of British doctors and nurses to the possibilities of medical sociology is most revealing.

allegiance to a fundamentally organic model and are, in many ways, the doctors' own creations.[33] However, the addition of social workers to the new health "team" represents a far more serious challenge to the doctors' leadership. Their ideology is fundamentally non-organic, their numbers are large, they work in many other settings beside the medial and their professional organization, at least in Britain, is increasingly strong. Since their ideology is in part psychotherapeutic, the main threat of medical imperialism may well come from them and not from the doctors who are likely to retreat even further into the organic specialism which they know and practise best – though even here social work ideology presents a major challenge to the form if not the content of the doctor–patient relationship since, unlike most medicine, it contains an explicitly theoretical approach to professional–client relationships.

(4) *Bourgeois freedoms*

The fourth and final restriction upon medical imperialism is the fundamental bourgeois emphasis upon the liberty of the individual subject. The state may have granted doctors a monopoly of practice in certain respects but it has given them almost no legal powers to constrain their patients' behaviour (Strong 1979). It may be up to the doctor to decide whether or not patients should receive treatment, but the latter typically reserve the right to decide both whether to seek it in the first place and, if offered it, whether or not to accept. Moreover, the belief in patients' rights in these matters is as central to many doctors as it is to the patients themselves. Many doctors see themselves as having only the most limited rights to intervene in alcoholism – if the patients reject treatment that is up to them (Strong 1978). Similarly an American study of genetic counsellors reveals that the majority believe that reproductive decisions were the clients' responsibility: the elimination of "bad genes" from the breeding population, or the economic burden on the community imposed by genetic faults were matters beyond their remit (Sorenson 1973). Medicine in this classic bourgeois version is a private contract between the doctor and the individual patient.

In the imperialist thesis, the fact of this freedom of choice is overcome by the argument that patients are addicted to medicine and cannot therefore be described as choosing the services which they procure. As we have seen, this assertion is somewhat dubious. The right to reject treatment or never to seek it in the first place means that patients can exercise their scepticism, and although some undoubtedly do not, it is clear, as I have

---

33 To take an extreme example, the first orthoptist was the daughter of the 19th century eye-specialist who devised the first mode of treatment.

argued, that most patients' use of medicine is still too moderate to be called an addiction.

The right to reject treatment also has important consequences when patients do appear for consultations. Medical sociologists have rightly emphasised the heavy control that is exerted by most doctors on such occasions. What has received less attention is the extremely polite manner in which they are typically conducted (Strong 1979). A fundamental premise of normal doctor–patient interaction is that, at least overtly, the patient is assumed to possess considerable moral character and competence. This gentility is the product of the patients' right to choose. Unless doctors are normally polite their patients will not return, thus harming perhaps both the patients' health and the doctors' income. Once again this constraint merely serves to reinforce the emphasis upon purely organic conditions, for it is only these which are morally neutral, or at least approximate to this state. By sticking with the more biological side of medical practice, doctors can avoid many of those topics which might threaten the surface gentility of the proceedings.

Finally it should be noted that, as before, there is an important difference as regards the ability to exercise patient choice between different types of medical system and this too has consequences for medical expansion. Whereas the British system minimises choice of doctor for those who do decide to seek treatment, the American system allows patients a very wide selection (though in practice this applies only to the rich). In consequence, the British system has been heavily criticised by such champions of the customer as Roth (1977). However, not only may such choice be delusory, as I shall argue in a moment, but the provision of choice, whatever its other advantages, is a clear incentive to medical imperialism.

A basic premise on which this expansion rests is, ironically enough, patients' own scepticism about medicine. For, although patients may have some general distrust of doctors, they normally lack the knowledge to pass correct technical judgements on the wisdom of any one doctor. Nevertheless, they still make such judgements for what else can they do? In a competitive market situation doctors can exploit this weakness by explicitly fostering the delusion of customer wisdom. The private practice style is one in which the doctor subtly indicates his own individual merit, flatters patients by treating them as particularly promising medical students and congratulates them on having chosen so well (Strong 1979). The personal charm, the lavish use of technical terms (displayed in the guise of enabling patients to make a better choice), the routine battery of impressive though normally useless tests, and the casual mention of colleagues in famous hospitals, all "prove" that you cannot get proper medicine unless you pay for it.

In such a pleasant ambience, it is only too easy for patients to be persuaded that they cannot be healthy unless they have regular check-ups, nor sane unless they see a psychiatrist once a week. One can even come to believe that only payment demonstrates a proper commitment to analysis. Moreover the financial power wielded by private patients can bend the profession towards their will (Strong 1979).[34] It is unhelpful to tell rich parents that their child is dim and more gratifying to talk of his "learning disability". Competitive private practice thus enforces product-differentiation and creates disease where none existed before.

Conclusions

The moral of this story is not that people in glass houses shouldn't throw stones, on the contrary, sociology and public health have heaved some most valuable boulders at medicine in recent times. Nor should my pointing to the phenomenon of sociological imperialism be taken to mean that its medical counterpart is either non-existent or negligible. The thesis of professional imperialism applies to all professions and most dangerously to those with great power – which medicine at present has and sociology has not. My aim has simply been to point out that sociology can have ambitions, too, and that professional hope may somewhat distort what are otherwise most valuable arguments.

In saying this I have normally adopted a *Guardian*-like editorial tone, "Yes, but on the other hand" has been my theme. I shall therefore close with something more dramatic and seek, for once, to chill the blood – though I shall begin, gently enough, with a mere summary.

When describing the practice of medicine, sociologists, much to the irritation of some doctors, commonly refer to the application of "the medical model",[35] or to a "disease ideology" which locates the aetiology and solution of problems at the level of individual biology. Medical irritation rests on an awareness of both the fractional nature of medicine and on the fact that this model, when considered as an intellectual theory, did not survive the 19th century in this pure and simple form. Nevertheless, though one may grant that sociologists' usage is perhaps misleading, there is a highly important sense in which, as we have seen, it remains true that what most doctors are interested in, are trained to deal with and have the facilities to handle are problems that are located within individuals, are preferably biomedical in nature and are capable of individual therapy.

---

34 See Freidson's distinction between client and colleague dependent practice (1970).

35 A good outline of this model can be found in Taber 1968.

However, the medical model which many sociologists represent as such a threat to the polity can in fact be shown to suffer from distinct limitations as a vehicle for empire-building. This is not to say that it precludes the illegitimate, or at least suspect medicalisation of parts of the social world. Certain kinds of expansion have clearly been possible within the limits that I have described. Psychoactive drugs provide a technique that does "work" in some sense and is compatible with the narrow constraints of the normal doctor–patient encounter. Bourgeois legal freedoms do not apply to all categories of patient; children, mental patients, prisoners and, to a much lesser extent, women are therefore more vulnerable to medical demands. Finally, new biological technologies with an important impact upon the social world may be developed which do not necessarily involve disease but are claimed as medical because of their bodily involvement. Modern methods of birth control are the obvious example here. Thus even within the constraints I have outlined medical imperialism is a far from negligible force. At the same time it can be argued that the more social model of illness, which many sociologists have recently come to favour, has potentially even more disturbing political implications and that the medical model is, in one sense at least, an important defence.

The first point to establish is that medical imperialism has no necessary tie to any one mode of doing medicine. Just as the cause of professional sociology may be advanced at different times by quite different kinds of sociology, so it is with medicine. At present the very predominance of an organic model of health and illness means that doctors, for all that the welfare state has helped them, are in fact excluded from the vast majority of political decisions, for these are deemed irrelevant to their competence. A social model of health is quite another matter. To quote another of social medicine's treasured dictums, this time by Virchow, "Medicine is a social science and politics nothing but medicine on a grand scale". Thus a fully social model of health, if implemented in any of the current forms of society, would require the involvement of social health experts in the whole range of industrial, housing, energy, and even foreign policy decisions, as well as a much closer supervision of people's nutrition, leisure activities, and so on. This strategy would dramatically lower the status of the currently prestigious branches of medicine such as surgery, but would entail an even more dramatic rise in the standing of disciplines such as epidemiology, public health, and health education who would now receive far greater political power than is at present available to any branch of medicine.

Moreover, there is no good reason to think that the shift to such a social model of health would avoid the detailed medical intervention at the level of the individual citizen which is the subject of so much criticism of the old "medical model". Indeed one may expect that a social model would call for intervention on a far more massive scale than anything required by organic medicine, for changing people's behaviour often requires detailed monitoring and supervision. Thus, not only was the creation of health visitors in Britain linked to the public health movement but any major expansion of the latter's power would almost certainly lead to a massive increase in both the number and powers of their associated health police.

The critics of the "medical model" tend to forget that its use, however barbarous on some occasions, has been liberating in others. In an alienated world, the sick role, far from having the entirely conservative implications which some ascribe to it, (Waitzkin and Waterman 1974) may serve as an individual defence and refuge. A fully social model, because it reintroduces human agency into health and illness, can serve, in a context where the state has still to wither away, as a means for an even more systematic oppression than is offered by organic medicine.[36]

---

36 See for example the measures to deal with alcoholics proposed by two critics of the disease model (Roman and Trice 1968; and the danger foreseen in the area of psychiatry by Leifer 1966). Zola himself (1972), is well aware of the dangers posed by the social model as are all those who write within the Hughes tradition. It is the more recent Marxist critics who tend to ignore this threat.

Chapter 6

The Rivals: An Essay on the Sociological Trades

One of the many problems that sociology faces is the sheer number of its rivals – unlike, say, physics, which may be reserved mostly for physicists, anyone can play. Not only are there competing social sciences, but everyone has to be something of a social scientist just to get by in this world. Everyone, that is, is obliged to gather data and test hypotheses. Although there may be more or less rigorous ways of doing this it cannot be denied that the central activity is the same.[1] Thus, as well as an ethno-methodology, there is an ethno-sociology, an ethno-psychology and so on.

There is also a third form of competition, one which comes neither from the academy, nor from the laity, one by which we are all influenced but which rarely receives the attention it deserves: novelists, journalists, film-makers and dramatists are, at least in part, also professional students of the social world. Their primary audiences may differ, as may some of their aims and, in consequence, their modes of analysis and communication, but quite a few of their findings and methods are the same, a fact which is all too often ignored, at least by ourselves – the consumers of our wares often make far less of a distinction. Here, as elsewhere (Bittner 1965), we seem to have been misled by an essentialist definitional procedure which concentrates on the differences between phenomena and neglects those other matters which they have in common.

There may, of course, be other motives in all this. We sociologists have had good reason to be stand-offish. To breach the university's walls and claim a serious place therein, sociology, like the other social sciences, has been obliged to draw a fairly rigid line. Its demarcation from those other professional analysts who cater to the mass market, has had to be made as severe as possible.[2] We have felt obliged to play up those special

---

1   Anyone who has reported their research findings to a group of those whom they have studied knows the problem. Living a life, for all its biasses, is a formidable method of data-gathering.

2   History and anthropology have not faced this dilemma quite so sharply. Since their wider audience is unfamiliar with their subject matter, they have

things which we alone do and to keep quiet about those which we hold in common. However, now that we have gained some sort of place within the academy, another possibility suggests itself. Might we not learn something from a closer look at our rivals' activities?

This is not, of course, a new suggestion and, to a rather limited extent, it is one which has already been followed. What I wish to argue here is that far more could be gained from a serious study of others' methods and findings. At the same time, such a study might throw an interesting light on the way we currently analyse our popular rivals. There is some evidence that sociology's analysis of professions such as medicine is biased by its own ambitions (Strong 1979b). How much more may we be biased against direct competition? How far, for example, are scathing exposes of media bias simply knocking copy (Anderson and Sharrock 1979).

What relevance has this to law and to medicine? Two answers may be given: first, just as they illuminate many other areas of social life, the methods and findings of our rivals may help us understand the work of the professions (to illustrate this, some of my examples will be drawn from medical novels; no doubt legal novels will be equally instructive); second, it is not clear how far we can go in understanding other occupations' behaviour unless we grasp that of our own.

Some Similarities

We may begin by considering some of those traits which, perhaps unexpectedly, the sociological trades share in common. Here, the first point to note is their mutual influence. On the one hand, large parts of sociology have grown directly out of the literary and journalistic traditions. The most obvious example is that of Park, a central figure in the Chicago School, who had been a journalist as well as having studied at Heidelberg (Dingwall, *et al.* 1980). But there are many other, rather more neglected influences. Steiner (1978) has argued that the study of both internal and external speech derives from the novel, and before that from the letter and the diary, and, before that even, from meditational religious exercises. Moreover, not only techniques but whole analyses have been borrowed. Trilling (1972) argues that Diderot was a crucial influence on Hegel. Likewise, Kumar

---

been able to lean heavily on the qualitative methods also used by the laity and by more popular commentators. Sociologists, however, since they have dealt neither with natives nor the dead, but primarily with living members of their own society have been obliged to use more quantitative methods to gain an edge over their competitors.

(1978) sees Dickens and other nineteenth-century novelists as centrally informing the sociological vision of the industrial revolution.

Similarly, although the ethnography of British rather than colonial life is only a recent development within academic sociology, the discipline having been associated with the statistical method from its earliest beginnings (Abrams 1968), there has been, for over a century, a major tradition of such work by novelists, journalists and social reformers (Keating 1976); a tradition which culminated in the work of Orwell, perhaps the most influential British social analyst of this century.

At the same time, one may, tentatively, argue that social science, in its turn, has begun to affect its competitors' production, at least in the United States. Two distinct trends may be discerned, though the same writer may work in both conventions. On the one hand, the growing cult of the fact may well account for the modern American cultivation of its opposite, the surreal fiction of Heller, Pynchon and Doctorow; if realism is captured by sociology, some novelists may take refuge in surrealism. On the other hand, there is the development of increasingly ethnographic forms and methods within both the novel and journalism.[3] Discussions of this hybrid, called 'faction' or 'the new journalism' by some (Kakutani 1980; Wolfe 1975), focus principally on the overlap and rivalry between the novel and journalism. One may also surmise a sociological influence. This emerges most clearly in 'Radical Chic' (Wolfe 1975) where Wolfe's ethnography is prefaced by a review of the sociological literature, but the genre as a whole, though typically lacking such overt ambitions, has some of the flavour of social science research. It emphasises lengthy and direct involvement with one's subjects, sometimes over a period of years; it places great stress on the recording of actual speech; and it stresses the need to consider the apparently trivial, the story behind the story, the background that is normally omitted from conventional journalism.[4]

This mutuality of influence is matched by a mutual ambition. Even if social analysis is something which everyone does, those who engage in it professionally are still tempted by delusions of grandeur. Indeed, perhaps the principal occupational deformation in the written arts, the social sciences and in journalism is the belief that one's particular profession holds the key to the meaning of social life. Though some apparently think otherwise (Runciman 1970), there seems little doubt that most sociologists have a very high opinion of their calling (Collins 1975). Indeed, there is a

---

3   See for example the work of Mailer, Capote and the anthology by Wolfe (1975).

4   There are of course important differences as well – particularly the aggressive stylistic flourishes developed principally by Wolfe.

touching tendency for each social science to assume that it, quite plainly, is the Queen of the Sciences.

This egocentric, if understandable, belief can be found elsewhere too. Poets seem no less ambitious on occasion. There is Shelley's famous claim, in 'A Defence of Poetry', that 'poets are the unacknowledged legislators of mankind', the equally grandiose claim of the French poet René Char, 'A chaque effrondrement des preuves, le poète répond par une salve d'avenir', which very roughly translates as, 'Wherever man's knowledge is found wanting, the poet sallies forth with a vision of the future' (cited in Steiner (1971)), and the German cult of the Poet or *Dichte* (Gay 1970). Journalists, likewise, scarcely seem reticent in their claims. Of course, just as sociologists and poets worry a lot about their actual influence, journalists may often see themselves as hacks and hackettes. Nevertheless, to call oneself the Fourth Estate is hardly unambitious, while the very names and nicknames of newspapers tell us much about their occupational pretensions – *The Times* (the Thunderer), the *Guardian,* the *Globe,* the *Tribune,* the *Observer,* the *Examiner,* the *Mirror* and *Le Monde.*

As this list also reminds us, journalists seem to worry as much as sociologists about their proper analytical role. Should one simply observe, examine, or, if a mirror, reflect the times, or, should one be a guardian or a tribune of the people? Similarly, just as sociologists or some of them, develop revolutionary tendencies from time to time, so too do poets from Wordsworth to Blok. More common, perhaps, is a desire to reform. Recent medical novels, for example, such as those by Shem (1980) and by Douglas (1977, 1980a, 1980b) share a suspicion of high-technology medicine and a desire to treat patients in a more humane fashion which is very close to their counterparts in medical sociology.

At the same time one may suspect that, despite these occasional ambitions, whether revolutionary or reformist, journalists, novelists and sociologists are typically analysts rather than practitioners. Advocacy is of course a central component in each, without which they would be weaker, but so, at the same time, is a certain scepticism and distance. Each is marked by an engagement with and a retreat from the world, a constant movement backwards and forwards which ends, if one stays in the profession, largely, though not wholly, in a withdrawal, for these are the picturing not the tinkering trades. Commentators who are too committed to particular types of action limit their appeal.

We also share, at least in part, a common location in the academy. Sociology has come very late to the university, compared with the other social sciences, and although it has found a base there in a way which the arts or journalism have not, even they have increasingly strong academic connections. Not only are there now departments of journalism and creative writing but the academy is now a central source of employment for many writers (as witness that modern phenomenon the university novel); its members and ex-members increasingly comprise the major audience for many arts; and, 'English' has become a theoretical subject like any other.

Since they are analysts not practitioners, sociologists, writers and journalists all have relatively weak professional organisations in bourgeois democracies though, given their different working conditions, the NUJ is much stronger than the BSA or PEN. They also share a common interest in free speech or, more accurately, freer writing. All three trades are vulnerable to censorship and where that is not practised overtly each, in their different ways, can be bought. Jobs, commissions, grants, pensions, patronage of one kind or another, all pose common dilemmas.

National traits are also important. Just as there are distinctive national sociologies, even if the differences are somewhat less marked than formerly (Shils 1980), so these are mirrored in the arts (and, to a somewhat lesser extent, in journalism). Shem's technique for describing the life of the junior hospital doctor, derives from that modern American surrealism described earlier, while Douglas's more restrained, more documentary style stems from the British tradition of Powell, Isherwood and Amis.

To this list of common origins and influences, of shared ambitions and institutions, one must also add a common interest in research, a keen theoretical ambition – on some occasions at least – and a fascination with speech and what it may reveal. Research is paraded as strongly by many journalists and novelists as it is by sociologists. Journalists conduct interviews, research documents, undertake joint projects with Insight teams and hire quantitative researchers to undertake polls. And so it is with novelists. Le Carré flies to Hong Kong; Arthur Hailey studies Ford and airport management; historical novelists like Farrell produce meticulous reconstructions of the Indian Mutiny and the Irish troubles; traditional crime writers check on poisons, and novelists of manners keep diaries to record events and people in much the same fashion as ethnographers.

Theoretical ambition is perhaps less obvious amongst journalists and writers but, in a way, this is no less true of sociology, where a lengthy tradition and major career constraints keep most research and theory well apart. For all this, some practitioners of each trade still manage to combine the two. One can, however, be misled here. Sociologists and journalists with theoretical ambitions typically announce these in a somewhat ponderous fashion. In the novel, by contrast, such aims may well be concealed. An example may, in consequence, be worth considering at some length.

Take, for instance, the series of twelve novels by Anthony Powell, *A Dance to the Music of Time*.[5] Many reviewers have seen this as a study of the author's times, as an amusing documentary record of literary and bohemian life in London from the 1920s to the 1960s, and so it is. However, more specifically theoretical concerns may also be discerned, though extensive theoretical passages are rare[6] (Spurling 1977). On my reading, the series is also a study of character, or characters.[7] What sorts of people are there in this world? How far do they change? To what extent is character immutable? These are the questions to which the series is addressed.

This theoretical concern is more readily seen if we consider the series, not as a piece of psychiatry or social psychology, the only social sciences to have considered character thus far, but instead as something more akin to interpretative sociology. Thus, while Freud receives some attention, as in Powell's respectful treatment of General Conyers, a late convert to Freudianism, his most favoured analysts are the English Renaissance writers on character, Aubrey[8] and Burton, who prefer a more naturalistic description of the range and variety of adult character. In line with this, his observations are drawn, not from the consulting room, but from the mundanities of everyday intercourse, while very great pains are taken to record only what the narrator directly observed, or had reported to him on good authority. He certainly engages in speculation as to what might have happened but treats it as such, continually emphasising that multiple interpretations of the data are possible, that there are many important matters to which he has not had access and that only limited and tentative conclusions may be drawn.

His method is to record what happens, over the course of sixty years of the narrator's life, to the large group of people that he meets and meets again during this period; what they made of themselves and what he made of them. This explicit treatment of his own life as data is further exemplified by his treatment of dialogue. Like several other British novelists in the realist tradition, he presents dialogue directly, and unadorned by any authorial comment. As in qualitative sociology, dialogue is seen as evidence and, therefore, to be presented and digested on its own. Interpretation and comment come either before or after the evidence, not during, and are explicitly defined as such. Dialogue is treated as an actual

---

5   Published in London by Heinemann between 1951 and 1975.

6   The most extended theoretical passage occurs perhaps in *Books Do Furnish a Room* (London: Heinemann, 1971) pp.153–4 and 157.

7   A useful guide to the characters is Hilary Spurling's *Handbook to Anthony Powell's Music of Time* (1977).

8   See also Powell's study, *John Aubrey and his Friends* (1980).

record of what happened, to be carefully distinguished from the observers' reactions and speculations.

Finally, he makes considerable use of 'natural experiments', the sociological, or in this case literary, device, of studying those natural contrasts which crop up from time to time. Two comparisons are central here, the first being those incongruous occasions, of which the book is full, when characters that he has previously encountered in quite disparate walks of life, happen to meet. A further, equally powerful device, is that of the Second World War. Prior to this, he has introduced a series of characters from a great range of settings. War-time mobilisation acts as a single institution which grades them all according to its distinct purposes, thus serving as an external check upon their nature quite separate from the whims of the observer and the contingencies of their previous situation in life.

It is therefore possible to see Powell as making a serious empirical and theoretical contribution towards the development of a sociology of character. Indeed, for those interested in observational methods, it is hard to see how a longitudinal study of any magnitude could be carried out in any other way.

One might, however, still argue that this work, and novels like it, merely ape social science conventions: that, whereas sociologists actually have research designs, cite data and distinguish between warranted and more tentative conclusions, novels are simply works of fiction, mere simulacra of the real thing.[9] There is, of course, something to this argument and some crucial differences between literature and social science will be considered later. For the moment it is worth concentrating on the shared concern for speech which is typical of both the written arts and, increasingly, of sociology.

For Powell, as for many modern sociologists, speech is the central data source, indeed the most characteristic human product. In consequence, both share a central belief in displaying speech as evidence. Of course, novelists have a license to invent their speech, and thus to heighten its

---

9 Clearly Powell's manner of handling dialogue cannot be a simple imitation of academic interpretative sociology, since no such thing existed at the time that he and various other British writers developed this mode. It seems more plausible to argue that both this style and sociology are joint products of a heightened consciousness of social science which affected British culture generally in the interwar period. See M. Lane, *Brave New Weltanschauungen: the intellectual context of sociology in Britain,* paper given at BSA annual conference, Lancaster (1980).

qualities for dramatic impact,[10] which is not granted to the journalist or sociologist. Whereas in sociology dialogue is a found object, produced ideally by forces external to the writer, it is the creation of literary authors. However, in several respects this divide is not as great as might appear. Not only is the method of demonstration the same but, given the research that novelists do, it cannot be claimed that their dialogue is wholly invented. Even the surreal speech that is so distinctive a feature of Orton's comedies was based in part on the systematic collection of real-life instances (Lahr 1980).

Moreover, the methods followed by interpretative sociologists in the selection and analysis of speech bear certain other important resemblances to those used by literary artists. If the sociologist is present at the moment of speech-production, whether as observer or interviewer, then he or she plays some part in the creation of the dialogue. Unless mechanical recording is used, sociologists necessarily invent at least some of what they report. Besides, though sociologists may not legitimately seek to heighten or improve the speech they collect, for purposes of quotation they certainly seek out the most concentrated, the most dramatic instances they can find. Finally, in informally analysing their material with colleagues, they commonly exaggerate for dramatic effect, using a whole range of literary devices. Often, it is only after the story or the joke that they realise that this was no joke, that this contained important elements of the truth. In the preliminary stages of analysis, dramatic methods can therefore play a central part in hypothesis-generation. If the quotation used by the qualitative sociologist is not too far from the heightened dialogue of the literary artist, it follows that, with only a little licence, one may use the work of at least some novelists much as one might use that of fellow ethnographers.

A personal example can be drawn from my own observational study of doctor–patient consultations (Strong 1979a). One of the central interpretative difficulties that I faced was the lack of comparable material from other studies. In particular, whereas I had fairly strong evidence that one particular set of rules, the bureaucratic format as I called it, was standard in NHS consultations and common in the American consultations on which I had data, what I took to be a further distinct mode, the 'charity' format, was used by only one of the American doctors in the study. Was this simply an idiosyncracy of this particular doctor, or not? Consultations with other doctors in Britain suggested that something like this format may

---

10 e.g. two junior doctors talking in Casualty,
    'Nothing in trolleys?'
    'No. So it's back to the suffering millions in triviatrics I suppose. I'm sure they just come in there out of the rain' (Douglas 1980b).

well have been fairly common in the past with the very poorest patients, while modern studies of casualty departments revealed that something approximating to it was still used with the most stigmatised of patients. I therefore included it as a separate mode although my analysis remained highly tentative. The following dialogue, however, which in certain respects closely resembles the charity format, suggests a wider incidence of the form, and in turn, a broader analysis of its origins:

Doctor: How long has she been ill?
Mother (M.): Five days now.
Doctor: *(Whispers to Feldsher)* Diphtheria. *(To Mother)* Why have you left it so long?
Grandmother (GM.): Five days, sir! Five days!
Doctor: Quiet, woman, you're only in the way! *(to M)* Why have you left it so long? Five days? Hmm?
Mother: *(Sinking to knees and banging head on floor)* Give her medicine. I'll kill myself if she dies.
Doctor: Get up at once or I won't talk to you. *(M. gets up. GM. starts praying).*
Feldsher: That's what they're all like. These people!
Mother: *(Furiously)* Does that mean she's going to die.
Doctor: *(Quietly)* Yes, she'll die.
Mother: Give her something! Help her! Give her some medicine!
Doctor: What medicine can I give her? Go on, you tell me. The little girl is suffocating, her throat is already blocked up. For five days you kept her ten miles away from me. Now what do you want me to do?
Grandmother: You're the one who's supposed to know.
Doctor: Shut up!

This dialogue is from a story by Bulgakov (1976). I have left the dialogue unchanged but removed some of the author's comments and set it out in sociological rather than novelistic conventions. The story was first published in Russia ten years after the revolution. Bulgakov had trained as a doctor and had spent 1917–18 working in a remote peasant community, an experience which formed the basis for a collection of short stories. Whereas I had seen the doctor who used the charity format as something of a villain, Bulgakov portrays himself as a hero in these stories and plainly expects his Soviet readership to do the same. I had explained the open abuse of patients in the charity format as largely the product of the doctor's belief in the idleness, immorality and stupidity of her patients; she was white, her patients black and poor. For Bulgakov, by contrast, though he certainly views his patients as culturally primitive, the point of such a style is to force the benefits of modern medicine on an ignorant, superstitious peasantry. Only by being so aggressive will his patients learn to consult immediately, to take proper precautions and so on.

Thus, this particular story ends happily. The doctor performs a tracheotomy, much against the women's will; the little girl recovers, and as the Feldsher remarks later, from then on his practice flourishes. The peasants believe he has performed a miracle and, thereafter, flock to him. He in turn comforts them as best he can with modern medicine. And here again there is a link. For, of all the doctors I observed, the doctor who used the charity format was the most concerned to emphasise the scientific basis of western medicine, not just to me but to her patients also. She, above all, was concerned to root out ignorance and dispel superstition.

Some Differences

Having argued that sociology is rather closer to journalism and the literary arts than some might imagine, I now turn to consider those differences that do, after all, divide them: in particular what makes social science scientific?

Perhaps the most central differences between the conventional literary artist and the journalist or social scientist is the very different nature of the truth which they claim to serve. The journalist and social scientist seek to establish that their claims are firmly based on actual incidents and specific individuals. Thus, even though they may for professional purposes, guarantee their subjects' anonymity in return for access, they nevertheless stress that behind the 'sources in Whitehall' or 'the people of Hicktown' there are indeed real people; thus establishing both their veracity and their morality. By contrast, artists normally strive, at least supposedly, for a general but not a specific truth, for a truth to life – however defined – but not a truth to particular individuals. Thus the morality of artists is often established in quite the reverse fashion to that of sociologists. Instead of guarantees that the story really happened, we get promises that it has all been made up. Here is an example, picked at random, of this somewhat implausible claim:

> The persons and incidents described in this book are fictional: any similarity to specific individuals and events is unintended by the author. The places too – with the exception of certain points of interest in New York – are imaginary and not intended to represent specific places.

Thus one exalts facts, the other the imagination; both conceal the extent to which they necessarily make use of the other's procedures. At the same time, such rhetoric does point to a very real difference. Gellner (1974, p.28) puts it this way:

> In any system of ideas or convictions, truth is the first and pre-eminent consideration, and its absence cancels any other possible virtues. This point may now seem obvious or even trite. Yet its sustained and ruthless application is anything but innocuous. It is radical, revolutionary and deeply disturbing. It requires that we look not to things, not to the world, but instead to the validity of what we *know* about things or the world. ... So real intellectual sovereignty lies in the norms of cognition ...

A sustained concern for truth therefore entails the public display of one's methods, for only in this way does one reveal not what one knows but how one knows it. And it is this public display which is the essence of science. For what is displayed can be checked by others, and, if possible, reproduced by them. Whereas writers and even journalists aim to construct individual works, works that stand on their own, the only novelty allowed the scientist is to be first. After that, ideally, everyone should be able to do the same. All they have to do is follow the methods. Scientists' methods are public, available to everyone after publication; those of artists are trade secrets, part of their mystery, and are typically concealed.

Here, then, is a vital difference. At the same time, one cannot go too far with this. Not only may some modern novelists display at least some of their methods, but it would appear that even the hardest of natural scientists fail to spell out all of the procedures which they follow in their research, indeed that they are sometimes unable to do so (Mulkay 1979). A central part of methods it would seem is tacit knowledge, developed and shared by those who work together but resting unformulated and thus unavailable to those without personal contact.

Finally, at least in the social sciences, there would seem to be strong social influences on which methods do get displayed and which are ignored. In sociology, for example, we are most explicit about those procedures which we ourselves have invented or developed, that is quantitative procedures. Most qualitative methods, however, since they pre-date the discipline, are largely ignored in qualitative reports. There has been little methodological writing about them until very recently; there are major researchers, such as Goffman, with many volumes to their credit, who have not published a single line on their techniques; and, while quantitative data are conventionally available to other researchers for re-analysis, no such traditions exists in qualitative research; field-notes, indeed are often jealously guarded.[11]

Science is therefore public, or at least normally strives to be. However, in another, crucial sense it is closed off from the world. Indeed, it is this central ambiguity in its relation to the world, and the specific form that this ambiguity takes, which is one of its most distinctive features. Its isolation from the world stems from the revolutionary nature of the search for truth. All radical movements, as Bittner (1963) notes, seek a unified and internally consistent interpretation of the meaning of the world. As such, they require for their survival and growth a fairly strict demarcation from the fuzzy, ad hoc and heterogeneous meanings of everyday life. An active segregation from the world is the standard radical policy.

However, the very procedures by which the radicalism so necessary to science is maintained, may also serve to limit and curtail scientific investigation. This problem is but one instance of the general paradox which confronts any kind of radical movement or occupation which is more than purely self-regarding. Radicalism can only be maintained by separation from the world and yet, where this outer world is still of interest to the inner group, whether as object of study or object of practice, it must also be constantly admitted, a process which continually threatens either the faith of the practitioner or the rigour of the analyst.

Since science's primary role is that of commentator rather than practitioner, the set of transformation rules[12] and practices by which the radical's dilemma is resolved have taken a special form. Whereas radical movements of a more practical nature often proclaim that they have found the truth and try to establish a world-order based upon this,[13] doubt is firmly institutionalised within the scientific realm. Science travels hopefully but rarely claims that it has arrived. It allows the world the chance of proving it wrong, though 'the world' can only do this on the scientists' terms.

To put this more concretely: scientists try to enforce a set of rules which place strict limits on the entry of the outside world into their realm.

---

11 There is, for example, no qualitative equivalent to the SSRC's quantitative databank. (Conversation analysts must be excepted from these strictures. Their special openness to other's analysis of their data stems, perhaps, from their use of group methods of training and analysis; from their reliance upon mechanical recording and from the novel character of their work – this is an original sociological method.)

12 This term is taken from Goffman (1961b) and refers to the procedures by which the outer world is transformed so that it may enter the world of conversational, or in this case scientific, discourse, in an appropriately dressed manner.

13 Contrast Baumann's (1976) account of conventional socialism.

Every scientific paper, be it ever so short and its subject ever so tiny, is nevertheless supposed, at least in principle, to make claims about and build upon, in a logical and verifiable fashion, our knowledge of the rest of the entire natural and social world; an ambitious aim. Thus, supposedly, nothing can be admitted to our writings unless it is capable of being checked by the reader, either via the presentation of original data and a methods section or through reference to other work which upholds similar standards. Everything else must either be explicitly held in abeyance or overtly assumed for present purposes (the *ceteris paribus* or *etcetera* clause in science). In this fashion the outer world is admitted to the corpus of scientific knowledge only after it has, at least in theory, undergone the most rigorous scrutiny; a scrutiny which is practically embodied in the use of external references by scientific journals. Moreover, every member of every discipline has a right, even a duty, to challenge, disprove or modify what has earlier been agreed or just taken for granted. Nothing is sacred, even after it has undergone positive vetting.

These sceptical, cautious and cloistered arrangements constitute the distinctive institutions of science which separate it from other more worldly activities. Within it, ideally, one's audience and judges are solely one's colleagues who, again ideally, have, like oneself, a purely disinterested commitment to truth. By contrast, sociology's more popular rivals are necessarily constrained by the requirements of their own, rather different, audience, the mass audience, whose interests are more practical, more ideological or more aesthetic.

At the same time, of course, one must remember that these are only idealisations. The peculiarly disinterested institution of science develops only in special circumstances and remains constantly vulnerable. According to Collins, the collegial pursuit of independent truth arises under the following three conditions: the development of an educational system large enough for teachers to become inward-looking; a relative autonomy from outside control; and some degree of internal differentiation within the school system – the key group in the development of science are those most insulated from the outside world, the teachers of teachers (Collins 1975).

But, even given these conditions, and the firm creation and institutionalisation of science, the outer world constantly presses upon it. Scientists face a constant struggle to segregate themselves from the inducements offered by governments, pressure groups and publishers, all of which may provide alternative sources of funding and prestige to those of their colleagues. There is a never-ending struggle to ensure academic control of, or representation upon, grant-giving bodies; to ensure freedom of publication – and to make sure that the line between academic and non-academic publishing is distinct.[14] A struggle that is made all the harder by the fact that, at least within the social sciences, the majority of academic practitioners have many other aims besides the scientific. The pursuit of ideological, practical and aesthetic aims dominates large areas of social science and constantly threaten the distinction between the different types of picturing trades. Just as journalists and novelists may have theoretical ambitions so, in their turn, academics often write with others in mind besides their colleagues. In actual practice, audiences, interests and markets overlap quite considerably. Nevertheless, despite such blurring, the constant academic struggle does achieve something. The peculiar cognitive emphasis of science is made socially manifest in that isolated collegial structure which renders science distinct.

The other features which are often claimed as defining characteristics are at once both subordinate to this and, on closer examination, clearly visible in many non-scientific enterprises. Certainly within science they are to be found in a highly concentrated form and used in a far more rigorous and systematic fashion. But the system and rigour is the product of the peculiar institutional and ideological form that science takes.

Cumulativeness, for example, the way in which scientists explicitly build, via references and reviews, on the work of their predecessors and competitors, although clearly a central feature of science, can nonetheless be found in somewhat different form in literary traditions. Not only do writers develop the innovations of their predecessors but they may also make more or less explicit references to their works, sometimes in highly elaborate forms. Thus the central theme in both the works of Steiner referred to earlier is the nature, and very recent decline, of classical literary culture which, for the classically educated reader, formed a complex web of allusions and developments.

Likewise, though Collins (1975) stresses as fundamental the scientific aim of explaining everything and of doing so via the method of controlled comparison, such aims and methods can, as we have seen, be found elsewhere. All radical groups have such an aim and the method of variation

---

14 See, for example, the sustained attack upon OUP by Marshall Sahlins (1979), which concludes: 'Like the marketing of automobiles or toothpaste, academic research is submitted to the one characteristic sense of criticism left to American society: Caveat Emptor. So the publishing decisions of academic presses, and ultimately the nature of scholarly research, are drawn irresistibly into the orbit of the average common opinions of the consuming public. It's a scandal.'

can be found in all who reflect upon the world; it is certainly central to Powell's method. What makes science distinct is not the unique possession of these features but the unique rigour with which they are pursued, even though not all scientists are as rigorous as they might be.

So it is also with quantification. Quantification, of a kind, can be found in every type of writing about the world, while qualitative work is still central even in the most mathematised of sciences. Certainly, sophisticated quantification is characteristic of science in an advanced stage of development, and even so-called qualitative sociology is increasingly far more quantified than its literary counterparts. Such developments occur, so Kuhn (1961) suggests, because of their advantages in settling disputes. By contrast, as Collins (1975) points out, more literary styles trade off an essential ambiguity. It is their very complexity and ambiguity of meaning which renders literary classics re-readable and thus classics. This same complexity and ambiguity creates the possibility of literary criticism as an organised enterprise. It is not merely that classics are ambiguous; it is also that ambiguous texts are more available for the debate which elevates literature to classic status. The clarity of science and the fuzziness of art both serve collegial purpose.

So finally, it is with literary style or dramatic mode. On the one hand, the best scientific writing is practical, precise and orderly, it is both usable and disposable. It serves, not as a monument to itself but as an aid to collegial communication. Once this has been achieved it can be dispensed with. Likewise, though there is some truth in Walpole's observation that 'the world is a comedy to those that think, a tragedy to those that feel', such genres are typically barred from science. At the same time, the distinction is not wholly clear. Sociology has both tragedians and comedians; scientific style also has its rhetorical side (Gusfield 1976).

Conclusion

Science is a particular tune played on a set of instruments which all of us share in common.[15] Some instruments receive far more prominence than they do in more everyday tunes, others get merely the lightest, occasional touch. Care, precision, consequence, reliability, parsimony, focus and contrast are turned up, emotion and prescription are turned down, though they never completely disappear. Within the austere collegial melody of

---

15 Indeed for G.H. Mead, research methodology was 'only the evolutionary process grown self-conscious' for it is an essentially problem-solving activity. 'The animal is doing the same thing as the scientist is doing.' See Reck (1964), ch.3.

science even the slightest emotional shading can have a suitably dramatic effect.

What renders science distinctive, then, is not so much the instruments that are played, for crude variants of these can be found wherever we look; nor even the particular tune, for everyone plays brief snatches of this from time to time; it is rather the sustained and collaborative elaboration of this particular melody in preference to all the others one might play.

For all its fragmentary ubiquity, getting to play this tune in any serious manner can be a most difficult task and in some areas, of which sociology is one, the band as yet plays in a rather halting and ill-coordinated fashion, while there is some confusion over the choice of instrument. However, the need for more practice should not prevent us, as it so often does, from listening to that same melody when it is played by our more popular rivals. They may play in a different key and with a somewhat different emphasis but the tune can often be heard all the same.

The very fact that some topics and methods are conventionally the preserve of artists has meant that many have shied away from them in their eagerness to establish their own practice as scientific. But dependence on a mass market is not always a bad thing. Scientists must proceed cautiously, moving ahead only with the assent of a fair number of their colleagues. Artists and journalists are not so dependent upon their colleagues' approval but can appeal directly to the laity. Sales are the only criterion. In consequence, they are freer to experiment with new forms and new techniques such as film, audiotape and video-methods that only now are inching their way into sociological approval.[16] The purity of science is brought at the cost of a certain conservatism.

What can we then learn from literature and journalism? Clearly the popular genres are normally restricted to the more descriptive or ethnographic side of social comment though, bearing Powell in mind, we should pay attention to their more elaborate theoretical constructions. As far as methods go, we may learn as much from their old techniques as from their new ones. Keeping a diary is still a profound method of studying daily life and one far too little utilised in sociology. And as for topics there is much to be learned. Such commentators can often gain access to many of the places which sociology itself is unable to describe by any except the most remote methods. Leys' (1978) recent account of China; Crouse's (1974) account of American presidential campaigns and the role of the mass media; and Wolfe's brilliant essays on such topics as navy fighter

---

16 Collins (1975) argues that, in fact, many of the most important contributions to the social sciences have been made by 'role-hybrids', that is by academically oriented non-academics, who bring to the academy empirical material and analyses which have, hitherto, conventionally been excluded.

pilots in Vietnam; all these represent areas to which sociologists would find access rather difficult. For in such work it is often the writer's special job, whether as journalist or as art historian/diplomat (Leys), or else their very fame as popular writers, that gives them their entry.

Sociology is also a lengthy business. Its characterisation as 'slow journalism', or the view of the latter as instant sociology, are both apt. We often take a long time to hear of what is going on in the outside world and when we do find out, it can take even longer to get into the field. Finding money, time, contacts and doing some reading: all this is a slow business. For a discipline which has made a speciality of the modern world we are somewhat at a disadvantage compared to journalists. The pressure for daily or weekly production may often trivialise their comments but it does keep them in touch with what is going on.

Artistic ethnographers also write about many subjects which sociologists find it practically difficult to investigate. The obvious example here must be that of the family, not one of sociology's high points but the setting for much of the greatest work in the novel, film and drama. Families, being private places, are rather difficult for the self-styled observer to cope with, but seem quite manageable for the more discreet artistic observer who, of course, only writes 'fiction'. Finally, there are many important topics in micro-sociology which till now have been far better explored by artists than by sociologists. Character, consciousness, emotion: all these have received a far more subtle empirical portrayal by our rivals and we have much to learn from them.

A moral: Our literature reviews should not ignore literature.

Acknowledgements

I would like to thank Sheila Adam, Janet Askham, Mick Bloor, Gordon Horobin, Klim McPherson, David Oldman, Bernard Smith, Clare Wright and Robert Dingwall and Phillip Lewis for all their comments and conversation.

Chapter 7

The Academic Encirclement of Medicine?

Though we all have need of doctors, the amount of faith we place in their advice seems to vary from age to age. At the moment, we live in an era of increasing scepticism. The cost, the effectiveness and the humanity of modern medicine are all the subject of controversy. Has bio-medicine really contributed much towards better health? Or is it mostly due to better nutrition, sanitation and housing? Do surgery or chemotherapy on a massive scale actually cure us or are they both ineffective and iatrogenic, producing rather than mitigating human misery? Does medicine free us from disease or does it serve as an instrument of social control? The new philosophy calls all in doubt.

The new philosophers are a mixed bunch – historians, lawyers, theologians, acupuncturists, ecologists, community physicians, faith healers, activists, statisticians and social scientists. One of the things we have in common, apart from an interest in health, is the hope that we might wax as conventional medicine wanes. How likely is this? This is the question that this paper sets out to explore, though it focuses on just one segment of the new philosophers, the non-medical academics and their aspirations to re-shape the course of medical practice. It asks what chance have sociologists or statisticians actually got to re-shape the medical world?

In attempting to answer this question, the paper is divided into five main sections. The first offers a quick historical sketch of the development of a scientific approach within medicine, while the second describes the rapid growth of various non-clinical disciplines with an interest in health and disease and their assault on the medical citadel. It focuses primarily on the extent to which they are accepted as colleagues by the medical profession and provides several reasons for thinking that the power of the non-clinical disciplines is growing, that some doctors welcome the prospect while others are somewhat alarmed. This interesting vision is then heavily qualified. The third section observes that, for all the extraordinary fragmentation of medicine into different specialisms, the profession has maintained a separate community, a solitary and isolated way of life which normally overrides the internal division of labour. To penetrate this is a hard task indeed. Moreover, as the fourth section notes, there is a variety of ways in which different disciplines relate to one another. Do any of us actually want to control medicine? Are many content with a more parasitic relationship? And if we do possess valuable knowledge, are there not ways in which medicine can learn from us, can use the knowledge we provide and yet still keep us at a distance and in our place? Finally the paper attempts to place these arguments in a wider political, economic and historical context, arguing that the relationships between medicine and the satellite disciplines are ultimately determined by much broader social forces. The analysis of inter-disciplinary relationships must venture far beyond the groves of academe.

The analysis is principally based on only two kinds of sources: general observation of medical sociology and community medicine, and recent internal discussions of the area within just three disciplines – academic medicine, medical sociology and medical statistics. It is based almost entirely on Anglo-American material. Things may be different elsewhere. Clearly, none of this will serve for a conclusion. It may, however, do for a beginning.

The Growth of Scientific Medicine

Scientific medicine, medicine based on the application of systematic observation and experiment to the problems of health and disease, can be traced back to the Greeks, the Chinese and beyond. In its modern Western form, its origins lie in the Renaissance. It was to prove, however, a difficult and prolonged delivery. The birth finally took place in the Paris hospital system in the first half of the nineteenth century (Shryock 1979). The techniques developed there and extended by the Germans formed the basis, both of scientific medicine and of a new division of medical and scientific labour; a set of approaches, disciplines and relationships which have been much elaborated but which have not yet, so far at least, fundamentally changed.

For all its eventual success, however, the new research-based approach took a long time to catch on. British medical practice took a distinctly lofty view of science compared to its German and American counterparts. Here, for example, is a physician reminiscing about his decision to accept a research chair in Oxford in 1938:

> So when the choice was offered, I became a professor, much to the surprise, indeed the consternation of relatives, friends and colleagues, who were disturbed that I should turn aside from the heights of consultant practice. (Witts 1971)

The special place that research occupies in modern medicine and the vastly improved power of the medical schools is a post-war phenomenon. The extreme rapidity of their post-war growth can best be illustrated by examples from the United States where the trend has gone further than anywhere else. Take, for example, the Department of Medicine at the University of Seattle: part of what is now one of the leading medical schools in America (Petersdorf 1980). In 1957 the department had 15 staff; by 1964 it had 12 full-time research staff alone; and by 1979 these had increased to 67. A similar expansion took place with graduate trainees; by 1967 it had already had 148 and by 1979 these had grown even further – to 265 in all. In 1964 the department had 53,000 square feet of floor-space, by 1979 this had become 160,000 – a figure to match that year's departmental budget of $33,000,000. The proximate cause of this growth can be found in the vast increase in the post-war funding of American medical research. As a proportion of GNP this increased from 0.06 per cent in 1950 to 0.33 per cent in 1974 and has fallen only very slightly since then. Overall, in the thirty years from 1950 to 1980, approximately $75 billion was spent on bio-medical research from public and private funds (Frederickson 1981).

The impact on medical training of these dramatic changes in research funding has, of course, been extensive. In most specialities, the hospital doctor who wishes to stay within the hospital is increasingly obliged to show evidence of personal research (*Lancet* 1980a). If he or she wishes to advance to yet more prestigious posts or places, further research is often necessary. The same does not apply to general practice but even so, its 'renaissance' has been founded on detailed research and the pressure for increased research here is undoubtedly growing. Moreover, the difficulties and necessity of keeping up with the ever-growing volume of research has led to successful campaigns for mandatory continuing education and re-certification in some specialities in the United States and such pressures are already felt, if to a lesser extent, in the United Kingdom and elsewhere.

This whole-hearted embrace of the academy and of medical science has brought the contemporary profession of medicine a vastly increased technical power and associated wealth, prestige and influence that are hitherto unmatched in its history. However, to embrace the academy may, in the long run, serve to diminish rather than enhance that power and influence. For control of the knowledge-base is one of the key sources of professional power (Parsons 1951, Freidson 1970). Medicine is increasingly dependent on its fellow-members of the academy for that knowledge. Hughes in a classic statement, described the claims made by the professions in thus fashion:

> Not merely do the practitioners by virtue of gaining admission to the charmed circle of colleagues, individually exercise the licence to do things that others

do not, but collectively they presume to tell society what is good and right for the individual and for society at large in some aspect of life. Indeed, they set the very terms in which people may think about this aspect of life. (Hughes 1958)

Medicine's claim to power lies in the claim to scientific knowledge of health and disease. If sociology, economics or statistics have serious truth to offer, may not they gain admission to the charmed circle of colleagues and set the terms in which others think about this aspect of life?

The Non-clinical Assault Upon Medicine

Take first the core of the traditional knowledge-base, bio-medicine. Despite the huge growth of academic medicine, there is a fundamental sense in which medical research has been, and continues to be, dominated by non-clinical investigations. Platt, after a review of many of the most famous medical advances, comments:

> Their [academic medicine's] contributions to the understanding of disease are established, real, and secure, and they have helped to make possible the deployment of the discoveries of modern medical science, both in relation to treatment and in diagnosis. Yet we must face the fact that these departments have not been responsible for, nor even seriously involved in, any of the discoveries in therapeutics or preventive medicine which I have just enumerated. (Platt 1967)

A recent, much more detailed investigation, a study of the origins of major advances over the last thirty years in cardiovascular pulmonary diseases (Comroe and Dripps 1976) shows that roughly two-thirds of the key contributions to major clinical advances came through basic rather than clinical research. Moreover, not only does academic medicine seem heavily dependent on non-clinical research but this dependence seems likely, at least on the basis of current trends, to increase. The last decade has seen a significant check in the growth of clinical research and in both Britain and the United States at least, academic medicine finds its recent eminence threatened (*Lancet* 1979; Rodgers and Blendon 1978). And this is not only simply due to the general decline in research expenditure. Wyngaarden, in a detailed analysis of recent trends in biomedical research training in the United States, has shown a precipitate decline in the number of M.D.s awarded NIH post-doctoral training grants and a continuing rise in the number of such grants awarded to those non-clinical Ph.D.s; indeed for the first time the latter are in the majority (Wyngaarden 1979). Likewise, a study of MRC research funding in the UK suggests that a similar trend can be discerned here also; even if it is not quite so marked (Booth 1980).

Two main reasons lie behind this continuing and apparently growing dominance of non-clinical scientists in the production of basic medical knowledge. First, natural scientists have in many respects a more appropriate training for basic biomedical research than clinicians, who require further education in order to compete. As the earlier quotation from Platt suggests, what most clinical researchers are best fitted to do is to spot new developments in other sciences which may have a medical relevance, and then learn how to apply them clinically. Doctors are best suited to applied, not basic science. Second, despite the rapid growth in medical manpower, it is often still far smaller than is needed to meet research demands in many new areas. For example, one recent estimate claims that the United States is currently training less than one tenth of the Ph.D. epidemiologists than it will need over the next decade (Detels 1979).

Just as important as this relative increase in numbers of natural scientists, there has also been a major shift in the post-war period in what counts as a topic for scientific investigation within medicine. The natural sciences have long been involved with medicine, but the 1940s onwards has seen the systematic application of a relatively new set of disciplines – the mathematical sciences, the social sciences and, most recently of all, moral philosophy. Mathematics and social science go back a long way in medicine (Shryock 1979) but their application on a major scale is new.

Two key trends may be discerned here. Traditionally, embattled clinicians have defended themselves against the claims of natural science by appealing to that central sense in which the practice of medicine is an 'art' or 'craft' (Avery Jones 1972). However, just as art has been captured by the academy – most serious art these days is practised by those who either teach in the academy or have undergone extensive academic training – so academics have begun to systematically record, measure and analyse the art and craft side of medicine. Sociological imperialism (Strong 1979b) is merely one part of a far more general assault upon the psychological, social, organisational, economic, political and ethical aspects of medicine. All aspects of medical practice are now open to inspection by the academy, indeed massive funds are available for this. Precisely because medicine is deemed so important, precisely because so much money is spent on it, all the problems which medicine has, both those which it sees itself and those which it produces for others, are now the subject of actual or potential empirical investigation. Nothing, it would seem, is too apparently trivial or obscure to escape academics and those gaps which presently exist will soon be filled, or at least touched on, given the academic prestige in delineating new topics of investigation.

This stampede into medical pastures is the more striking given the small scale of the social sciences prior to the second world war and their relative neglect of medical matters. Somehow, apparently medicine was seen as dealing with natural rather than social affairs (Ehrenreich and Ehrenreich 1971). Things soon changed and, although American sociology was perhaps the first to enter the field on any scale (Bloom 1978), economics, though starting later, has made more serious inroads, at least in the United States. Sociologists may now get the occasional article in *Annals of Internal Medicine* but economists appear regularly and on the most weighty of topics in the most prestigious of all medical journals, the *New England Journal of Medicine*.

Matters are somewhat different in Britain, for most of the medical schools and the medical journals have still to accept social science in any but the most bowdlerized of forms. Things may, however, be changing. Social science is on the curriculum of every medical school bar Oxford. Health economics has grown rapidly here and is now undergoing a period of self-scrutiny similar to that undertaken by medical sociologists a few years back (Engleman 1980). Likewise, the recent publication of the 'Black Report' (DHSS 1980) and the major series which the *British Medical Journal* has now devoted to health economics (Mooney and Drummond 1983) suggest a new and more serious approach to social science.

The second major area of invasion is that of the mathematical sciences and, here, two particular threats are posed to medicine. First there is computer science, which, according to some (*Lancet* 1975), represents a systematic and growing threat to the traditional practice of medicine. Computers can take faster and more accurate histories than doctors in many respects, and may also produce better diagnoses and prognoses. Such work is, however, largely at an experimental stage. On the other hand, however, there is medical statistics which has already mounted a major challenge to traditional medical practice. Statisticians' role in medical research is not simply limited to a brief period of statistical advice. They have an increasingly important role as general advisors on research design and on the interpretation of research. Moreover, the randomized clinical trial, the most important method in the evaluation of medical techniques, was invented by statisticians; has since been applied to ever-larger areas of medicine – in the United States in 1975 $641.8 million was currently being spent on a total of 755 (Office of Technology Assessment 1978) trials; has still to be applied to most medical therapies – one estimate suggested that between 80–90 per cent of all procedures have not been so evaluated (Bunker 1978); and, it is argued by some, should in the future be mandatory in the introduction of all new surgical as well as drug therapies (Bunker 1978).

The success of statistical imperialism has two obvious causes – the increasing importance of medical research and increasing consumer and financial pressures for evaluation. But it also derives from internal divisions within medicine. The issue here concerns the sheer organisational demands made by modern clinical trials. In areas where improvements in therapy are likely to be only small and this applies to many areas, clinical trials are only successful if carried out with very large numbers of patients. Most such trials, since they are organised by just one or two clinicians, do not meet this criterion (Tate 1979). The only solution therefore is either to aggregate the results of many different trials, or else, and this seems the current trend, to move towards large multi-centre trials. The sheer difficulties of co-ordinating large numbers of independent and to some extent rival clinicians, grants the statisticians a central role. They alone, as outsiders, are 'above' the clinical wrangles and can emerge as designers, controllers and independent arbiters.

In summary, it is hard to think of a single major academic discipline which does not now have a medical interest. What then will become of medicine, if it loses, or has lost control, of all its fundamental knowledge-base save that of clinical observation, and even this may well be threatened. Can real power, such as medicine has enjoyed, be sustained, if its own knowledge comes from biology, chemistry and physics, and if every aspect of medical belief and practice is now open to systematic and public investigation by other disciplines?

Already, slight but very definite cracks have begun to appear in the bastions of professional, as opposed to trade union, medical power; that is, in the colleges or faculties which organise and collectively embody each medical speciality. The Royal College of Pathologists already admits those without medical qualifications; there are serious current proposals to found an American College of Epidemiologists open to clinicians and non-clinicians alike (Lilienfield 1980); some British Community Physicians are calling for social scientists to be admitted to the Faculty of Community Medicine (Acheson 1980). A recent *Lancet* editorial summed things up this way:

> If pathology and community medicine seem to be working in the direction of welcoming scientists who are not members of the profession – what about other specialists? The links, for example, between physics and radiology, or between physics, pharmacology and anaesthetics, are clear. Can the Colleges reasonably expect to continue saying 'We cannot do without your expert advice and help but you may not eat at our table?' (*Lancet* 1980b)

Although the academy and medicine are now firmly in one another's embrace, it would, however, be naive to assume that we can talk of academic instead of medical dominance. The relationship is, and is likely to remain, a good deal more complex. Two major qualifications must be made to the story; the complex nature of interdisciplinary relationships and the solidarity of the medical profession.

Fratricide in the Academy; Solidarity Within Medicine

First, and most obviously, the various academic disciplines with an interest in medicine often have little in common besides that interest. Outside that area they too are often rival empires and, within it, they still fight over the pickings that medicine has to offer. Medicine may be encircled but the academy has no disciplined army, and is instead a motley collection of fractious and independent tribesmen, who spend as much time fighting each other as they do fighting medicine:

> Great battles are fought over what subjects should be taught. The alley-cats of psychology, sociology, epidemiology, statistics, anthropology, communications studies, computer science and even general practice and community medicine are hardly visible for flying fur in the scrap for time and status. Meanwhile the lions and tigers of medicine – surgery, anatomy, physiology and the like, count their blessings and guard their cubs (*BMJ*: 1980).

If the academy is divided, medicine, by comparison, is united. Indeed, there are good grounds for arguing that, despite all its divisions, fellow-feeling within medicine is considerably higher than in most other occupations. It is essential not to under-estimate the extent to which the medical world is still closed to outsiders, despite its long association with and inter-penetration by science. Even the natural sciences have only just gained a serious foothold in perhaps the most traditional of the medical crafts, surgery (Woodruff 1977) – the previous major incursion here, that of anaesthesia, was shunted sideways and made into a separate, lowlier discipline. Similarly, statisticians, though far better entrenched than sociologists, still feel excluded and their work under-valued (McPherson 1972). Even in the apparently simplest matters, change has been and is likely to remain slow, as Birtley ironically points out:

> Academic staff have not always been made very welcome in London's teaching hospitals, but that is now a thing of the past and my spies tell me that now even non-clinical professors are everywhere, allowed to eat in the consultant's dining rooms, if they wish to do so (Birtley 1980).

Unfortunately, we lack any detailed ethnographic study of the relationship between clinical and academic disciplines. There is nothing, for example, comparable to Rushing's brilliant study of the relations between psychiatrists and the other professionals practising in mental hospitals (Rushing 1964). Even without this, one may still point to a number of factors which foster clinical solidarity. All occupations, all groups indeed, develop ways of cherishing members and excluding outsiders but in medicine these have been taken to very special lengths, for if printers are the aristocracy of labour, with traditions and privileges going back to the very beginning of industrialization, then doctors, along with lawyers, are the professional aristocracy, whose traditions go back even further.

One obvious point to note is medical income. Mick presents evidence that the American health sector has the most sharply divided income of any industrial sector and the same seems likely to be true of the United Kingdom (Mick 1978). Moreover, although his analysis applies only to health practitioners, the income of non-clinical academics also lags well behind that of clinicians, once the latter's training is completed. Doctors are better housed, have bigger cars, take costlier holidays, have more expensive hobbies. Thus, whatever else separates them they have a common interest in the maintenance of their income and what it can buy.

But money, of course, is not the only thing which gives doctors their distinct identity. If it were, there would be little to distinguish them from, say, senior managers. Equally, or perhaps even more crucial, is their distinctive education. The nature of medical training has long been a favourite topic among medical sociologists. However, the focus here has been on how initiates *become* doctors, we have rarely asked the equally important question of how, as it were, they stay that way. Four factors seem particularly important here.

First, as compared with those who study non-clinical disciplines, medical students have, from their very first day, joined a club which virtually guarantees them future and life-long employment. Whereas only a few sociology or physics students go on to become straight sociologists or physicists, most medical students go on to become doctors. The profession keeps a watchful eye on the number of entrants to the market and ensures that there are lucrative jobs for all. The current outcry over medical 'unemployment' is somewhat touching and largely artefactual.

Second, as in all successful re-socialization programmes, the initiates are physically separated for lengthy periods of time from the outside world. Medical trainees are typically based on a separate campus; required to work long, a-social hours; and often obliged to live on the premises. In such a situation, like other members of total institutions, they have no one to fall back on but each other. The two big differences, however, from the scene which Goffman paints are, first, the eventual rewards and, secondly, the way in which trainee medical staff are rotated rapidly, both from one branch of an institution to another and from institution to institution (Goffman 1961a). In this their training resembles that of army officers or oil company executives and like them they acquire a loyalty as much to the profession as to the particular locale in which they are currently based.

Not only are medical trainees isolated in this fashion but some of the experiences which they share are of a most unusual kind: highly dramatic, personally testing and emotionally charged. Inexperienced young men and women are suddenly thrust into the most intimate matters of life and death, of hope, tragedy and trauma and given a central part to play. Like those who have experienced battle doctors share a bond which it is hard to communicate with outsiders (Shem 1980). Of course, most medical practice is far less dramatic and even that which is is must necessarily become fairly routinized with time. Nevertheless, this initial experience is a powerful one and reinforced by the special role into which patients cast their healers. Every novice teacher is surprised to find that their pupils treat them as possessing knowledge, indeed, some never get over the shock. How much more powerful then is it to be treated as a healer, as one who cares, knows and acts when others are at their most vulnerable? As a subject for study, medical charisma is as neglected by doctors as it is by social scientists (Kosa 1970; Brody 1982), but as an object and product of practice it is experienced and acted out daily by every clinician, even if direct medical consciousness of its power and shape usually fades once the novelty has worn off. It seems unlikely that the individual and group consequences of systematic and routine treatment by others as authoritative, caring and charismatic are unimportant.

All professions which practice with human subjects elaborate and cherish what one may see as a clinical myth, a mystique of practice. What is involved here is that special knowledge, those tricks of the trade, that gallery of types of client, those special incidents – funny, tragic or bizarre – which can be learnt only by doing, by experience. To call it myth is not to deny its very firm rooting in reality. Those who have never practised will never know, or so it is often claimed, and those who no longer practise are in danger of forgetting. In consequence, all members of a profession, whatever their current work, are obliged to pay lip-service to the clinical myth. Psychiatrists lecturing to surgeons tell jokes about the problems they share in common and the things that happened to them when they, long ago, were part of a surgical team. Community physicians who no longer practise clinical medicine still tell stories of the patients they once saw. In this doctors are no different from social workers or teachers, each of whom have their tribal loyalties. What may, perhaps, render that of doctors even stronger is their special isolation, the unusually dramatic nature of at least part of their work and that special charismatic status which people still grant them, however much – as people have always done – they also cast doubt on their competence and integrity from time to time.

Finally, doctors form a separate social as well as occupational world. They often inter-marry, or at least choose nurses as partners, and there are sufficient numbers of them in most places as well as sufficient contacts, both through lengthy job rotation and through the complex referral network, to find friends as well as colleagues among the medical ranks. Medical jargon provides a rich source of metaphor through which insiders may jokingly analyse the world's events and diagnosing pathology among friends, acquaintances and those seen in the street or on television, gives endless hours of amusement.

The Diversity and Ambiguity of Inter-disciplinary Relationships

If the academic penetration of medicine has been a somewhat dilatory affair, a vegetable passion, the slow pace is not simply a matter of medicine's stubborn resistance. Of equal importance, perhaps, is the ambiguity of the academy's aims and interests. Imperialism, whether geo-political or disciplinary in nature, is a complex matter and empires may expand or defend themselves against other's expansion by a variety of different means. Direct control is not the only aim, interest or outcome.

Four general types of inter-disciplinary relationships may be discerned: masters and servants; colleagues or collaborators; parasitism – where one discipline lives off the funding, concepts or data provided by another but pursues its own quite separate aims; and finally, occupational imitation, that is, the situation in which a discipline borrows the concepts and techniques of another, but keeps them firmly under its own control. Any two disciplines may, in some aspects, display any or all of these types, while any individual relationship between members of two disciplines may also contain its own special mixture.

(a) Master and slave. The role of servant or slave and, by extension that of master, would seem in the long run to be incompatible with the traditions of the academy. Nevertheless, as in the case of medicine, where one discipline has financial and political resources denied to others, the latter may well find themselves reduced to servitude, though occasionally rebelling from time to time and proclaiming that they are, or should be, the masters now (Strong 1979b; 1983b).

(b) Colleagues. The role of collaborator and colleague is the more normal aspiration of the under-dog (Robinson 1973), though the extent to, and manner in, which it is claimed, varies. For example, whereas many disciplines aspire on occasion to be the Queen of Science, statistics sees itself rather as Consort of all the sciences, possessing as it does, an unusual capacity to work with many, very different, disciplines:

> it is next to impossible to do good work in statistics without first-hand knowledge, preferably well up to date, of applications and the best possible discipline for a statistician, one uniquely available to him in the scientific community and one which is the peculiar glory and challenge of his professional life, consists in bouncing his statistical ideas off the critically receptive minds of colleagues whose specialties are not his own (Healey 1978).

The role of collaborator does, however, seem to imply just a little more than is conveyed in the above quotation. The classic distinction drawn by Straus between sociology *in* and *of* medicine (Straus 1957), can be found repeated, in different ways, in a variety of non-clinical disciplines (Campbell and Wiles 1976). What seems to be at issue here is the right of the particular disciplines not just to aid in projects which are of interest to clinicians but to take an independent part in the formulation and design of new projects. In medical sociology this often means working by oneself, though taking advice when necessary from doctors and others. In statistics it more normally represents a closer form of collaboration but one that nevertheless goes beyond simple statistical advice. To cite another medical statistician:

> First, and I think highest in the statistician's order of priority, are the genuinely collaborative projects in which the statistician play an essential role, finds stimulating problems to surmount – and I do not mean merely mathematical ones – and is a joint author in publications (Armitage in Spencer *et al.* 1970).

However, one must be careful to note, where the collaborator has such a degree of independence others may see it as motivated more by imperialism than by collegiality. Thus one clinical epidemiologist has written of 'the takeover of epidemiology by biostatisticians' (Orchard 1980) while other clinicians have feared that the problem was far more general than this:

> It is not only epidemiology which has felt the heavy weight of the statistician. Disquiet has also been voiced at what is perceived to be attempts by statisticians to dominate, for example, cancer research and there is no shortage of other examples ... the recognition that the control of information is power has not been lost on the computer-empire builder (Payne and Stafford 1980).

In other words, any one mode of relationship always has the potential to turn into something quite different and, given this, claims to be engaging in one mode may be no more than rhetoric, or at least may be regarded as such by the more suspiciously-minded. Finally, one should note that collaboration can result in the creation or attempted creation of an entirely new discipline formed out of parts of the contributory disciplines. Molecular biology is a spectacularly successful example of this in the medical field and may be contrasted with the failure of a similar attempt in the area of alcoholism.

(c) Parasitism. If the second type of relationship, collaboration, has distinctly symbiotic overtones, a third type may be seen as a form of parasitism. In its crudest form, one discipline or profession, while claiming to serve the interests of another, uses this liaison to divert funds, posts, etc. to its own exclusive purposes. A nice example of this relationship is Greenberg's account of the way in which Soviet and American high energy physicists played upon military and civilian ignorance to fund even bigger and better machines. The arms race was thus paralleled by a race to build the biggest accelerator (Greenberg 1969). Not all sciences can live off defence budgets in quite the same way and for sociology, and perhaps other disciplines too, our equivalent of the arms race is the public's fears about their health and their belief in modern scientific medicine. Certainly micro-sociology, feminist sociology and the sociology of the professions have all benefited greatly from medicine in recent years. It is a cleaner trough than 'defence' and one from which many disciplines may sup.

This is, of course, not to say that such work is necessarily immoral. All research applicants are obliged to claim to serve some higher good beyond that of the discipline's development. Moreover, there are good arguments to be made that basic research may and sometimes does lead to important developments within medical practice. All that is meant by 'parasitism' is that other disciplines often have no wish to control medicine. Insofar as it provides them with a suitable status and resources to carry on their own work they may well be content. Indeed, for a discipline to remain a distinct entity, some distance from others seems essential. Medical sociology is looked down on by those sociologists interested in 'theory' and, likewise, there are strong tensions in statistics between those who favour its empirical applications and those more interested in 'pure' theoretical development. Insofar as every science constitutes a kind of game, with its own internally derived rules and sets of interests, the famous toast, 'Here's to pure mathematics. May it never be of use to anyone', must strike a chord in parts of every academic discipline.

(d) Inoculation. The final type of relationship to be considered is one where a discipline borrows the techniques and concepts of another but puts them to its own uses and without employing members of the discipline from which it has taken them. Such inter-disciplinary borrowing is, of course, rife. Elton (1969) points out that historians have been borrowing from sociologists in this fashion for the last sixty years. Many disciplines can readily tolerate such borrowing. Indeed, one might argue that the resources which individual disciplines do get are in part dependent on the extent to which their ideas have generally permeated throughout the intellectual realm. It has been argued, for instance, that the massive creation and expansion of British academic departments of sociology which took place in the 1960s was merely the culmination of thirty years of steady growth in quite separate realms (Burns 1979). However, there is one sense in which this borrowing may well represent a threat. A discipline whose expertise is borrowed by many other separate disciplines is under serious challenge. For example, just as statisticians' collaboration may represent a threat to medicine, so other disciplines' parasitism may well threaten it:

> Without the involvement in other subjects via personal contacts and conferences, we may find whole fields of application slipping away from the professional statistician. This happened to some extent in psychology and may now be happening in some aspects of ecology and planning (Curnow in Spencer *et al.* 1970: 160).

To those, such as statistics, from whom much is borrowed, the strategy may, sometimes, come as a threat, but for the borrower, particularly where this is done on a massive scale, borrowing acts as an all-round defence against the encroachments of other disciplines. Such a strategy is often alleged to have been pursued by history. What counts, at any one point, as a sensible topic or a plausible explanation within history is heavily influenced by the findings of and changing trends within social science. Nevertheless, or precisely because of this, many historians remain suspicious of those from whom they borrow and, indeed, doubt whether a science of the social realm is even possible.

Something like this strategy has also been pursued in medicine, though on a much larger scale, given its greater wealth, and in a somewhat different fashion, given its natural science leanings. Thus, as new sciences have developed or have produced medical applications, so they have been incorporated within medicine, and this at two levels. On the one hand, they have gradually been introduced, in some form, into the undergraduate or pre-clinical curriculum and on the other hand, small groups of post-graduate clinicians have been trained in more advanced work and research. It is through this latter group that the work of non-clinical research has been mediated. Platt, (1967) saw this process as 'bridge-building' and Christie has provided an eloquent medical apologia for such work:

> Another type of specialist that is appearing in teaching hospitals comprises those who have specialized both in their clinical and in their research interests on one particular organ such as the heart or thyroid. They know more about the clinical aspects of their work than most physicians and more about the physiology and pharmacology than most physiologists or pharmacologists. They are particularly well equipped to exploit new discoveries for the benefit of the patient without the delay that was characteristic of the past. Sir William Osler in his Harveian oration in 1906 had this to say about Harvey's great discovery: 'There was nothing in it which could be converted immediately into practical benefit, nothing that even the Sydenham's of his day could take hold of and use.' 'One of the functions of clinical scientists is to prevent that kind of delay'. (1969)

All this may be true, but what is in one sense a bridge, may also act as a barrier as well. By training selected members to act as specialists in all the various sciences by which they are now surrounded, medicine has ensured that these sciences are kept at arm's length, that their interpretation and application is under medical control. In other words, there is a process opposite but complementary to that which Hughes noticed in the treatment of 'dirty work' (1958). All professions try to offload the latter onto other, more junior occupations; a tactic at which medicine has been remarkably successful. At the same time, we must also notice just how successful it has been at capturing and colonising parts of much more prestigious work as well; thereby retaining overall control of its chosen field. By imitating and appropriating the work of those disciplines which now produce most of its fundamental knowledge-base, medicine has successfully inoculated itself against this very immediate threat. Whether this will prove so successful in the long run cannot yet be known.

To say all this is not, of course, to allege that clinicians' main concern has been to defend their empire. Those who have learnt new sciences have often done so in the face of much clinical opposition or scepticism. Moreover, sciences eager to gain a foothold in that empire have been only too willing to lay on courses to train doctors in their skills. However, one must still include some element of intent. For inoculation has been the strategy, not simply with regard to the sciences, but to all supervisory or regulatory groups as well. The call for better management of health services has led, in Britain at least, to the training of clinicians in management – the modern community physician. When governments attempt to manage medicine, medics, in their turn, may turn into managers.

Conclusion

Social scientific predictions have an unhappy track record. It is always wiser, if less fun, to keep quiet about one's interest in the astrological side of the discipline. The trends discussed here are merely hints and possibilities; hardly actualities. Nevertheless, aside from the purely sociological interest of making patterns of the complex relations between disciplines, the argument may still have some relevance for the student of contemporary medicine. The scientific revolution in medicine is still young and medicine itself has been seriously respected for no more than a century. There is plenty of time as well as plenty of scope for change.

At the same time, the academy is not the only body which currently seeks to participate within and perhaps control medicine. The sheer size and impact of modern medicine have rendered it an object of interest to many other marauding empires besides that of the University. The self-interest of the modern State in medicine is now a commonplace. Two equally important but insufficiently analysed empires also deserve a mention – Law and Capital. Kennedy's much acclaimed Reith Lectures were little more than legal imperialism in populist clothing. Consider the following interesting quotation:

> I would not regard it as a bad thing if more law suits were brought against doctors or hospitals in, for example, cases in which a patient in a mental hospital was treated without consent. In this way the law would come to the aid of the inarticulate or helpless who otherwise might remain neglected and forgotten. Equally, it would not be a bad thing in a case in which the full implications of a particular form of treatment were not explained to the patient, or were discussed only with relatives or with the patient's spouse. Such action would, in my view, lead to a healthier respect for the patient's interests than at present seems to exist. And it would tend to ensure that standards of practice were established which met the approval of outsiders and were adhered to (Kennedy: 1980).

If the Law claims to offer a solution to some of the medical consumer's problems, capital claims to provide others. As medicine, and not just illness become increasingly seen as problematic, every kind of outsider rushes in with a patent solution – academics are not the only ones to claim to know the answers. Here is the solution to the growing financial costs of modern medical practice as offered by the vice-president of a Wall Street brokerage firm.

> Forget about ... (this) ... cost-containment stuff. What we're getting is the beginning of real competition and major shake-ups in medicine. There are now about 200 investor-owned so-called minor – emergency clinics [he said,

Noting that] they're popping up like fast-food franchises [he added that] the economics of these high-traffic, walk-in physicians' offices – many located in shopping centres – isn't all that different from the hamburger and chicken business. With about 2000 square feet, they can gross roughly $600,000 a year, which is average for a fast-food outlet ... the notion of a continuous relationship with a family physician doesn't make sense for most of America any more. People move too much ... and they're conscious of marketing, promotion and pricing. The price of these clinics is usually set just a bit below a visit to a conventional doctor's office. (Greenberg: 1980)

Two final cautions. First, there is an important sense in which we have been here before. The current wave of criticism of medicine; our doubts about its effectiveness and humanity; our interest in social rather than biological explanations of health and disease: all these received an even more powerful expression in the first half of the nineteenth century. Just as some modern epidemiologists have come to have doubts about the effectiveness of much of modern medicine, so the *therapeutic nihilists* of the nineteenth century applied statistical methods to the cures of their day, to blood-letting and the like, and found them wanting (Shryock 1979; Starr 1982). And just as modern statisticians, social scientists and community physicians have proclaimed the importance of social as much as biological factors in the production of health, so in the nineteenth century, doctors such as Virchow, engineers such as Chadwick, teachers like Shattuck and nurses such as Nightingale proclaimed the importance of social and environmental reform (Shryock 1979). So strong indeed was the hostility to conventional medicine that when the British government created the first National Board of Health, not a single doctor was appointed.

Yet though the first wave of therapeutic nihilism had a major effect both in creating a new, more sceptical medical practice and in the founding of modern public health, its impact receded with time. For all the criticism which they had faced, doctors, aided by natural science, went on to a vastly increased prestige. Bacteriology, surgery and then chemotherapy led the way. Might the same fate lie in store for the second wave of therapeutic nihilism which we are currently experiencing?

Now turn to consider the case of France, in many respects the birthplace of modern medicine, the place where the key scientific innovations were made. It was French doctors and scientists who first began the detailed pathological investigation of tissue, who put disease classification on a new footing by systematically combining both clinical observation and post-mortem findings, who first showed a clear link between social class and mortality, and who developed both modern bacteriology and physiology. Yet despite the international influence of French medicine in the nineteenth century, the local impact of some of the later discoveries of French medical science was extraordinarily slow.

Thus, Jamous and Peloille (1970) suggest that serious reform in French academic medicine has only occurred when there has also been a crisis of legitimacy within the wider State. On their analysis, the three major changes in the government of academic medicine over the last two hundred years can be linked, in turn, to the rise of Napoleon, De Gaulle's accession to power and the events of 1968. However pressing the need for reform, however widespread the general agreement that something must be done, nothing was in fact done until the wider political structure was itself undergoing drastic change. Those in charge of medicine had too strong a vested interest in the status quo to modify its structure in any serious way. Claude Bernard and Louis Pasteur might have revolutionized medical science but they were not doctors and the full impact of that revolution was not felt in France itself until 1958; only then were physiology and bacteriology wholeheartedly admitted within the teaching hospitals – up till then the central medical exam had consisted entirely of anatomy and pathology and the clinicians had maintained an almost complete dominance of the curriculum.

This extreme example of clinical dominance may, perhaps, owe something to the extensive medical penetration of French politics – there were 72 doctors in the National Assembly of 1898 (Zeldin 1973). However, since the creation of the National Health Service in Britain was also the product of a major shift in governmentality, the same argument may well apply here also. Thus, in conclusion, although clinical rule seems likely to be increasingly shared, which branches of the academy partake in that rule will be heavily determined by much broader changes in the polity and economy of individual countries. Those new disciplinary imperialists who seek to challenge clinical rule rely, in the end, more on external than on internal sponsorship and depend as much on the wider success of their patrons as on their own academic efforts.

Acknowledgments

I would like to thank Sheila Adam, David Armstrong, Paul Atkinson, Nick Black, Robert Dingwall and, above all, Klim McPherson for their help with this paper – though I am sure they would still quarrel with parts or all of it.

Chapter 8

Doctors and Nurses[1]

General management means, above all, micro-management: the organization, coordination and close monitoring of the frontline. The whole rationale of the Griffiths reforms lay in the proposition that there was something fundamentally wrong with the old nature and organization of the clinical trades. So our story focuses only on the aspects of those trades that presented major problems – at least in managers' eyes – for the creation of an efficient and effective service.

This is not, therefore, a rounded picture. Our topic may be doctors and nurses, but our perspective in this chapter is solely the management point of view. Moreover, our portrait is a collage and not a picture of a particular hospital, district or service. We have drawn on many different speakers to create a composite account. That account is based on the comments of a wide variety of managers (using a broad definition) – of general managers and nurse managers, of community physicians, treasurers and chairmen. Such managers had one thing in common: they had survived, sometimes profited from, the Griffiths reorganization. So these views on the clinical trades are the views of those who – for the most part – were committed, or not wholly opposed, to the major changes that had taken place. As such, the picture they painted was often selective, deliberately drawn to illustrate the worst, not the best, of medicine and nursing – the horrors that justified, so they held, the radical Griffiths reforms.

In giving their diagnosis and speaking of their many frustrations, most of these managers drew on twenty years or more of health service experience, on widely varied careers that had taken them through very different positions and highly disparate locations. But, despite the great variation in their backgrounds, there were some very striking similarities in their analysis of the problems posed by clinicians. An ex-administrator, now a tough general manager with decidedly Thatcherite tendencies, could hold remarkably similar views – in certain key respects – to a manager who had pioneered the professional development of nursing. Of course, there was sometimes much less unanimity over the solutions that might be necessary. None the less, many of the complaints about the clinical trades – at least as they were currently organized – were very much the same.

---

1 [Editor's note: co-authored with Jane Robinson.]

This is a backroom view of the NHS[2] and its management. Those we observed, heard speak or talked to ourselves were often outspoken. Why quote these selective, often satirical, necessarily distorted tales? Like a play, our story has several acts and each tries to balance or complement those that have gone before; each part must be interpreted in the light of the whole. Thus, our aim in these opening chapters is not to be fair to doctors and nurses but to present, in its most vivid form, the new managers' case against the old ways of running the clinical trades, the moments of anger, frustration and despair that led people from many different backgrounds to feel that change was urgently needed. Other points of view come later on.

Medical Individualism, Medical Power

We begin, then, with the managers' indictment. Take doctors first. The old NHS specialized in macro- not micro-management, in the shaping of broad structures rather than individual action. At the micro level, doctors were left free to run things in the way that they wanted and the power of medical syndicalism meant, so the new managers argued, that a rampant individualism reigned throughout the length and breadth of the service. Consider this reflection by a doctor turned manager on his ex-colleagues:

UGM: The planning system exists in the NHS simply to legitimize developments which have already taken place ... I'm a child psychiatrist and one of the things I've learnt is that it's almost impossible to get children to do what you want them to do – they're very like doctors ... One hospital administrator said to me the other day that he was answerable to 96 doctors who were answerable only to God – and four of them didn't even accept that!

---

2   List of abbreviations: CNA Chief nurse advisor; CNO Chief nursing officer (CANO in Wales); DCh District chairman; DFD District finance director; DDR District director of research; DGM District general manager; DMO District medical officer; DNE Director of nurse education; DNS Director of nursing services; EAG Educational advisory group; ENB English National Board; GP General practitioner; HAA Hospital activity analysis; HSR Health services researcher; INT Interviewer; ITU Intensive therapy unit; MAC Medical advisory committee; MC Management consultant; NHS National Health Service; NMPAC Nursing and midwifery professional advisory committee; PSGM Private sector hospital general manager; RGM Regional general manager; RNO Regional nursing officer; UGM Unit general manager; USVPM American hospital vice president of medicine.

Medical individualism was exemplified in every type of decision made by doctors. Consider, for example, the huge range of variation in medical treatment decisions, variations which, as these extracts indicate, were a key topic in the management conferences which surrounded the introduction of Griffiths:

RGM: There was a study in our region of cataract surgery. The variation in length of in-patient stay for the operation was between three and twelve days, with a mean of four days. Yet for private patients the mean was just two days! When we challenged the twelve-days man, he said it was to ensure high quality of care – yet his private patients were only staying two days.

HSR: What about surgical output? If you look at the data from trauma orthopaedics, the discharge rate by whole-time equivalent surgeons varies from 0 to 1,000 annually. Of course the data may be ropy. But the probability is that some surgeons are lazy and some are not ... We have very diverse ways of working in the NHS! And they can't say they're off attending Royal College meetings. Most of those who attend are the hard working surgeons ... Another example. The death rate from cholecystectomy [surgical removal of the gall bladder] in 51 districts varies from ½ to 4 per cent. Is this just because HAA is inaccurate? I'm not saying it's all poor performance. On the contrary, we have some super performers – but we also have some very poor performance and this question must be addressed. It's what I call grasping the Normansfield nettle.[3] A lot of people know what the problems are but they refuse to do anything about it. I recently did a report for a health authority and they refused to officially accept the data on surgeons' workload as they said it would be too hard to handle! ... I'm tired of facing my neighbour over the fence who's been waiting four years for an operation. The medical profession has been very slow on accepting measurement. Some things are superb; for example, the routine inquiries into maternal mortality, but in many other things they have been very slow – peri-operative deaths for example – very slow to come forward.

Medical individualism was equally apparent in the distinctive way in which doctors' participation in management decision making was reported. Decisions by the professional advisory committee might carry little weight with any particular doctor unless he or she was also on the committee:

CNA: They [doctors] may meet together but there is no entity and the real danger I've found, the real problem, is that you send them a paper, you

---

3 See Martin (1984).

attend the meeting – I've done this on our policy on resuscitation [that] nurses will initiate emergency resuscitation, including defibrillation – yes, the medical advisory committee agree to all these things in the meeting, all the people who are there do. And then you find that they don't disseminate the information through their organization, so the people who are not there don't know that the committee has agreed that on their behalf. They don't have any true representative authority, they are not delegates in any sense, they are not mandated. And you find that two or so years on, you are still quarrelling with individual practitioners ... 'I'm not going to allow my nurses to put a defibrillator on my patients.' 'But doctor, you might be fifteen miles away, up in the hills. Would you rather your patient died?' ... You know it's hard work.

The only way round this problem of representation was to include everyone on the advisory committee, but this too had its difficulties:

DGM: They won't allow either me or the deputy DGM in there and there are 50 people on the medical advisory committee! John [chair of MAC] doesn't believe in small, exclusive committees!

This lack of interest in corporate decision making was equally reflected, so managers argued, in many doctors' ignorance of management issues, in their inability to understand the new management proposals and in their unwillingness to play any part in such matters unless they were paid extra, something that rankled with other staff whose salaries were far smaller:

DGM: Doctors only operate inside their own environment. A friend of mine, the DGM from X district, said that doctors were very intelligent but very poorly educated!

DGM (ex-doctor): You'd be surprised how ignorant doctors are about these things. I bet half the doctors in this district don't know what RAWP is.

DGM: Doctors in the acute unit think that Griffiths is the worst thing that ever happened to them because we've appointed a doctor as UGM and they can't understand how one of their own colleagues can be making decisions – particularly when it conflicts with the medical executive machinery.

Asst UGM/DNS: We have a [mental handicap] unit meeting once a month. We set aside a Friday afternoon to informally discuss issues that arise ... We haven't called ourselves a formal administrative group because, if we do that, we have to pay the consultant to do it and – OK, it's a very small amount of money – but we feel very strongly about it. Likewise we've devolved the drugs budget to the hospital manager because if we'd given it to the consultant we'd have to pay him.

DGM: [We spent] half an hour [at the medical advisory committee] on whether there should be free sandwiches in theatre.

Moreover, not only was there little sense of institutional responsibility among some doctors, or so it was claimed, but some doctors were engaged in ruthless competition with one another for more power and resources. Thus, the clinical stress on patients too often meant a partiality for the patients of the most powerful clinicians:

DGM: In general, the quality of medical advice from the medical executive committee is insular and acute biased.

DMO: The surgeons are saying, 'You can't cut beds, you can't do that. It'll mean waiting lists.' And I say to them, 'What do you mean? If you've got a dementing 86-year-old granny, we haven't even got a service, let alone a waiting list.' But they don't understand.

Indeed, this competition for clinical resources proceeded, so it sometimes appeared, almost regardless of any financial or institutional constraints:

USVPM: In the States – and I imagine here too – you measure your importance [as a hospital doctor], even your sexual virility, by the number of beds you have.

UGM: The acute hospital can't be contained. It's running away with money at the moment. There's a half million overspend. The new cardiac surgeon has been told not to take on more than four patients a week and he simply refuses to do this. They've told him not to anaesthetize patients unless there is a bed in intensive care, but he insists on doing it anyway.

Such problems were multiplied in medical schools. The technical and imperial thrust of acute medicine increased dramatically in teaching districts. University doctors had very special powers. Indeed, they not only dominated the old administration but they could stand up to the new general management in a manner that was impossible for any other branch of the medical trade:

CNA: The UGMs realize now that the issue is getting hold of the doctors ... the real problem over there [the teaching hospital] is that there are far too many doctors and far too many sub-specialty doctors, some of whom have only got half a dozen beds ... and they all want to expand. If you take university appointments into account, over in X wing there are almost as many doctors as there are nurses!

MC: It was largely the London teaching districts I was working in [before]. Bureaucracy was everything. There were little empires, office politics, hospital versus hospital, consultant versus consultant. You'd do a plan. Everyone agreed to it but no one had the political backbone to do it. And yet these same weak people were the same ones who'd go bleating in public about cuts! Any idiot can close a ward. The skill lies in putting them to more effective use. But expediency and pragmatism are the name of the game in too many places ... Most teaching hospital consultants are pretty much the same.

DNS: One of the big problems is that I'm not sure the new UGM has any more control over the medical staff than the old unit administrator had – because half the doctors are not employed by the hospital but by the university and yet he's still supposed to manage them.

CNA: I had tremendous support from the Dean and from the consultants. [When the DGM had wished to abolish the senior nursing post at district.] The Dean said, 'Don't worry, there's no way we'll let them get rid of you' ... and I still manage the nursing budget – the teaching hospital unit wanted me to do this. [Almost no other CNAs retained the nursing budget post-Griffiths.]

Thus the individualistic ethic of medicine allowed the most powerful individual clinicians to dominate service priorities. At the same time, although doctors might be in fierce competition with one another for resources, this was a game they played among themselves. Faced with an outside challenge, they closed ranks. For managers, the huge emphasis on the right of individual doctors to take their own decisions too often meant a tacit agreement to the following code of professional ethics: to support one's colleagues whatever they did, simply because they were colleagues; to use Buggins' turn as the main principle for the allocation of new equipment; to ignore anyone who was not a member of the brotherhood:

DGM: We had an outbreak of some resistant infection. We had to close several wards. There's nothing new about that. But we got into a debate with the consultants who said they couldn't direct junior doctors to wash their hands – they were going from one patient to another in ITU and not washing their hands. What the doctors wanted to raise instead was food and cleaning.

DGM: A lot of doctors have a loyalty to the organization, but a number do not. I find it rather irritating and distasteful that clinicians are willing to knock this organization – but you don't hear a peep out of them that the private hospital down the road transfers loads of patients to us and wouldn't accept an AIDS case. Privately, among friends, one suspects they moan to each other – but you don't hear a peep out of them in public. Nurses will criticize the hospital they work in, but there's not the same hypocrisy.

CNA: I have grumbled at them over some of the things they have done. They are very bad at purchasing equipment ... they are very loath to say, 'You can't have that', so when it comes to actually allocating resources, they don't feel able to tell any other [medical] discipline [this] ... I keep telling them we can't afford it and they have really got to do better than this ... [It's] 'You scratch my back, I'll scratch yours' ... it is very difficult because of course they immediately say, 'We have clinical autonomy'.

DMO: The only reason I'm treated with just a bit of respect in this district by the consultants is because I once was one [he had been an anaesthetist] ... Doctors as a group are an absolute shower really. They're worse than any other occupation in terms of selfishness.

Given the enormous power of medical syndicalism, many of the old health service administrators had, so it was argued, simply given in. Even in the new era, many consultants expected to be dealt with individually at the very highest level. Particular consultants might try and do deals at any time and with anyone – with managers, with other trades, with the chairmen, with treasurers over breakfast. Moreover, the medical demand to go right to the top, the assumption that all managers, no matter how senior, were there to serve them individually, carried over even into the private sector:

DNS: Consultants try and solve everything by themselves ... In the past, they just nobbled an administrator and went off on their own to do some *ad hoc* planning. Not all administrators did this but some did, because this way they didn't get any aggravation – no doctors bursting through their doors demanding to know what was going on. Doctors nobbled nurses in exactly the same way. In the acute unit, it was all *ad hoc* planning led by individual consultants just nobbling administrators and nurses ... there were endless little deals going on all over the place ... and deals could get passed without being debated at all by the unit planning group! Doctors just manipulated the administrator and things happened without anyone else knowing about it!

DCh: What does a non-executive chairman do? One is constantly taking the temperature – being an open door. I would say that never a week passes without two or three people – usually doctors – coming to talk.

DFD: The DGM has just had this row over how many pacemakers are to be bought – in the past the consultants simply bought as many as they wanted. I had a consultant on the phone at eight o'clock this morning, he rang while I was having breakfast. Fortunately Bernard [DGM] had rung me over the weekend to brief me. The consultant was seeking a statement of our general policy here – but he didn't tell me what had happened or warn me he was seeing Bernard again later on today. He was just trying it on.

DGM: What's the difference between the behaviour of clinicians in the private sector and the NHS?

PSGM (from an American-owned private hospital): It's a Jekyll and Hyde thing, the same person in different guises! They do bring over into the private sector some of the old bad habits – and we have to educate them! The first year of our operation I got calls from doctors phoning me, the managing director! They were trying to go the back door route …I had to repeat over and over again, 'There are no special funds in my back pocket' …You [NHS managers] have got a tougher job, there's no doubt about it, OK?

Nursing Hierarchy, Nursing Subordination

If managers' main problem with medicine was its rampant individualism, many of their problems with nursing were quite the reverse. While medical syndicalism was the exemplar of the potential power of a profession, nursing was organized on quite opposite principles. Yet despite this fundamental difference, the principle on which nursing was based still created huge problems of management. Where doctors exhibited an excess of individual initiative, too often nurses had no initiative at all. For all the attempts to create something closer to a profession, many managers still felt that key aspects of nursing were dominated by an outlandish sense of hierarchy. A quasi-military discipline could extend throughout nursing, to every level of the organization:

DMO: Nurses took the wrong turn at the very start of nurse management. They should have taken the professional role. What we need is nurse practitioners equivalent to the hospital consultant who, like doctors, would have peers. They could be managed either by nurses or non-nurses. But, instead, nursing got trapped in the strange blind alley of a hierarchical system where to get any money you had to go up the bureaucracy. But nurses are basically staff, not line.

INT: Why didn't you appoint a CNA but rather let one be elected by the NMPAC?

DGM: The previous CNA had had a bad effect on nurse management all the time that I'd been in the district. I felt I had first to get the nurse managers' confidence back. It's taken nurses some time to realize what peer group support is. They've needed time to develop their confidence

... The main people imposing a hand-maiden role on nursing having been nurses themselves ... And it's not just oppressing other nurses. There's also been some oppression of the domestics. We've got a little problem there at the moment.

CNA: You haven't asked me anything about relations with the RNO ... The meetings are dreadful! We're simply told what to do. They're a replica of the old NMPAC here. It's the sort of meeting you always send a deputy to if you can!

DNS: [It's being] ... afraid of failing, that's what I think is the biggest thing with nursing staff. They are so used to being criticized if they lose a pill or somebody has happened to miscount them – and then they have to report it. And they are so used to being told, 'How could you let that happen, nurse?'

DNE: Most nurses come in with a do-gooding personality. The trouble is they don't ask too many questions. This is the hidden curriculum in nursing – open doors for your seniors and don't sit too close to them!

Moreover, although there was a radical internal reform movement within nursing – led by the Royal College – to create a proper nursing profession, comparatively modest attempts at professional development could still meet considerable opposition, not just from outsiders elsewhere in the service, but from senior figures within its own ranks. Many nurse managers, so it was held, positively enjoyed bossing their subordinates and had little interest in actively soliciting their junior staff's opinion or seriously enhancing their technical skills. To do so was too threatening to their own status:

CNA: They [the district's DNSs] don't accept, in my opinion, the professional role. One of the things we have strengthened is the nursing and midwifery advisory network – or at least we've tried to strengthen that – and it's interesting that some of them [DNSs] are not particularly interested in trying to get feelings from the grassroots staff.

DNS: There was fantastic opposition to our sister development programme at middle management level. The nursing officers blocked every move.

DNS: Most senior nurses are so concerned to deliver nursing services that they don't think how to develop nursing. Perhaps it's because they're so hierarchical and insecure. It's a particular style of management.

CNA: Despite two or three years of really hard work, there are still signs of real backwardness ... still some nurses who don't understand anything about professional responsibility. That woman in the meeting today who wanted auxiliaries to sign for everything! She's a clinical tutor.

This hierarchical world could extend, so it was argued, deep into some nurses' private lives and personality. In those parts of the country with expensive housing, the closure and sale of nurses' accommodation (one item in the new NHS policy) presented major problems in retaining staff. None the less, some managers were glad to see the old nurses' homes abolished. Nurses who had lived there for years could become institutionalized, as could those who worked too long in the same place:

DNS: There are a few nurses there [nurses' home] who've been there over twenty years and don't know any other world. It's dreadful. They go very peculiar.

DNS: The problem with mental handicap hospitals is that some of the managers are as institutionalized as the patients. You see that woman over there? She's forty now and she's been here since she was fifteen.

DNS: There have been two big recruitment surges into mental hospital nursing: one in the inter-war years during the period of high unemployment; the other during demob at the end of the war. Mental hospital nursing lent itself to the military model. It was an institution for the staff as well as the patients – and the superintendent physician was the commander.

All these factors, so managers held, had a further consequence which distinguished nursing quite dramatically from medicine. The elaborate hierarchy, the lack of any developed sense of professional identity and the initiation into submission from the earliest years meant that nursing was extraordinarily weak in the face of external opposition. Nursing might be huge in number, but there was relatively little occupational solidarity – some for example rejoiced in the demotion of the old nurse managers at district and region:

CNA: The divisions among nurses are its weakest point. Nurses shouldn't laugh at the fact that X district has managed without a CNO [as some members of the audience just had].

RCN representative: The key point made by Jean [the CNA who was the previous speaker] is that there are groups of speakers who are not supporting their CNO. We're much more cruel to each other as a profession than the other professions in the health service; indeed than most other professions I know of.

As a result, where nurses often found it hard to oppose the new management, DGMs had to proceed much more gingerly with doctors:

DNS: All too often in nursing, you start out with the support of your colleagues and when you get to the chairman's door and knock on it and say, 'We're all saying, "No!"' you suddenly find there's no one with you!

DGM: The capacity of nurses to screw the system is much less than that of doctors.

INT: What is it doctors have got?

DGM: Clout. They have the best trade union in the world and a capacity to retreat into professionalism that no one can challenge. There is immense group loyalty. Normansfield was a classic example. When the chief was suspended, they all came out in sympathy, but when he was shown to be culpable, nobody said a word ... [By contrast] ... we had a nursing officer suspended for unprofessional conduct – this involved transactional analysis of a very brutal kind and coercion of junior staff. The union went to the paper and said they wouldn't have it, but the campaign rapidly dissipated – the bulk of staff just weren't interested – yet this was where nurses were strongest.

Finally, some nurse managers noted that although nursing possessed its own elaborate hierarchy which stretched, since 1974, through every management tier, its place at the highest levels was very far from secure. However formidable an RNO might appear to a ward sister, her position was far weaker than her colleagues' and rivals':

RNO: The doctors here [community physicians] have ... got all the medical contracts – several thousand of them. We've not got this ... If you count up all the numbers [of staff at region] there's fifty people in personnel; fifty people on the medical side; a hundred in the treasurer's department; three hundred in administration – and two in nursing. That says it all. [This was after a post-Griffiths reduction of several posts on the nursing side but still gives a reasonably accurate picture.]

DGM (ex-nurse): The big advantage that the medical profession have got over nurses is that there's powerful professional advice at the regional level – and there are regional [medical] specialities too. Neither is true in nursing. How far is the problem in nursing the fact that it lacks a powerful input at region, so as a result the districts can't get started?

There was, then, a quite extraordinary contrast in managers' eyes between the individual power of doctors and the collective feebleness of nurses; between medicine's influence at the highest levels and nursing's notional representation; between doctors' fierce syndicalism and nursing's massive internal hierarchy. But having drawn that contrast, it is also crucial to see that the two are very intimately linked. Nursing's hierarchy stemmed not so much from within nursing itself, as from the many powerful forces – medicine, gender and the demands of an extremely labour-intensive industry – which had created, shaped and controlled the nursing trade. The effect of these three closely interlinked forces was to powerfully subordinate the entire occupation. As a consequence, it had reproduced internally the structure of its external domination. Tight control from without meant rigid hierarchy within. Though many deeply resented it, nurses had been – and mostly continued to be – the handmaidens of the medical profession, a servant class:

DNS: Doctors want a handmaiden. This is what they want. One consultant moaned to me the other day about the need for change. In the past, he said, his tea and toast were always ready for him when he came to the ward! I thought, 'I wish I'd known that before!'

DGM: Some people – the chairman of the medical advisory committee, for example – don't want thinking nurses. He believes that all nurses are good for is powdering the patients' bums!

DCh: Lots of doctors regard nurses as fodder for bossing around and nurses – well, I don't know if it's natural or not – but some nurses have a desperate desire to be subservient!

Even the most senior nurses could be patronized – or bullied – by some members of the medical profession. The following speaker recounted her arrival eight years previously at one of Britain's more famous teaching hospitals:

CNA: Within a fortnight I was summoned by the medical executive committee to account for my being appointed. So I went before them. I had to wait for twenty minutes and the person who went in before me was the DNS for the acute hospital and she was just berated. They were incredibly rude. She was reduced to a quivering wreck. It was obviously a common practice in the past to call matron to account ... They felt they had every right to ask me to account for yet another post in nursing administration and just what was I doing ... I was there three-quarters of an hour and they berated me one after another – things like, 'We don't want American-style academic nurses coming here' ... though *afterwards* one or two individual consultants came up and wished me good luck. [Original emphasis]

Managers, in their turn, might simply reflect medical attitudes. Doctors were the real bosses and their values could permeate the entire organization, affecting the new management quite as much as the old:

UGM (ex-nurse): We had this one-day meeting and Jim [chair] said that only doctors and administrators would be UGMs. He said that all the posts were sewn up and that they wanted a GP for the community – they were interested in X – who was quite keen. I told him that I wanted to be a general manager and he said, 'That's funny, I'd never thought of you as a general manager! We'd not thought of having any nurses as general managers in the authority' ... Jim said that the only way to lick management into shape was to get professionals into management and by professionals he meant doctors! ... What he failed to realize was that nurses are managers ... I have never been so angry in my life!

Most doctors and health care managers were, of course, male, most nurses, female. Such institutional stratification was regularly reinforced, so some female nurse managers reported, in their interaction with other staff

Asst UGM/DNS: My appointment to the local medical committee was for six months in the first instance. When that six months was up I raised the matter as no one else had and offered to leave the room while they discussed it. They said there was no need and the chairman made the typical remark which you learn to ignore that they had to keep me on as I was prettier than the rest.

CNA: Before the interview [for DGM] the chairman said to me, 'You don't want to be a general manager do you?' I said, 'Yes, I do'. But I kept my application in – I wasn't going to be put off by sexist talk ... The interview was a shambles. The first question was, 'Could I manage as a nurse and a woman?' I said, 'Well, I manage half the labour force already, so I don't think the other half will be a problem!'

CNA: Don't get me wrong. I'm no feminist [but] ... he [doctor/UGM] is sexist and an autocrat ... He is utterly condescending towards me as a nurse and as a woman. On one occasion when I asked what my role was at a meeting, he said, 'You're down to do the flowers, dear'.

Such an attitude towards women could, of course, also be held by male nurses and men held a very high proportion of the most important jobs within nursing. Likewise, given the cultural power of conventional gender roles, such attitudes were not confined solely to men:

Male CNA: It's most important not to react to this [the lower status of the CNA] like a little girl.

Male CNA: What I always wanted to say to them [other CNOs in region] is, 'Come on boys, get stuck in!'

DDR (and nurse): Of course, there is also the gender thing. I am the only woman with a senior appointment at district level. I wrote a letter for the DGM the other day and gave it to [general typing services]. When it was returned to me the secretary had typed in 'Mrs Frances Smith'. I said to her, 'But I told you to put Director of Research at the bottom' and she said, 'Oh! Will you be able to sign it then?'

Medical Science, Nursing Ignorance

One key contrast that managers drew between medicine and nursing thus lay in doctors' individualism and nurses' subordination (both internal and external). But to fully grasp managers' views of their position within the health service – and their complex relation to one another – one further distinction must be made. While all doctors were educated, most nurses were not. Medicine was backed by several hundred years of scientific investigation and its students had received a university level education for over one hundred years. By contrast, nurse training was mostly a matter of discipline and routine, but not of science. The radically different education that each trade received was a fundamental factor in their respective organization. Medical syndicalism rested on medical knowledge; nursing hierarchy on nursing ignorance.

Since medical training and medical science are so familiar, there is little point in describing them here. The hidden world of nurse education, however, needs more detailed investigation. None the less, to make the contrast between these sharply separated trades, it is worth stressing just how centrally medical syndicalism rested on doctors' intimate links with science. Doctors were in charge of a remorseless drive for technological advance; an advance which, as things were currently managed, only they understood. All other health service staff, however nominally powerful, depended on them for enlightenment:

DCh: I'm absolutely delighted with the medical staff; absolutely delighted that they're going to have a serious think about where this new technology will take us. Only they can tell us. They're the only ones who know.

For all this particular chairman's delight, such technological progress often generated vast costs, many of them potentially unnecessary; or so many other managers argued. New, highly expensive techniques exploded across the medical world in a largely unexamined fashion, propelled by an extraordinarily potent mixture of individualism, personal ambition, scientific interest and concern for patient welfare:

USVPM: As for new technology, we [doctors] don't know how to introduce it and we never have. Everybody's got to have it before it's been scientifically proven.

Asst UGM/DNS: A gastroenterology consultant has been putting awful pressure on the nursing staff, so I saw him [about this]. He said that he used to be able to endoscope only a couple of patients in a morning. Now he's got better he can do six! So now he's endoscoping everybody! It's absolutely rocketing. There's a much more accurate method of diagnosis now, of course – but no one's done a study of what percentage are negatives. So now we can have twenty or thirty 'scopes in an afternoon. My endoscopy department used to be part of outpatients. Then we gave up two theatres for this. There was minimal staffing available but the consultant said that was fine – he didn't need any more staff or equipment. But, of course, as soon as he was in, he demanded lots more staff and lots more equipment. This is his philosophy. Get in first and then make your demands!

Thus, doctors' individual power rested crucially on their monopoly of medical knowledge. In turn, the lowly place that nursing held within the NHS rested, for all its enormous size, on nurses' bio-medical ignorance. For a hundred years, most student nurses were primarily viewed as just cheap ward fodder and their education came a long way second to their work (Dingwall, Rafferty and Webster 1988); indeed, as many nurse managers argued, it might hardly be taken seriously at all:

DNE: When I was a student [twenty years ago] I wondered why all the tutors wore a corset. Then I found out that if you got a back injury they made you a tutor!

Most nursing schools were in fact tied, until relatively recently, to the specific manpower demands of particular hospitals, to the service of local doctors and to the views of the local matron:

DNE: Nurse education was traditionally very medically oriented. The consultants controlled the curriculum in the past. They marked the papers, set the exams and chose the students.

DNE: In this district there used to be five separate schools of nursing, one for each hospital! When the 74 reorganization came a DNE was appointed to look after all the units and she was responsible to the CNO; so the school became autonomous and independent – before that the results used to go straight to matron.

Despite such changes, students were still used heavily as cheap ward labour. Moreover, the extraordinarily complex funding arrangements for nursing schools still reflected the domination of particular service demands:

> DNE: Money comes from all sorts of places ... the EAG for statutory training, the ENB which pays for teachers and non-staff costs, the regional post-basic training budget and the district budget for in-service training and clinical practice development – which makes life complicated because teachers are paid under different budgets. At one stage you weren't even encouraged to allow a teacher to be paid from more than one budget – pathetic. It's easing up a little now. It was EAG at region that was fussy. District wasn't as bad. But you still have to keep an eye on this. For example, if I have a vacancy in statutory training which it's fundamental to fill, I couldn't transfer someone from a post-basic course. It's daft. In A and E training, it would make sense to employ someone with this skill to teach at all levels – but I can't ... The statutory training expenses for students who are leaving the base hospital for training in things like obstetrics, psychiatry and community work – this goes to EAG. But if they're being moved for service reasons, nursing has to claim from district. It's a bizarre system. It wasn't designed. It just growed like Topsy!

Thus, though nursing education had begun to achieve some independence from local medical and nursing demands, there were many unsolved problems. One fundamental difficulty was that training depended on tutors who were no longer in clinical practice – and were thus remote from the practical concerns of the service:

> DNE: Unlike most other professions we have a division of labour between the teachers and the practitioners. This is very unhealthy. Neither can survive and grow without the other. This is the key problem. We need to do both.
> DNE: [All] this changed over the sixties and seventies. Now nursing is completely detached from the medical profession – which is good and bad. No matter what people say about medical staff, they are realistic. Nurses, particularly teachers, sometimes don't talk about reality at all.
> DGM: I guess nurse tutors are amongst the worst really – in terms of thinking they know a lot (about the NHS) – but actually they are on the side, they are peripheral to what is going on.
> DNS: The real thing is partnership. The most difficult thing [in this district] was to develop links between the school of nursing and the service side. No one does that. The DNE sabotaged everything ... If you can't do, then you teach – that's still fundamentally true, which is why it's so

difficult to recruit a tutor like Joan, because most tutors don't teach clinical practice. It's not the fault of the tutors. It's the system ... Despite all the good developments here, we're still working round the school of nursing.

The problems caused by such divisions were compounded, so many nurse managers argued, by the weight of the past, by the sheer novelty of nursing's attempts to develop its own serious educational traditions and by the extraordinarily low standards from which many of the new schools had started. The most basic reforms were still desperately necessary in some places:

DNE: This school was in a diabolical state when I arrived [two years ago]. It was threatened by the ENB with closure in a year. They had good staff but no curriculum. No one knew what to put in the timetable. There was no defined philosophy, no aims or objectives. People just did what they had done in the past. They thought there was no time to plan – and although they did have some planning meetings, no action was ever taken ... My predecessor – who was retired [by the DGM] – just used to put his feet up and watch television. He had a set in his office! He should have been shot.

Even the most active proponents of professional reform might have real doubts about the time it would take to change nursing education. Project 2000, for example, was a radically new proposal, which came from the ENB, the body that set standards in English nursing education. It aimed to take nursing students out of the wards – at least at the start of their training – and make them full-time students in nursing schools that were linked to the rest of higher education. Some observers, however, were sceptical. If, for example, nurses could cling so fiercely to their old-fashioned uniforms, what chance was there of fundamental educational reform?

ENB representative (speaking to a meeting of CNAs): Well I've seen Project 2000 and I can promise you that by the year 2000 we will have got rid of the hats!

Moreover, even in those schools where major reforms had taken place, many nurse managers still had grave doubts about what was actually being taught. Some argued that in their desire to break with the past, nurse teachers had devised curricula with little relevance to practical nursing care. Cut off from the ward and filled with lofty occupational ideals, nurse educationalists had become trapped, so they felt, in a professionalizing project to ape medicine, forgetting, while they dreamed, what nursing actually involved:

DNS/Asst UGM: Nurses have lost credibility because they have left the bedside. I argue with Virginia [DNE] for hours about this ... our nurses are not being trained to give basic nursing care. They're trained to be mini-doctors. I want basic nursing care ... I want toilet care – that's what I want. We are building nurses now who think that bedpans and cups of tea are not nurses' jobs. I'm sorry to say this. You hear it from doctors all the time that you can't get nurses to give basic care nowadays. What they want to do is intubation. I get very irritated when people talk about non-nursing duties. We've pushed up the entry requirements far too high so that a lot of girls who'd make very good nurses can't gain entry. Girls with two A-levels are a very good thing for the profession – as long as they'll change beds.

The tensions over quality, the division between educators and clinicians and the arguments over the pace and direction of reform were reflected in the mixed views held by some nurse managers of the professional accrediting body, the ENB, and the new methods which it promoted. The introduction to the curriculum of 'nursing models' – abstract sets of principles shaped heavily by social psychology – appealed strongly to the educationalists. They certainly made a change from the more military methods of the past. But many nurse managers still had doubts about the adequacy of the new techniques, as the following discussion reveals:

CNA 1: They [ENB] used to check the dust on the lockers and if there wasn't any they'd say the training school was OK. But now they check the wiring diagrams [nursing models]!

CNA 2: The real problem is that the nurse tutors don't understand the models themselves. They simply learn them off by heart and then teach them by rote to the students ...

CNA 1: The ENB's advice is crass, they've got no understanding of the service ...

CNA 2: In the last two years – and for me in my experience, for the very first time – the ENB advisors have got real credibility. But in general, I agree the ENB has very low credibility ...

CNA 3: The problem is that even before the ENB, the GNC was a load of rubbish ...

Qualifications and Conclusions

Our aim in this chapter has been to capture a few simple stereotypes of the clinical trades, to distil service managers' views of the worst organizational attributes of medicine and nursing – the features that made radical reform so essential in their eyes. In the crude model presented here, the two trades had a strange symmetry, each being a bizarre reverse image of the other. Doctors were men and nurses were women. Doctors were small in number but possessed extraordinary power. Nursing was vast in size but amazingly weak in influence. Doctors were educated and nurses were ignorant. Doctors were wealthy and nurses were poorly paid. Medicine had a vast scientific base, nursing had hardly any. Doctors were independent professionals, possessing a fierce autonomy in their clinical judgement; nursing was not a profession and was notorious for its hierarchy, indeed, for an almost military discipline. Doctors were famed for their solidarity when threatened, nurses renowned for the ease with which they gave way. Doctors were to be skilful, nurses were to be virtuous.

The managers from whom this collage has been drawn were of many different types. Some came from administration, many others came from nursing or medicine. Whatever their origins, there was often remarkable unanimity in the problems they perceived. None the less, our telling of the story has necessarily been selective. We have had to abstract key themes from many different accounts; not every manager would endorse the views presented here. We have also had to simplify. In striving for a few essential features, we have ignored the many local variations that occurred throughout the NHS. Several qualifications should, therefore, now be made.

The first concerns the character of doctors. As we have seen, doctors came in for a good deal of abuse from many managers. Some doctors, so they argued, were selfish, egocentric and greedy; highly aggressive on their own account but always willing to cover up for each other. 'An absolute shower really', as one doctor and manager put it. But, as that doctor also added, this applied to their properties, 'as a group'. At an individual level, many doctors could be fine fellows.

So, for all managers' fierce criticism of doctors, their comments were often balanced by some positive remarks. The CNA who denounced doctors' inability to establish a group policy on defibrillation ended her story by saying, 'But having said all that, they're good chaps really'. Most managers took similar care to qualify their criticisms. As we have also seen, there were some very 'hard working surgeons ... some super performers' and 'a lot of doctors' who had 'a loyalty to the organization'. The problem for managers lay, for the most part, not in doctors' individual attributes but in their properties as members of a profession. Moreover, even at the group level, their attributes might vary. The management consultant from outside the NHS who had been so angry with doctors in teaching hospitals found his colleagues in a non-teaching district far more reasonable:

DFD: On first working for the NHS, I thought I'd find a lot of people who cared enormously but who needed active leadership. This district is like this ... The consultants here are mostly OK. I've found them positive, constructive.

A second qualification concerns the character of nursing. As the reader may have noticed, many of the fiercest criticisms of nursing came from nurse managers. Griffiths was not the only reaction to the failings of traditional NHS management. Nursing too had produced its own internal reform movement. The 1974 reorganization offered the chance for nursing reformers to found a proper nursing profession modelled on medicine. If some of the nurse managers created at that point simply continued the old hierarchical ways, others used the new powers of the CNO in quite the opposite direction – to foster, not stifle, professional development. The old military discipline was breaking down (Robinson, Strong and Elkan 1989). Systematic clinical research had begun and in some areas nurses had been encouraged to treat each other – and doctors – as peers. Here, for example, are three quotations from nurse managers who had systematically tried to develop a new and radically reformed model of nursing.

CNA: I've just finished three years' research into fractured femurs which shows that there's been a dreadful quality of care – so I had to give a talk to the orthopods and their post-graduate students ... The research nurses had followed up one hundred patients over time. I showed the doctors that we just weren't getting them to move, we weren't giving them enough fluids ... They've asked me to give a paper on it at their national conference.

CNA: Nurses have become very articulate. We've learnt a lot in the last ten years. We've moved away from being the doctors' handmaidens. There's been the funniest row in antenatal care. It's a real cattle market down there. So we said that whoever actually sees the patient – even if it's the doctor – has to do everything, including the urine! I've had a doctor on the phone to me saying, 'Your nurses said they're not our handmaidens!' I said, 'Quite right too' and put the phone down.

CNA: I got permission to set it up [new ward] as an experiment to see if we could get better care cheaper through a mixture of primary nurses, support workers and clerical help for twelve hours a day ... The philosophy for nursing care [that we want to test in this experiment] is that registered nurses do the nursing. They have individual responsibility for individual patients and everything flows from that. You unbutton the whole of the existing system, including the shift system. You give primary nurses control of the resources and they determine how their patients will be looked after and how their support staff will be used.

In short, just as many doctors were not egocentric and selfish, so many nurses had begun to develop their education and challenge their subordination. Thus, in focusing deliberately on the worst attributes that managers saw – and trying to list these in some systematic fashion – we have painted an essentially timeless portrait of the clinical trades. We have gone for stark contrasts and ignored the internal changes that were slowly occurring within both medicine and nursing. Radical developments in science and technology and the huge growth in the size of acute hospitals were both modifying the traditional models of practice and imposing their own fundamental pressure for a more corporate view of health care organization:

DCh: The sheer diseconomies of scale [of the modem hospital] are very important – and the complexity of modern care. Hospitals used to be far simpler places. Our smaller community hospitals have no problems ... High-technology medicine has changed the relationship between doctors and nurses.

DNS/Asst UGM: They [doctors] think the return of the matron would bring back organization – but it wouldn't. The NHS has never been organized right; it's a myth. In the days they're quoting, patients with coronary thrombosis stayed six weeks – now it's ten days. So you can't have that old leisurely pace. Certainly in the past the cleaners and the porters did as they were told. The discipline was very rigid. But the same was true with the medical staff. Junior doctors never stepped out of line. But they do now. The whole idea of discipline has changed ... [Hospitals have too] ... they were very much smaller ... You didn't have the big DGH. Only psychiatry had the giant institutions. In years gone by, a general hospital had 200–300 beds ... Another thing, of course, is the growth of specialities that just weren't present in the forties and fifties – renal transplants, cardiac surgery, oncology units and so on ... Twenty-five years ago a matron in an acute hospital didn't have to worry about staffing in ITU ... Specialization puts a huge strain on resources. ITU costs a vast amount of money to staff ... Nursing now is much more technical than it was. The amount of skill a trained nurse now has to have has more than doubled since I was a student.

But, having said all this, it is important not to take such qualifications too far. Our account has largely set aside the important differences that existed *within* nursing, *within* medicine and *between* different districts. It has focused, instead, on managers' views of the worst of the clinical trades. The accounts we have chosen are, no doubt, both lurid and selective, but there is still good reason to take the main thrust of the charges seriously. Such views were held by many different sorts of manager, both with and without clinical backgrounds. Doctors might be slowly moving towards a more corporate view of things but they remained, so it was argued, individualist at heart. Though its force might vary from one doctor and one institution to another, medical syndicalism still blocked most attempts at corporate planning and allowed the minority to dictate to the majority. Nurses' education might be slowly improving but most nurses remained poorly trained and subordinate. Some nurse managers had initiated professional development, but nursing could still, on occasion, be fiercely hierarchical. The internal attributes and external relationships of each trade might be gradually mutating under the powerful influence of wider social, economic and scientific change, but there was still a very long way to go.

PART 3
Models, Methods and Methodologies

PART 3
Models, Method and
Methodology

Chapter 9

A Methodological Appendix to *The Ceremonial Order of the Clinic*

The subject of this book concerns those rules which make up the bureaucratic format; but finding rules in interaction and, more especially, keeping them alive in captivity so that others may see them too, presents considerable difficulties. A brief account of these difficulties and of the various ways of tackling them may therefore be necessary, at least for the sceptical or technically-minded reader.

The method of data collection used in this study was primarily based on observation. Observation, or the systematic recording of behaviour, has several advantages over interview data in the study of social rules. First, interviews are no guide to actual behaviour (Cicourel, 1964; Phillips, 1971). Many of the studies of doctor–patient relationship, since they are based solely on interviews, are purely accounts of attitudes. As Stimson and Webb's (1975) study has shown, there is no necessary relationship between what patients do in medical consultation and what they say they do in another context. (In group interviews women recounted heroic tales of their personal combat with their doctors, but no such behaviour was actually observed in GPs' surgeries.) What people say depends very much on what questions are asked, who asks them and the general sense of the occasion. Even where rules are accurately recounted – and interview methods allow no clear check on this – it is still impossible to determine how such rules relate to actual behaviour. For no rule specifies the grounds of its own application. That is, to use a rule one also needs a further set of rules to say when, how and in what circumstances the rule is to be used. These rules of thumb are rarely spelt out formally, save in legal proceedings. Aside from these difficulties, there are good grounds for arguing that people are incapable of immediate recall of many aspects of their behaviour. It is not merely that our accounts are guided by our prejudices or immediate circumstances but that we fail to notice much of what we do, for we attend only to those things that concern us most. As Fingarette (1969) has argued, there is no need for us even to be conscious of following a rule in order to actually do so. Interview data therefore contain a strong bias against the routine and the non-eventful.

The strategy that was followed in this study was therefore to observe and record the behaviour in question systematically and then to engage in detailed analysis and exemplification. This has certain advantages for both researcher and reader. For the researcher it provides a source of data which, unlike pre-coded material, is independent of the analysis and can therefore be re-read or re-played as a check against that analysis. Similarly, in so far as examples of data are provided in the text they provide readers with the possibility of independent checking.

Certain difficulties still remain. The method is highly labour-intensive and thus, like informal interviewing, does not permit of ready generalization, though this difficulty may be surmounted if other comparable studies are available (Becker, 1969a). More crucially, there are major problems involving the accuracy of note-taking, the detection of rules in observed interaction, the quantification of such phenomena, the influence of the observer upon the recorded material and the general difficulties of analysing qualitative data. Each of these matters deserves some attention.

Recording Interaction

There is a variety of procedures for recording interaction, each with its own advantages and disadvantages. Audio or video-tape offer the possibility of highly accurate recording but are obtrusive and pose major problems for transcription. The pen and paper method used in this study is, by comparison, extremely inaccurate; much that is spoken is lost and much that is recorded is no doubt altered. At the same time however, it does enable the relatively easy study of a very large number of cases and it is this which justifies its use in the present study. To have transcribed and analysed a mechanical recording of over 1,100 consultations, some of them up to an hour long, would have been a forbidding task and yet, unless one had gathered some such large body of data, there would have been an insufficient number of 'deviant cases' for analysis – and as we have seen it is the exceptions which prove the rule.

Moreover, this rather crude method of recording seems relatively tolerable for the somewhat gross matters with which I am here concerned. To illustrate the broad components of a role format, one does not require the same degree of accuracy in recording as is necessary for those concerned with the minutiae of conversational analysis, where the precise sequence and phrasing of word and gesture is essential to the analysis.

Quantifying Qualitative Data

My central assumption here is that it is illegitimate to attempt to count social phenomena more precisely than lay persons are themselves able to.[1] An examination of everyday counting practices soon reveals that the kind of things which human beings are able to count with any ease, and in which they may reasonably expect others to arrive at a similar total, are remarkably limited. They belong solely to the world of objects. We count cars, meals or bathrooms, but counting actions or emotions seems to be a much trickier business. To say, 'I had a good day,' I is a meaningful statement but to attempt to quantify its good aspects in any precise fashion is not possible.[2] Under inspection, 'good' things have their 'bad' side too; every silver lining has a cloud. In consequence it would be entirely bogus to quantify many aspects of the data which I have described here. Nevertheless, following Douglas (1971), I think there can be an important degree of certainty over people's typical meanings. Indeed, organized life would be impossible if this were not the case. A limited version of counting is thus often possible, using quantificatory statements such as 'always/typically/rarely/never'.

The reader will therefore have found a mixture of kinds of quantification within the book. On some matters, for example the number of foster-mothers or cases seen in a clinic, I feel able to be precise. For many other matters which deal with actions rather than objects and where far more judgment is therefore necessary, 'typically' or 'rarely' seem more sensible terms. For a few kinds of action I have in fact used numbers. Where these were extremely unusual and I had only a limited number of cases to study, it seemed reasonable to risk a little more quantification. Since these cases could be analysed in considerable detail, terms like 'three', 'four' or 'five' have sometimes been used. I cannot really claim to know that there were exactly three, four or five instances of X or Y. I have used numbers here because these were highly infrequent happenings for which I was specifically searching, and any possible examples of which had been given a good deal of thought. Such numbers also have, I confess, a rhetorical significance. 'Look, I could only find five!' sounds more convincing than 'I found very few exceptions' .

---

1   My stress here is upon capacities, not upon actual counting practices, for clearly there may be some things which people could count if they so chose but which only social scientists have any interest in. Moreover, there are some tribes where arithmetic is so under-developed that the precise counting of anything stops at a handful.

2   See the marvellous critique of 'quantophrenia' and the rise of the accountants in social science in Sorokin (1956).

The Influence of the Observer

One objection that is commonly made to studies such as this is that although observation is undoubtedly a more direct way of studying action, the presence of the observer changes the action in a way that interviewing does not. Since all action is oriented in some way to the immediate social context, it is undoubtedly true that the fieldworker changes that situation. However, there are good grounds, at least in the present study, for arguing that such effects were minimal. First, as Becker has emphasized, the daily business of life has to get done, and in clinics there was no other time or place for it to be done:

> The people the fieldworker observes are ordinarily constrained to act as they would have in his absence by the very social constraints whose effects interest him; he therefore has little chance, compared to the practitioners of other methods, to influence what they do, for more potent forces are operating (Becker, 1969b, p.43).

Second, such a presence was by no means strange. The medical settings that were studied here were highly public places with nurses, students, other staff and sometimes other patients all watching the action or overhearing parts of it. Fieldwork was not uncomfortable since there were so many others engaged in somewhat similar activities. Thus, staff rapidly became used to the presence of researchers and treated them as part of the furniture. Some of them indeed, despite being told otherwise, seemed to think that only the patients were being studied.

As for the clientele, it must be remembered that all of what they said was for the record, regardless of the record made by the researchers, for doctors themselves routinely made notes on what was said by parents during the consultation. It is quite likely that had there been no audience and no note-taking at all, conversations might have taken a somewhat different turn. Parents might have found 'personal' and emotional matters somewhat easier to raise, and they could well have felt more relaxed and been more informal. However, such constraints were in the nature of the settings, they were not imposed upon them by the research.

Understanding Action

Yet another problem which plagues both the writer and the reader of sociological work is the ambiguity of human action. How can we be certain that such and such really did mean what I say it meant? This difficulty is heightened when the reader is presented with mere snippets of data, abstracted from the context in which they occurred – a procedure which is clearly essential when data are long and monographs are short. As we shall see, there are special difficulties involved in interpreting the kind of data considered here. For all of these reasons some comment is needed on the solutions that I adopted.

For some writers the difficulty of providing guaranteed interpretation of any datum has led to their rejection of all conventional sociological description. While it is certainly true that all hitherto existing sociologies have failed to provide any sure method for overcoming the ambiguities of meaning in social interaction, it would be absurd to argue that such inquiry was thereby invalid.[3] The relevant arguments could and unfortunately do fill many volumes. Two brief points may be made here.

First, although misunderstanding is commonplace in daily life, it is clear that most action is premised upon the assumption that a correct interpretation of it is both possible and likely, at least where the participants are familiar with the situation. Indeed, action is constructed very precisely so that it can be correctly interpreted by the competent insider.[4] Thus for the outsider who wishes to understand what is going on, the principal method of arriving at this is to try to become competent, to immerse oneself as fully as possible in the situation; which is, of course, the procedure adopted in this study.

3   Some authors have been so disturbed by the failure to generate foolproof interpretive methods that they have abandoned all interest in conventional subject-matters and concentrated solely on analysing the methods that are used in everyday life to this end; their hope being that here at least some certainty is to be found. The more optimistic of them have an essentially Cartesian strategy. They have deliberately suspended belief in all the things that sociologists normally claim to know, hoping that if some small area of life can be found about which knowledge can be truly guaranteed, then a proper sociology might eventually be constructed on this firm basis. While this quest for certainty has produced some brilliant studies of lay methodology and the structuring of talk, the larger programme is surely a delusion and is likely, for all its rigour, to go the way of the many previous attempts to find epistemological bedrock. The best we can hope for in this world, even if we study practical reasoning, is a plausible story.

4   Paradoxically, if competent insiders could not normally grasp the meaning of events, deceit would prove a most difficult matter. Its ready accomplishment depends on others both continuing to operate with the premise that things are as they seem and possessing the skills to interpret things in the normal fashion. Sudnow (1972) gives a nice example of this in his paper on glancing. As he shows, it is a central property of social scenes that they can be understood at a glance, at least by those familiar with them. They are indeed skilfully constructed in order that insiders can so read them, and dissimulation merely uses the same procedures to different ends.

One further source of help is also available. Since misunderstanding is still a common occurrence, whatever the participants' competence, they are obliged to take the possibility of failure continually into account. Indeed, in responding to one another we openly display that we have understood the previous speakers' meaning in order to establish our reply as a relevant one.[5] Thus the students of interaction can be guided in their reading of these matters, not just by their familiarity with the scene but by the readings displayed by the participants. Neither procedure guarantees an objective interpretation, but the use of both may help to generate a substantial measure of confidence in the analysis.

So far, so good. It must be noted, however, that the extent and manner in which meanings and understandings are displayed varies greatly, and this may add considerably to the difficulty of the analysts' task. In any interaction a large number of different things are conveyed and some are much more liable to misinterpretation than others. The main reason for this is simple: participants typically differ in the extent to which they have shared membership in the various social worlds under discussion.

To take the example of doctor–patient consultations: it is notorious that certain messages are extremely difficult to convey. Doctors, for instance, often experience great difficulty in understanding the world in which their patients live and may operate with a set of stereotypes quite inappropriate to that world (e.g., see Macintyre, 1977c).

By contrast there are other matters in which both doctors and patients typically share some competence and about which they can communicate with facility. Such would seem to be the case with the matters under consideration here. That is, with the exception of some of the Puerto Rican patients in the American hospitals, all the adult participants in these medical consultations demonstrated considerable awareness of the rules of the ceremonial order of clinics.[6]

---

5   See Goffman (1981b) for an elaboration of this point. Some may object that, although this is true, one cannot have any proper confidence in the readings one makes until the procedures by which meaning and understanding are displayed have been fully analysed and are available to the sociological researcher. The weakness in this argument is that there are no good grounds for restricting it to sociologists; and applied generally it becomes ridiculous. If this were in fact the case, no one could become competent in any social sphere without formal instruction in ethnomethodology. If the laity can acquire a working competence in these matters, one sufficient for their purposes, I see no reason why constructive sociologists cannot do the same.

6   Quite why this is so is beyond the scope of this monograph. It is not surprising that doctors and therapists should have this facility, since this is their daily task, but parents' ability here poses more of a problem. The competence shown by the great majority of parents in this study would seem to derive from three

This shared competence can present considerable analytical difficulties, greater perhaps than those found where misunderstanding is common. For where both parties are insiders, communication as to the nature of the world they share is typically indirect and allusive and, although meanings and understandings are certainly displayed, this is normally done in the most delicate of fashions. In such cases rules are spelt out only in special circumstances, as when, for example, they have been broken or when outsiders are present. Since this is done only to the deviant or the ignorant, to name a rule is to name a person and must necessarily be done with discretion if one is not to formulate oneself as incompetent or offensive.

In consequence, although I have quoted several examples in which rules were actually spelt out, these occurred but a mere handful of times. Since rules were openly formulated only in special circumstances, such occasions cannot be cited as direct evidence of normal rule use but are instead something different: acts of teaching, warning or attempted mitigation.

This general absence of relevant formulations in the interaction means that we are faced with a paradox. Interviewing generates spoken or written statements of rules, either made by or agreed with by the respondents. These can be openly displayed and sometimes even counted by the researcher. However, there is no way of knowing how these rules relate to and are used in actual behaviour. By contrast, the observation and recording of relatively trouble-free interaction provides extremely rich data on 'what happens', but few if any occasions on which we may actually see or hear the rules being followed.

Quite what the rules are is therefore unclear at first. This difficulty is compounded by two further features. For a start, the same rule may be embodied in a great variety of very different behaviour according to circumstance. I have already noted how no rule contains within it the further set of criteria for its application on particular occasions. Observation certainly permits the researcher to gather extensive data on the differing ways in which the same rule may be applied. But since rules are not

---

main sources. First, certain of the rules relate to identities which are in standards use in our culture, e.g., our images of mothers, fathers and childhood. Second, as I suggest in chapter 8 [of *The Ceremonial Order of the Clinic*; see also chapters 3 and 4 of this volume Ed.], it seems likely that the bureaucratic role format is, with minor modifications, in standards use across large areas of medical practice Most parents will therefore have had considerable experience of the form. Finally, it is also likely that the bureaucratic format found in medical consultations has a good deal in common with those used in many other types of service relationship, though so far no detailed comparison has been made between these. (But see Bigus 1972; Wenglinsky, 1973).

normally formulated during action, still less their rules of use, seeing the same rule across a wide range of encounters presents considerable difficulties, as does the display of that rule in its various natural habitats so that others may see it too.

The other difficulty is this. Following a rule concerns the omission of certain behaviour as much as the commission of other behaviour. Here not even the acts, let alone the rules, are directly audible or visible. Absences are as important as presences; but to notice that the dog did not bark in the night is often a most difficult task and one that is even harder to prove unless one can display all of one's data.

Understanding and Formulating Rules

There are certain solutions to the problems of finding and displaying tacit social rules with the use of observational data. These procedures were used in the analysis of the material discussed here and inform the logic, such as it is, of its presentation. Apart from the special case that I have already cited where rules were already spelt out, six types of data have been presented to warrant the finding of a particular rule, though, given the limitations of time, space and enthusiasm, not all six have been listed for every rule.

First, I have given examples of typical and entirely routine uses. I hope this gives the reader some flavour of standard usage but it does not, as we have seen, necessarily display that this was indeed the rule being followed in the behaviour cited. Nor does such quotation adequately establish just what was omitted. For these purposes a second type of example is necessary. Although this book is principally concerned with the nature of the bureaucratic format in medical consultations, the rather different behaviour found in the other formats, when contrasted with that found within the bureaucratic type, gives a much clearer indication of the basic rules within the latter.

This contrast may illuminate just what is involved by the rules of the bureaucratic format, but it leaves untouched the problem of demonstrating the range of these rules and their universal application within this range. The scope of the rules has been shown first by a consideration of their outer edges, the limiting cases in which they do not apply. These form a third type of data. One analytical strategy in these cases is to show that, although these are counter-examples, they are produced by very special circumstances and occur only within these.

To demonstrate that the rule was applied consistently, apart from these special circumstances, has required a fourth kind of data. This may be divided into two types. First, one needs a selection of examples which display a cross-section of the kinds of occasion on which the rule is necessary. Second and more importantly, one requires a detailed consideration of those situations which would seem to threaten the applicability of the rule. In other words, to establish a rule's universality one needs to examine those occasions on which it is most seriously tested. For example, in analysing the rule that the doctor is always the expert, the crucial test becomes what happens when the parents do in fact possess medical knowledge.

A fifth type of data has concerned the extent to which the rule varies systematically in use. So far I have considered only the problems of finding and displaying the most general form of a rule. But rules vary in their manner of use according to circumstances, and this too must be demonstrated. For example, all parents were treated as if they were moral, loving, intelligent and honest; but as regards their competence vis-à-vis the child there were important differences. Mothers' competence was totally assumed; that of fathers was openly questioned.

A final and sixth type of data has come from the discussion of these rules in interviews with doctors. Such data present considerable problems for analysis if the researcher has no other; but, taken together with the other data sources that have been outlined, they act as both a check and a useful guide.

The Generation and Testing of Hypotheses

A brief comment is necessary about the way in which the ideas in this study were produced and tested. There are various systematic methods for analysing qualitative data, and the procedure used here was a mixture of that which Glaser (1964) has termed the 'constant comparative method of qualitative analysis' and the method of 'analytic induction' as described by Robinson (1951), Cressey (1971) and Bloor (1976b). Both are alternatives to the hypothetico-deductive or 'big bang' mode of analysis that is normally used with pre-coded data. In this latter mode one systematically deduces a set of hypotheses from a body of theory and attempts to falsify them at one go. By contrast, analytic induction attempts to relate the process of generating propositions more closely to the data. Explanations are tested out all the time, trying them on one case to see if they fit, then moving on to another, and so on. Where the proposition does not cover the particular case, it may be reformulated or else the phenomenon redefined until a universal relationship is established which fits all the cases.

For its successful use the method of analytic induction requires a precise formulation of at least part of the problem. However, the research described here had initially no one focus but several overlapping ones. To begin with

I had no intention of studying the doctor–patient role-relationship since I held 'role' to be an old-fashioned and exploded concept. It was only at a late stage in the project and as a result of writing on various other themes that I became convinced that there were clear structures here. Making up one's mind as late as this has important disadvantages. If I had discovered this earlier on I could have designed the study far more systematically to test my propositions. Since I did not, I was faced with a dilemma. On the one hand, I needed a method that would enable the generation of a coherent set of ideas but that would also, at least initially, leave matters somewhat open and offer scope for modification. On the other hand, once I had a series of propositions, I required a method that would enable me to test them in some relatively adequate form.

In consequence, I began the analysis with a method that had a strong resemblance to the 'constant comparative method' proposed by Glaser. He argues that

... in contrast to analytic induction the method is concerned with generating and plausibly suggesting (not provisionally testing) many properties and hypotheses about a *general* phenomenon (Glaser, 1964, p.438).

As its name implies, this method consists of comparing each datum with a given selection of categories and seeing whether or not it fits. Once one has coded for a category several times and developed a more sophisticated version of it, one then codes only if the datum that is being examined points to a new aspect of the category. The only exception to this are categories of great theoretical interest but of which there are very few examples. If the datum fits under none of them, then the categories are modified or an entirely new one produced. The aim is to bring whatever initial ideas one has systematically to the data, and in the process of this to see what new ideas can be generated. Once all the data have been examined, the material relating to each is systematically scrutinized and further sub-divisions or re-groupings made, as items are found to differ or cluster together.

In my use of this method I made one important modification. This process of hypothesis generation was carried out on only one half of the data, with most of the material from the American hospital and most of that from the Scottish neurological clinic being excluded. Having completed the initial analysis of the first half of the data, I then re-organized my basic categories according to my current ideas, re-analysed the coded data and wrote a first, though only partial, draft. This provided me with a systematic set of propositions which I was then able to test by analysing the further half of my data. Where these did not fit the argument was amended. This latter step rendered my analysis, in this instance, more akin to the method of analytic induction.

Chapter 10

Natural Science and Medicine: Social Science and Medicine: Some Methodological Controversies[1,2]

1. Introduction

(A)   Over the last 100 years or so, Western doctors have grown used to using science, natural science, to assist them in their art. Thus, though medicine itself is not a science but a technology, it has come to rest increasingly on a natural scientific basis and, correspondingly, large numbers of clinicians have themselves trained to become natural scientists. Even surgery, perhaps the most traditional of all areas of practice, has seen the rise of 'surgical science'.

(B)   This application of natural science to a traditional craft has had striking successes; results which have led some doctors to hope that social science might in its turn show equally dramatic improvements. But this later marriage, though it has its moments of bliss, has proved a somewhat tempestuous affair. The relationship with natural science has not of course always been smooth. We may reasonably doubt whether it has achieved all that some have claimed for it, while there is clear evidence that the application of science has caused as well as cured many illnesses – not that iatrogenesis is anything new in medicine. Nevertheless that there has been success, and on a major scale, is conceded by all but a very few. By contrast, social science has met with no such general acclaim. Of course, the relationship is still relatively new and it does have its fervent supporters; however, it seems unlikely that it will settle down in anything like the same smooth pattern of the earlier marriage. Indeed, looked at from the viewpoint of natural science, the only science with which most

---

1   [Editor's note: co-authored in with K. McPherson]

2   Originally prepared as a Joint Background Paper for Section G. *Seventh International Conference on Social Science and Medicine*. Leeuwenhorst. The Netherlands. 22–26 June 1981.

doctors are familiar, social science, both in and of medicine, does have
some odd, indeed worrying aspects:

(i)   The very first lesson that doctors have to learn about, for example,
      medical sociology, is that there is no such thing, or at least not in the
      sense in which one may speak of say biochemistry. There are, instead,
      medical sociologies and if you dislike one you may pick another.
      Put another way, and perhaps more contentiously, social science has
      multiple paradigms – unlike natural science which does not, save in
      the rare and normally fairly brief period of 'revolution', when a new
      paradigm overthrows an older one. Indeed, it was his surprise and
      puzzlement on first encountering social science that led Kuhn to coin
      the notion of paradigm (Kuhn 1962).

(ii) Not only are there multiple paradigms within any one social science
      but, with one or two unimportant exceptions, there also seem to be no
      clear disciplinary boundaries. Thus the doctor who asks 'What does
      medical sociology know about X?' may well be told, 'We sociologists
      haven't actually looked at that yet, though we undoubtedly should
      and no doubt soon will, now you've mentioned it. However, if
      you are interested in X then perhaps medical geography, social
      administration, medical anthropology, medical psychology or health
      economics have looked at it, though I don't know anything about
      them'. In other words, the doctor is confronted with a long string of
      disciplines, most of whose names are a mystery, whose topics and
      whose paradigms often overlap, and yet whose practitioners know
      very little about each other.

(iii) Since social science disciplines have grown up in an *ad hoc* way in
      response to a great variety of practical social problems and since no
      one methodology has achieved any clear domination, the adherents
      of each can believe that they possess the real answer, the one which,
      given sufficient time, effort and money will unlock the door to
      the study of human behaviour. Those whose methods more nearly
      resemble, at least superficially, those used in the natural sciences, can
      readily see themselves as the only true social scientists, the rest being
      mere journalists: while those whose methods stand furthest from the
      natural science may argue that since the study of humanity requires
      very different procedures – or so they believe – those who ape the
      methods of natural science are simply sufferers from scientism, not
      true scientists: these latter being, of course, themselves.

(iv) Moreover, even in the most confident paradigms or disciplines, doubts
      may creep in about the scientific status of it all. While some, such as
      economists, are fairly confident that they are indeed a science, it is

nevertheless rare to find individual economists, who are completely willing to describe themselves as scientists. The discipline may be but they, it seems, are not. By contrast, within natural science, though there may be some dispute as to whether X or Y is a 'rear' scientist, that scientists exist is not in dispute and the term is one to be used with pride.

(v) Natural and thus medical science is of course heavily involved in the moral and political world. Medical scientists have strong personal and cultural values which shape their research interests. New discoveries such as the birth control pill may facilitate widespread changes in behaviour and new techniques such as renal dialysis or heart transplantation create new categories of choice and thus moral dilemma. The origins and uses of science are by no means neutral Nor, it would seem are the methods of that science; experimentation on both human and animal subjects is a matter of considerable ethical debate. More generally, the ecological movement has called into question the whole meaning of humanity's relationship to nature (Ashby 1977). Nonetheless, despite these important caveats there is a strong sense in which the findings of natural science are held to be neutral or amoral; whether we like it or not that is the way nature is. But no such consensus exists over the findings of social science. Many social scientists of course claim that their work is neutral but these claims are strongly contested by other commentators, both lay and professional, who delight in exposing the hidden values in supposedly neutral work. The multiplicity of paradigms is matched by a multiplicity of values, indeed particular sets of values often seem to coincide with particular paradigms.

(vi) By the standards of the natural sciences the actual product delivered by social' science looks very disappointing. There is simply no social equivalent of, for instance, the radio, which developed from physical theory first elaborated at the same time as Marx developed his theories. Social science, it would seem, cannot offer doctors the equivalent of penicillin or the sulphanomides. Moreover most of what it does offer lacks any serious mathematical base; has only the most dubious experimental base, if it has any at all: is often banal and can often be criticised quite adequately by the laity as well as by the professional, for the boundaries between social science and commonsense or practical knowledge are often hard to draw – a worrying position for a supposed science.

(vii) All these problems are thrown into sharp relief when the attempt is made to put social science in the medical school curriculum. What is taught depends, to an alarming degree, on just who is hired to teach it. Moreover, teaching medical students social science does not seem the easiest of work, for such courses are routinely accused of being not just irrelevant – a common enough accusation in medical schools – but also of being vague, banal, over-complex and politically biassed.

(C) In consequence, many doctors, and medical scientists even more so, are extremely suspicious of social science. Indeed, those disciplines such as economics which pride themselves on being rather nearer to natural science than some of their colleagues, are often held in especial scorn by natural scientists, who see them as distinguished merely by their presumption (Ravetz 1971).

For natural scientists, the term 'science' is not something to be granted lightly. Whereas to the outsider, the central position and power of natural science within modern society may seem virtually unassailable, to practising natural scientists things can look very different. To many of them, the creation of science was a bitterly fought struggle against the forces of human unreason and superstition, a struggle which still goes on today. Science, on this view, is a fragile creation of the human spirit, and one that is continually threatened, both internally, from inferior products or even deliberate deception, and externally, from the ignorant and unworthy, from the folk-sciences and pseudo-sciences. They believe, in other words, in a kind of Gresham's law of science – that good science is continually in danger of being driven out by bad science. Natural science had a mighty struggle to get established in medicine, and still has many bitter disputes in the battle with 'clinical experience'.

(D) All this raises several important questions: What can social science learn from natural science that may render it more adequate, or at least more humble? Will social science remain in this 'immature' state or can we reasonably expect it to develop in time to resemble something more like natural science? Can such inchoate and inconclusive knowledge be of any serious use to doctors? Ought anything so vague be allowed to contaminate the good name of science? And finally, is this picture of social science entirely fair – has it some other virtues which deserve commendation?

To answer any of these questions requires that for the moment we leave aside any detailed consideration of the special properties of social science and the human social world, though these will certainly need attention, but concentrate initially on the special properties of science itself. Only when we have grasped these can we consider social science.

(E)   Before we begin, however, it is essential to stress that although much has been written about these topics, there are no clear answers to them. The intellectual division of labour itself generates mutual incomprehension, as does the vast size to which the academic empire has now grown. Four points should be noted:

(i)   Natural scientists rarely know much, if anything, about social science and the same is true vice-versa; each side's image of the other derives mostly from folk-science. Even philosophers and historians of science tend to specialise in one or the other.

(ii) The natural and the social sciences are each so vast that those who know much beyond even their own sub-discipline are rare.

(iii) Those whose profession it is to be the specialists on ideal methodology, primarily the philosophers and statisticians, are held by many working scientists to be sufficiently removed from the rather grubby realities of scientific practice that their pronouncements must be treated with reserve as well as respect.

(iv) Finally, there is, as we shall see, an important sense in which the constitution of science is open and to be determined by empirical investigation. There are certainly stringent scientific standards but there is also continuous debate as to whether these are adequate or appropriate.

It is therefore only too easy for the most rigorous of scientists to be biassed and ignorant about the worth of their colleagues in other disciplines; a point which is nicely illustrated by considering just which social scientists have and have not been elected to the Royal Society, the most ancient and prestigious scientific body in Britain and one with a highly select and self-selecting membership:

"Apart from Sir William Petty among the founding members Malthus was an FRS and so were Sir John Simon and William Farr among the ethnographers and Jevons and Sir Robert Giffen among the economists. But the list does not extend to Marshall, Keynes, Malinowski, Radcliffe-Brown or Evans-Pritchard. This can largely be explained by the extent to which the work of those included was of a statistical or experimental kind ..." (Runciman 1970).

If the Fellows of the Royal Society can make mistakes then so can we. Moreover, in such a vast and complex field, any account as brief as this must necessarily be crude and highly compressed.

2. Some Links and Similarities between the Natural Medical and Social Sciences

(A) The first point to stress when contemplating the gap that separates the natural and social sciences is that, for all the huge size of the gulf, there is an important sense in which the two are often closely inter related, and can be seen as part of the same ideal programme. This programme goes under a variety of names – the unity of the sciences, methodological monism, naturalism – and has been formulated in various somewhat differing ways since the beginnings of modern science in the seventeenth century. A crude specification of the core doctrines, would include the following: causal explanations may be given for all phenomena including the actions of human beings, for we too are part of nature; that physical determinism holds everywhere, for the laws governing physical matters are universal laws; that science forms a unity whose different parts or levels are interconnected, or put another way, though phenomena in any one area may have a partial independence which requires detailed consideration of the special features of that area, we may also rank areas hierarchically and talk of levels, with one level setting the preconditions for phenomena at another level if not actually determining them i.e. the doctrine of reductionism.[3]

(B) Now clearly not all scientists, whether natural or social, believe in all the features of this programme, for its particular manifestations, rather than the crude summary given above, are highly complex and there is a good deal of practical dispute. However, although it has received some important challenges, these have up till now all been largely rebuffed – at least to the satisfaction of most scientists – and the programme continues to inform and inspire their daily work. Inspiration is perhaps the key word here for the unity of the sciences is not, it must be stressed, a practical

---

3   Reduction is a boo-word for most social scientists, so the term must be introduced with some care. We are not here arguing for a strong version of reductionism, i.e. that macro-sociological statements can ideally be reduced to psychological statements and the latter to physiology and so on. Three points may be made here. First, any crude attempt to deny the partially independent reality or macro phenomena is clearly absurd and, indeed, this is not a normal part of the doctrine of reductionism which recognises that each level contains phenomena which have their own separate existence. (See Brodbeck in Blaug 1980: 14.) Secondly, since there are good grounds for holding that determinate laws in the style of the natural sciences can never be produced in the social sciences – a point discussed in detail later – there can be no straightforward extrapolation from lower to higher levels. Thirdly, as a corollary of this last point, the analytic strategy of breaking things down into their component parts may sometimes be of less heuristic value in the social sciences than in the natural sciences.

achievement but an extraordinarily ambitious ideal and an ideal whose adequate realisation under the special conditions found at any particular level requires arduous work and debate. All present achievements, however impressive, are merely provisional.

(C)   As part of this programme, the social sciences share a number of more specific doctrines and institutions which have been elaborated in the attempts at its implementation. Since it has proved rather more difficult to elaborate this programme in the social sciences, these doctrines and institutions lack the degree of solidity and precision found by their more secure brethren and are, therefore, rather harder to discern. Nonetheless, without some grasp of these common features, as well as their attendant difficulties, social science cannot properly be understood:

(i)   There are first of all, some shared methods – to give just one example; the case-study method, which is central to clinical medicine is also a standard part of ethnography, history and management science. There are also, of course, many special techniques of investigation used by the social sciences which are not found in the natural sciences, though these differences are no greater, perhaps, than those between the natural sciences. Moreover, there is a fairly general agreement that, regardless of any differences in technique, *all* sciences should share a common method of proof or validation. Quite what this should be certainly changes according to the fashions in the philosophy of science. Nonetheless as these change so too do both natural and social scientists. At the moment some form of Popperianism is in vogue.

In recent times the only serious challenge to this doctrine of the unity of methods of proof has come from the German hermeneutic tradition. This has both emphasised the social scientist's special status as an insider, a member of the same species – something which enables an intuitive grasp of social action – and stressed that the meaning of action cannot be grasped without an attempt at such intuition. However, although one can make a strong case for 'Verstehen' as an important and distinctive technique, it is hard to develop any serious case for it as a method of proof and indeed social scientists rarely do so. Those who do believe fundamentally in the distinction do not become social scientists but turn, perhaps, to religion or the arts. (Thus our argument becomes, not that the unity of the sciences is certainly correct, merely that social scientists tend to think it is.)

(ii)   Since the unity of the sciences is fundamentally, an ideal, to believe in it is to treat the most rigorous models of scientific explanation, such as those offered by physics, as heuristic devices. These can still direct research in the more complex and 'softer' areas of enquiry, such as biology and the social sciences, even if the same level of rigour cannot be attained within them. Put more generally, as by Gellner (1974), epistemology is fundamentally a normative not a descriptive enterprise. Such ideal norms are practically important because the level of rigour that can be attained in any one science is an empirical question i.e. only sustained inquiry will reveal just what can and cannot be said. What was thought impossible in one era may turn out to be quite feasible in another. Rigorous norms enforce both an essential scepticism and a continued search for better means of proof.

(iii) This ideal programme is embodied in a set of distinctive social institutions. To grasp these we must understand first that science is a radical movement (Bittner 1963, Strong 1983b). That is, just like religious or political radical movements, science seeks a unified and internally consistent interpretation of the world. Such a quest is always difficult, for the ideal is constantly threatened by the fuzzy, *ad hoc* and heterogeneous nature of the outside world as perceived in daily experience. Thus, like other radical movements, science must segregate itself from that world in order to survive. However, the ways in which it does this are shaped by two further characteristics which give its radicalism a very special form.

Unlike many radical religious movements, science does not simply ignore the world but makes it the central object of its studies; the world cannot be avoided but must be studied and explained. Thus the world is admitted within science, even though it must be transformed via precise and public rules to gain that admittance. Thus, for instance, journal publication in both the natural and social sciences is ideally governed by the following procedures: compulsory and precise reference to other scientific literature; a public description of some of the methods pursued in the research; a display of some of the data that was analysed; assessment by external referees.

Secondly, and this time unlike many radical political movements, there is, ideally, as little dogma as possible. Scepticism is a prime virtue. Every member of every discipline has a right, even a duty, to challenge, disprove or modify what has earlier been agreed or just taken for granted. Nothing is sacred, even after it has undergone positive vetting. And this applies not just to individual works but to whole paradigms, even to the corpus of metaphysical doctrine, such as the belief in causality, that constitutes the heart of the programme of science. Thus, for example, the hermeneutic critique of the unity of science is still a legitimate enterprise and one from which social science has gained considerably. Many of the features of the social world noted by writers within the hermeneutic tradition have been incorporated within social science, even if its metaphysical programme has been largely rejected.

Of course these institutions are fundamentally ideal – in actuality they are not always effective, for the world continually presses upon science however hard it tries to keep its distance. Social science, in particular, faces two especial difficulties. The existence of multiple paradigms means that it is harder to agree on standards for journal publication; and, more importantly, since social science is necessarily much closer to the lay world than is natural science – a point which we shall argue later – it can far more readily be compromised by that world.

(iv) The fact that social science has multiple paradigms and natural science, at least normally, does not is no decisive barrier to social science. In the Kuhnian version of science, proper, serious and sustained scientific investigation i.e. 'normal science', can only begin when a single paradigm has conquered a field. By implication, normal science cannot exist in areas like social science where a variety of paradigms co-exist. To argue thus, however, is to ignore three important points.

First, on a strict definition, paradigms are incommensurable with one another. However, whether all the different schools or traditions in social science are in fact so completely distinct is a moot point.[4] The requirements of incommensurability are tough and perhaps rarely attained. Moreover, it can be argued that until recently it was in most schools' interests to maximise their differences and minimise just what they shared in common. When the total market for social science is expanding rapidly such a policy can pay handsomely. By contrast, when times are hard a more ecumenical approach is to be expected – particularly from the hardest hit.[5]

---

4   We do not intend, however, to argue that the difference between contending camps in the social science are no greater than those in natural science. This is clearly not so. Our point is merely to argue that there may well be good sociological reasons why these important differences have been exaggerated. Note also on the subject of these differences an important point made by Kuhn – just prior to his work on scientific revolutions – that the harder it is to quantify, the harder it is to provide decisive settlement of disputes (1961). This alone might explain a good deal of the differentiation of social science into fiercely contending camps.

5   Thus we might currently expect the popularity or a strong, incommensurable version of paradigm to be waning in the social sciences as we huddle together in

Secondly, it can be argued that the normal pattern of the growth of knowledge in natural science is somewhat different from the way Kuhn has portrayed it:

> ... to a very considerable extent, scientific knowledge has developed by the identification and detailed investigation of phenomena which have not been known to exist previously or which have not been studied before in any depth. The *typical* pattern of growth, then, in science is not the revolutionary overthrow of an entrenched orthodoxy but the creation and exploration of a new area of ignorance.

One may plausibly argue that the same pattern of growth is typical also of the social sciences. Medicine, indeed, is an excellent example of this, for the social scientific investigation of medicine is largely a post-war phenomenon and prior to this virtually no one had been interested. Once the field had been identified, however, there was clearly room for massive expansion.

Finally, even if we grant some validity to the multiple paradigm model of social science it can still be argued that individual paradigms may and do generate their own research programmes and that, within these, a normal social science takes place which bears a striking resemblance to the internal dynamics of normal science as specified by Kuhn, i.e. problems central to the paradigm are empirically investigated, new methods developed, hypotheses refined, and progress in understanding is developed. At the same time, just as in natural science paradigms, each paradigm tends to throw up anomalies which it finds difficult to explain in its own terms; such anomalies leading eventually to the demise of the old paradigm and the establishment of a new one; one which tackles the same problems but from a new and more encompassing point of view.

(v) So far we have touched on the public face of science and the important similarities between the public face of both natural and social science. But there is also a private face, one which does not normally appear in the published work of science and is absent from most philosophical or methodological accounts. In this private sense, science is a craft, dependent on a vast amount of tacit knowledge, of informal rules-of-thumb (Thomas 1979). And in this respect also natural science is much like social science.

(vi) Finally, and this is an important source of unity for the medical and social sciences, not only are all the sciences, ideally interconnected but biology and social science are both fundamentally *historical*

---

the dark. (See the parallel analysis for religion in Berger 1967).

sciences. In summary, then, the social sciences have rather more in common with the natural sciences than a casual inspection might lead one to believe. Likewise, the difference between the various social science traditions has, perhaps, been exaggerated a little. However, it must still be emphasised that there remain important differences in these, respects and we now turn to consider why this may be so.

3. Why Social Science has Special Characteristics

(A)   To grasp humanity's distinctive features it is necessary to place the species in an evolutionary perspective. The following account is based, rather loosely, on Mead's attempt to do this (Mead 1938, Reck 1964, Miller 1973). Human social science, from this viewpoint, faces several distinct problems:

(i)   The problem of understanding our selves. If we ourselves are the subject, the scientist has some clear advantages compared to other areas of investigation. At the same time, however, human beings have a notorious capacity for self-deception and for disagreement. Even if one did produce a correct theory could one actually persuade everyone else of its correctness? Moreover, understanding ourselves is not as easy as it might seem. Each of us has a different self and the capacity for extreme self-differentiation is one of our species distinguishing characteristics, while social scientists, so far at least, belong to singularly unrepresentative strata and cultures among our species.

(ii)   With humanity, argued Mead, evolution has become self conscious. But a species that has the capacity to understand both itself and the rest of the world – and we are the first to at least potentially do so – necessarily stands at the end of a long line of evolution through physico-chemical, geological, biological, archaeological and historical time. We are therefore extraordinarily complex and still rapidly evolving creatures.

(iii)   To grasp how both we and the world are determined in any systematic sense requires an unusual ability to escape those determinations – or some of them at least. And clearly, a creature with a capacity significantly to ameliorate its determination is a hard creature to which to apply a deterministic analysis. It is therefore not so much the high rate of change which renders the study of humanity so specially complex – after all the flu virus changes rapidly also but – rather, the cumulative profundity of that change caused by our ingenious capacity to turn both nature and society to our own advantage.

(iv) Our extraordinary advantage in the struggle of all living things for mastery of their environment stems from two distinct but perhaps related developments. On the one hand, there is the development of the capacity to create tools, that is, objects which systematically extend our body's capacity physically to manipulate the material environment. On the other hand, the development of language and thus of a special form of consciousness and communication, enables us, first to single out and reflect in great detail on our modes of engagement in the world, and second, to engage in particular projects to understand and alter those modes of engagement, both the collective thought and the collective physical efforts of tens, hundreds, thousands, millions, even billions of members of the species.

(v) However, although these capabilities certainly enable human collaboration on a vast scale they by no means guarantee it. On the contrary, as we have also implied, language and tools give humans such a flexible relationship to both their natural and their human environment that an enormous variety of types of individual, types of relationship, types of institution and types of society become possible.

(B) All this has major consequences for the ideal programme of science when applied to human beings. We shall single out three problems for especial consideration:

(i) The *segregation* of the scientific from the everyday world, so necessary for the pursuit of this radical enterprise, is simply not feasible in anything like the rigid fashion that is found in the natural sciences.

(ii) The doctrine of *reductionism* faces major problems.

(iii) The doctrine of *determinism,* likewise faces great difficulties.

We shall not, however, argue that in consequence the programme must be abandoned, merely that its implementation for the human social sciences requires especial care and will not achieve the same form as that possible within, say, those fields where essentially closed systems operate.

4. The Distinctive Relationship of Social Scientific and Lay Theories

Since human beings possess tools and language they can and do both reflect and experiment on both their own nature and that of their environment. There is, therefore, an important if limited sense in which we are all 'researchers', 'scientists' and 'theorists' and were so long before the creation of modern science. This fact has important consequences for both natural and social science in medicine. Both confront developed, in some instances highly developed, lay systems of medical thought and practice. Moreover, it is impossible to segregate them completely from these lay versions; rather, they co-exist in complex interaction: some scientific theories have their origins in lay theories; some lay practice is in advance of scientific discovery e.g. the recent flurry of interest in non-Western medicine; and finally, the results and findings of science are fed back into the world and modify it accordingly, for once evolution has become self-conscious, even if only to a limited degree, then that new consciousness in turn helps to shape future evolution. Natural and social science when applied to medicine modify both the evolution of our own species and that of others.

(A) The special closeness of the lay world

Natural science for all its deliberate separation, is still intimately bound into the lay world, but social science enjoys or suffers from an even closer relationship. Problems, conflicts and misunderstandings are generated both by its special closeness and yet also by those occasions when it, nevertheless, breaks from commonsense. We shall begin by considering five problems engendered by its special closeness: the conceptual problem; the problem of professional competence; the problem of morality; the problem of history; and the problem of methods. Then, in the next section we shall turn to the special difficulties created by distance.

(i) *The conceptual problem.* Beginning with closeness, the most important feature here is the obvious fact that lay theories, or more prosaically, lay meanings, are partially constitutive of the social world. In Thomas' famous dictum, 'If men define situations as real, then they are real in their consequences'. This places human social scientists in a very different relationship to their data from that experienced by natural scientists:

> Consider the electron ... there is no question of the electron characterizing its own behaviour in some way or another which antedates the arrival of the physicist: and thus there can be no room for us to mischaracterize the behaviour of the electron as a result of failing to understand the logic of its own characterization. But this danger is just what social scientists are exposed to as soon as they venture beyond the mere cataloguing of what people say about their activities ... (Ryan 1970).

In other words, social scientists, whatever their interests must at some point engage in a measure of *dialogue* with those whom they study. Yet this was one of the central points on which the natural scientific revolution of the seventeenth century broke with the past. Older, anthropomorphic versions of physical science e.g. astrology and alchemy saw human meanings in the physical world and held that the investigator must correspondingly engage in dialogue with it (Ravetz 1971). The notion that this world was however, in one vital sense, meaningless was central to the scientific revolution and gave us our modern meaning of 'natural'.

Given the importance of this break with anthropomorphism in the later success of 'natural' science, this strategy has, from time to time, been tried in the realm of human affairs – most recently in Watsonian and Skinnerian behaviourism in psychology. However, despite very great effort and some useful spin-offs, the project has never met with any major success, for it ignores the nature and centrality of language in human society (Taylor 1964). Thus, though the' attempt is almost certain to be repeated at some future date, it is hard to believe that it will meet with any greater success.

In consequence, human social science seems necessarily stuck with an, at least partly, anthropomorphic view of human beings – though the precise relationship between social science categories and the categories used by the subjects of that science is highly problematic and the cause of serious dispute in every social science, be it economics, sociology or anthropology. Is it sufficient for a theory to explain a collection of observed social facts or must it also be subjectively adequate i.e. correlate at some point with the consciousness of those whose behaviour it studies? And if so how is this to be done?

None of these questions admits a ready answer. In consequence since social science seems to be closely tied to lay thought, some of its branches both have and will continue to have a rather more philosophical cast than many areas of natural science.[14] For problems of conceptualization, the key subject-matter of philosophy, are thereby made central to the enterprise; a fact which renders them woolly in some natural scientists' eyes. (Moreover, one may note, philosophy is also likely to be more prominent in any area of science where there is no agreed methodology.)

(ii) *The problems of professional competence.* Insofar as it deals with actors' knowledge, then, as the discussion of electrons implied, social science faces a series of challenges that natural science does not. First, it is quite possible, indeed only too common, for the subjects to be better informed about some relevant matters than those who are studying them. Thus not only may social scientists be wrong, a familiar enough story after all in natural science, but what is less familiar, the subjects may turn round and actually prove them to be so. Thus doctors, patients, nurses and so on may all at times, and quite reasonably, ridicule social science. Even if that social science is correct, if it deals with matters close to lay knowledge it runs a further risk; it may simply be banal. This time, our medical audience may cry 'but we knew that already'. And this too is not uncommon.

Moreover, what is known already may not simply be trivial matters of fact available to anyone in that setting who is more than half-conscious. The capacity to make certain types of fairly accurate and insightful generalisations about human behaviour is a fundamentally human capacity, not something that has developed only with the advent of professional social science. It is something that all of us possess. Indeed, we could not lead our ordinary lives unless this was so. Some grasp of certain crude principles is essential.

Such principles can become highly refined in the work of those who reflect deeply upon them. Burke presented his ideas as 'the late ripe fruit of mere experience' (Burke, in O'Brien 1968) and such ripeness is scattered throughout both the oral tradition and world literature. Thus it is that some doctors or patients may value social science but feel that there is often as much or more to be gained by listening to a wise friend or colleague, or by reading Tolstoy.

Of course, these rival commentators, whatever their quality, do not work within a scientific tradition. As such their analyses remain typically unsystematic and lack, mostly, any rigorous methodology. Nevertheless, although the possession of the latter marks social science off quite distinctively from common sense, there is still a vast gap that separates it from natural science. Natural science, as a matter of daily practice, produces explanations that are quite outside the realm of everyday discourse. By contrast, social science rarely, or perhaps even never, comes up with entirely new explanations. Its role instead is to describe the social world far more rigorously than would normally be attempted and then adjudicate between competing lay theories of those events; to decide in some systematic way just which out of several lay versions is, or are, plausible and to what extent.

The social scientist therefore routinely faces serious competition of a kind that is almost unknown in the natural sciences. Moreover, this competition occurs not just in the production of explanations but in the production of descriptions also, for the modern social world is full of professional social commentators who work beyond the academy – journalists, film-makers and writers – all of whom also make a living out of social analysis. Such commentators may still lack the complete rigour of the social sciences, nevertheless, in certain areas at least they offer a powerful challenge and one that social scientists commonly ignore (Abel 1981). 'A review of the literature', too often means a review of the social science literature, or some of it, the thoughts and observations of essayists, novelists and journalists being largely ignored.

Thus it is that in its efforts to make itself distinctive and, supposedly, more scientific, social science has often ignored the qualitative methods used by other types of commentators on social life, save in history, where such methods pre-date the creation of modern social science and in anthropology, where the problem of meaning is posed so starkly that qualitative methods seem only natural. The very power of the lay tradition of analysis has served to blinker the scientific tradition.

A related argument may, perhaps, explain the fetishisation of the term 'theory' in the social sciences. What social scientists mean by theory often bears, as we shall see, little relation to natural scientists' use of the term. Indeed social scientists' constant use of the term is a great puzzle to natural scientists for it looks so little like natural science theory and so much like common-sense or aphorism. The explanation plainly rests both in the scientific aspirations of social science and in the strong analytical abilities of social scientists' subject matter. 'Theory' is a term used mostly to demarcate what we do from what they do and, at the present stage, conceals perhaps rather more than it explains.

(iii) *The problem of morality.* The very closeness of social science to lay concepts and theories renders social science a thoroughly moral enterprise in a way in which natural science is not, for all its various involvements with the social world. For the categories with which we view the social world are thoroughly imbued with morality.

> Moral concepts change as life changes, I deliberately do not write 'because social life changes', for this might suggest that social life is one thing, morality another, and that there is merely an external, contingent, causal relationship between them. This is obviously false. Moral concepts are embodied in and are partially constitutive of forms of social life. One key way in which we may identify one form of social life as distinct from another is by identifying differences in moral concepts (Macintyre 1967, see also Taylor 1967).

Thus there can be no completely neutral language with which to describe the social world. Of course many social scientists strive hard to choose concepts which sound as neutral as possible and, for a time, and in certain instances, such efforts may meet with a fair degree of success. Nevertheless, as a moment's historical reflection will indicate, there can be no absolute achievement here. Some concepts which seemed perfectly neutral to one generation are revised by the next. Likewise, though many minor terms may go unchallenged there is continuous, often passionate debate around more central terms such as 'class' 'intelligence' or even 'society'.

It follows, therefore that the concepts which social scientists use to describe medicine are necessarily evaluative. This, it might be argued, should cause no great upset, since the fundamental categories such as 'disease' and 'death' with which natural science operates in medicine are also profoundly evaluative. However, although this is indeed true, they happen to be concepts for whose use there is a quite remarkable consensus across peoples and cultures, a consensus which is based on a predicament common to all of us, whatever and whoever we are. Our embodiment is a precondition of all other types of action. In consequence, however varied their institutions and values, all cultures share fairly similar opinions about the value of health. Is it for this reason that organisations such as the Red Cross, the Red Crescent and the WHO are so readily accepted across national boundaries.

Although both natural and social science share this common evaluative base when dealing with medicine, natural science stays pretty much within this, whereas social science strays further and further from it. Thus topics like the way in which consultations are organised; the arrangement of health services, the availability of service X as opposed to service Y, the organisation of the health professions and so on; all these can be characterised in different ways, according to our different values and, accordingly, are so characterized. Thus the essential closeness of social science to the lay social worlds which it attempts to describe and explain, necessarily means that it imports the values either of those social worlds or of the social world of the researchers.

Of course, all this would be solved if social science could be naturalised in the way in which physical science was in the seventeenth century and biological science was in the nineteenth. For another way of making the point that morality and human meaning are inextricably interlinked is to note that the seventeenth century revolution in physical science challenged not just the notion of dialogue with the physical world but conventional religious notions of morality – as of course did the Darwinian revolution of the nineteenth century. However, although first the physical and then the biological realm have been stripped of most vestiges of morality, it is hard to conceive of this as a possibility for the realm of human social affairs. For the evolutionary process itself has created a species in which morality is an intrinsic feature of its mode of life. A social science which takes evolution seriously must therefore take morality seriously. Once you have language, you also have morals. Once you have language you have different points of view and when you have different points of view you have different moralities. Social science cannot therefore be morally neutral. Even a Martian social science of human life, since it presupposes a Martian language, would be shot through with Martian values.

To say that any piece of social science is necessarily prejudiced is not, however, to say that it is all equally worthless. The problem of prejudice in social science has been tackled in four main ways. Some social scientists have tried to be as open as possible about their own values. Yet others have tried to be as neutral as possible. Both groups, meanwhile, have tried to expose the values and prejudices implicit in each other's work. Finally, and just as importantly, social scientists as a class have been subjected to moral criticisms from the laity. And through this process of both internal and external criticism, considerable progress has been made. For example, most modern social scientists are far more aware than they were fifty years ago of the biasses induced by class, racism, nationalism, colonialism, sexism and professional imperialism. Thus while it is true that values are not something that can be overcome or abolished within the social sciences, it is possible, though with considerable effort to mitigate some of their more seriously biassing effects.

(iv) *The problem of history.* Mitigating the effects of bias, whether due to differences in morality or simply a lack of information, is, however, made significantly harder by what may be termed the problem of history. Over the last 50,000 years or so the human species has undergone cultural evolution, differentiation and imitation at an extraordinarily rapid rate. Indeed the rate of change, and profound change at that, is ever faster. It is, in consequence, extremely difficult for social scientists to escape too far from the prejudices and perspectives of their own position in time and space. Obviously astrophysicists and biologists face something resembling this problem when they consider the evolution of the universe or of species. However, the profundity of the changes in human social evolution and the speed at which they have occurred in recent times puts social scientists in a far more difficult position.

The problem of the limitations imposed by one's own position in space can be overcome by comparative study. The social science of medicine is therefore full of studies comparing differences by class, gender, culture, nation, tribe and so on. Nevertheless, such studies are still only at an exploratory stage. There is for example no serious medical equivalent of Weber's comparative analysis of religion; or more recently, of Barrington Moore's comparative analysis of the origins of dictatorship, and of Anderson's comparative analysis of different types of state.

Such studies will certainly come and their current absence is perhaps largely due to the relative novelty of serious interest and research in the social side of medicine. However, even though their presence will contribute enormously to our understanding of medicine, major interpretative problems will still remain for the problem of time is far more difficult to overcome. Historians can certainly tell us of the medical past, though most social scientists at present ignore this, but they, like other social scientists, can have little notion of the future and yet this is essential for a proper understanding of many phenomena, McNeil writes thus:

> It seems likely that the change in ordinary, everyday human experience and habit implied by wholesale flight from the fields will alter society as fundamentally as it was altered when men ceased to be simple predators and began to produce their food. If so, it is difficult to overemphasize the historical importance of the industrial revolution and impossible to believe that the social organisation and styles of life that will eventually prove to be best attuned to industrial economies have yet emerged (McNeill 1979: 425).

It follows that though we can, through sustained effort and comparative study, escape some of the biasses of our particular culture, class, occupation and sex, there are other biasses which only time and the presence of a different historical standpoint can reveal. Moreover, it is crucial to note, when the historical process does enable a new evaluation to occur, social scientists are not the only people to benefit from this. Sexism, to take a recent example, is not something which social scientists alone have discovered.

Medicine, also, is an excellent example of how social scientists are as trapped by the conventions of their time quite as much as are the laity. For all that one may plausibly argue that health, disease and medicine are central features of every human society, social scientists expressed almost no interest in them at all until very recently. One looks in vain for guidance to the eighteenth and nineteenth century classics. Medicine only became problematic for social scientists when it became problematic for the rest of society. Moreover, there is some evidence that once medicine was an object of study, that changing social science formulations of and critiques of medicine were very closely matched by changes in the medical profession's own internal analysis and critique (Armstrong 1982). Thus, history provides one further reason why social science can never escape too far from commonsense.

(v) *The problem of method.* Finally, the very closeness of social science to social life means that just as there are no morally or politically neutral concepts with which to describe the social world, so also there are no neutral techniques with which to investigate that world. Research techniques are themselves social products; their use is a special form of social act and they have their own social meanings and consequences. The behaviour of electrons or cells may certainly be modified by research techniques and the same is true of the subjects of social science. What renders the latter different, however, is their capacity consciously to modify their behaviour to match the research context. We shall briefly consider three notorious consequences for social science methods:

(a) The problem of *quantification* – precisely because human behaviour is so flexible and individual, given our capacity to create our own meanings and to manoeuvre backwards and forwards within a context, the quantification of that behaviour has proved a task of some delicacy. For one has first to decide whether this action here is the same as that action there; often a singularly difficult task. Of course, some things within the social world are relatively easily counted – human beings themselves, as in say a number of patients; their gender; their age; the numbers of goods and services that they use, as in say the use of drugs, the availability of bodyscanners and the number of visits to the doctor that they make; and, finally, their money, for money is a medium specifically created to be a neutral medium of exchange, to solve, at least in part, the variability of human meaning and valuation. But human transactions with one another – what happens for instance when a female patient in her sixties visits a doctor, receives a bodyscan and pays a fee – all this is far harder to quantify. Likewise, many concepts that are absolutely fundamental to the social science have proved extraordinarily hard to quantify in any very satisfactory fashion. Class and power being two notorious examples (Runciman 1970).

Despite these great difficulties, enormous efforts have been made to improve the level of valid quantification within the social sciences, and important progress has been registered. This advance will undoubtedly continue. However, it has been hindered, and will continue to be hindered, by four recurring dangers. First, the great complexities which beset the qualification of human action have led many who pursue 'naturalistic' methods of inquiry largely to ignore the quantitative possibilities within this area, indeed to style themselves, misleadingly, as 'qualitative' researchers. Such researchers are in danger of removing themselves from science altogether. By contrast, two other types of sin beset those who strive for as much quantification as possible. There is first, the constant danger that the attempt to impose measurement on relevant data leads to purely artefactual results – a major problem with questionnaire methods as is indicated by the old tag that attitudes are what attitude studies measure. Secondly, there is the danger of getting carried away with mathematics. Here, the assumptions necessary for the mathematical model are often so far removed of the real world that the model is merely a toy with no practical use. Finally, all those who attempt to quantify the social world in any serious fashion, are in danger of forgetting just how vast is the gap that separates their own feeble achievements from those that are routinely made within the natural science.

(b) The special nature of human consciousness puts *experimentation* in an even worse state than quantification. First the resulting complexity of human social behaviour renders controlled experiment problematic at any but a micro-social level as there are far too many interrelated variables for experimental control to be achieved. But, second, even where experimentation is possible, experiments are still social occasions with their own appropriate behaviour. Subjects can and do modify their behaviour to allow for the fact that this is an experimental situation, a condition which holds true even if the actual point of the experiment is concealed from the subjects. It is, therefore, often not clear how far one can extrapolate results from experiments to other, different forms of behaviour. This does not render experimentation useless, indeed much valuable work has been done in social psychology using this technique, but it does mean that its results are often equivocal. Once again, advances have been made but progress is slow compared to the dramatic success of the experimental method in the natural sciences.

(c) Finally, one may note somewhat similar consequences both for *prediction*, normally a key weapon in the scientific armoury, and relatedly, for the possibility of establishing *scientific laws* of the kind found in physics and chemistry. Macintyre puts it this way:

> According to the conventional account ... the aim of the social sciences is to explain specifically social phenomena by supplying law-like generalisations which do not differ in their logical form from those applicable to natural phenomena in general. ... This account seems, however, to entail – what is certainly not the case – that the social sciences are almost, or almost entirely, devoid of achievement. For the salient fact about those sciences is the absence of any law-like generalisations whatsoever (Macintyre 1981).

Likewise, and precisely because of this, the social sciences have a pretty dismal record of prediction. Economists and demographers are particularly notorious for their many failures here – but this is merely because they have cast their predictions in a precise, quantified form; something which sociologists typically avoid. Two important questions follow. Why has this failure occurred? And what can we reasonably expect of generalisation and prediction in social science?

The sources of systematic unpredictability in human life lie, for the most part, in those special features of the human social condition that we have already discussed (Macintyre 1971, 1981). The acquisition of language and thus of reflexive thought creates the possibility of radical conceptual innovation – and this, by definition, cannot be predicted. Likewise, the complexities of the self mean that none of us can predict our own future decisions and even though we can partially predict those of others, the fact that we cannot in turn predict our responses to others decisions, introduce a further element of unpredictability. Most important of all perhaps is the game-theoretic nature of social life and the special nature of that game; features which add extraordinary complexity to human action. By this is meant first, the indefinite reflexivity of human interaction – 'I know that you know that I know' etc; second, the fact that deliberate deception and concealment are central to human action: and thirdly, and fourthly, that there are two crucial ways in which the games of life differ from monopoly and football – in real life there are normally several games being played at any one time, not just one, and, moreover, in each of these, there is often no determinate group of players or area in which the game will be played. *Post hoc* analysis may certainly reveal a specific set of games and players on that particular occasion; but here one can be wise only after the event. At the time these issues are still open. The final source of systematic unpredictability is, of course, pure contingency – Napoleon had a cold at Waterloo.

All this is not to say that human life is totally unpredictable – far from it – for there are, at the same time, several sources of systematic predictability in our affairs. Nevertheless, generalisations in social science, and thus predictions, can never hope to match the precision found in the natural sciences. What can we then reasonably expect of generalisations in social science? Macintyre, from whom the above account is drawn, argues thus:

> It seems probable that they will have three important characteristics. They will be based on a good deal of research, but their inductively founded character will appear in their failure to approach law-likeness. No matter how well-framed they are, the best of them may have to co-exist with counter-examples, since the constant creation of counter-examples is a feature of human life. And we shall never be able to say of the best of them precisely what their scope is. It follows of course that they will not entail well-defined sets of counter-factual conditionals. They will be prefaced not by universal quantifiers but by some such phrase as 'characteristically and for the most part' (thus) 'the generalisations and maxims of the best social science share certain characteristics of their predecessors – the proverbs of folk societies, the generalisations of jurists, the maxims of Machiavelli' (Macintyre 1981: 99).

(B) Yet social science also breaks from the lay world

If there are many problems caused by the necessarily intimate relationship of social science and lay analysis, quite other difficulties are due to the fact that social science, at certain crucial points, necessarily breaks with lay models of thought. Social scientists are, therefore, in the unfortunate position of being criticised both for being banal and for being unintelligible. There is little expectation that natural science will make obvious good sense; indeed, almost the reverse is true. We expect physics, nowadays to produce bizarre and mysterious phenomena. But social science, in some way or another, is usually expected to conform to commonsense. Now of course a social scientific explanation which in no way related to any part of commonsense experience would indeed be a puzzling event, given all that has been argued about the necessary closeness of social science to lay thought. Nevertheless, even though it may always, at some later date, be incorporated into lay thought, social science must often break with lay thought, and does so for several different reasons:

(i)   For all that has been said of the importance of human meaning, a central topic in all social science disciplines is that of the *unintended results* of human action. Indeed, for some disciplines, those which concentrate mostly on the aggregated results of many thousands or millions of human actions, this is their principal topic:

> He (the demographer) like the economist, takes for granted the conceptualization of the world employed by the people whose behaviour he is studying, and seeks to elicit the consequences of their behaviour which they generally neither forsee nor exercise any control over. Although it is true that population trends, like the growth rate of the Gross National Product, have their roots in the intended behaviour of individuals, it is not the case that they are themselves intended, and for the most part they can be studied without attending to the intentions of anyone (Ryan 1970: 158).

For all the success of this programme, one obvious problem that it creates is that its results may be unrecognisable to those whose actions are thus aggregated, they may feel that they have become, 'merely a statistic'. Thus, to take a medical example, it appears that surgeons are not particularly interested in work which considers how regional rates of operation vary according to different supply factors. Their own work may have been aggregated to produce those results and the supply factors, insofar as they are effective, will have been so only through their own actions; nevertheless, the overall results are far too remote from their own consciousness of surgical decision-making for them to have any serious impact on most surgeons. They cannot see themselves in the figures. Put another way, it is hard for human beings to recover their own intentions in work that focusses on unintended results.

(ii) Moreover, much the same problem is faced even by that work which concentrates on the micro-level of human behaviour, for there are powerful arguments to suggest that human beings often have very little awareness of crucial features of their own actions; that their consciousness is systematically skewed. It is now a truism in the social sciences that what people say bears no necessary relationship to what they actually do. We are all of us now well aware of the distortions produced by repression, ideology, and self-deception. Simple forgetfulness also needs a mention. What is perhaps, most crucial here is the fact that each of us is simultaneously engaged in the world in a great number of directions and, yet, consciousness can only focus on one thing at a time. Since we have, therefore, to select, we focus on those modes of engagement that are most problematic to us and ignore the rest (Fingarette 1968). In consequence there are vast numbers of skills and practices which go simply unnoticed by us, actions which we certainly perform and yet which are not 'intentional' in the sense of our possessing a conscious intention – even though we may certainly be held accountable for them.

To return to our surgical example. (One must quickly add, lest surgeons feel they are being picked on, that there is no reason to suppose that they are any different from other human beings.) First, surgeons may be unaware of the influence of certain long-term and relatively unchanging supply factors on their own decision-making criteria.[6] For they may long ago have adjusted those criteria to match supply and are likely to notice only the more immediately pressing question of whether this particular patient meets those criteria. Secondly, there is strong evidence that even when considering their own criteria, they are only aware of certain features of these; that other parts are completely taken-for-granted, so routinely are they used (Bloor 1978).

Finally, there is evidence that just as they may lack consciousness of certain important determinants of their decision, so too they may over-rate others – and for much the same reasons. Factors that give them little immediate trouble are ignored, while those that do cause this may have their importance considerably inflated. It is a standard finding within social science that doctors and surgeons dominate most medical consultations. However, precisely since their power rests on such a firm base, medical staff would seem to take their dominance for granted. What they complain about, rather, is threats to that domination i.e. patient pressure, a factor which looks, so far at least, to be a fairly minor influence on most surgical decision-making, even in areas such as tonsillectomy where it has traditionally been seen as highly important (Bloor 1976a).

One important appendix must be added to the argument above. That human beings can and do ignore many features and consequences of their action is obvious. But, as we noted earlier things can change. Where an issue becomes politically relevant, then lay consciousness may suddenly focus in great detail upon it. At which point, continuing with our previous example, surgeons may well start inspecting their actions more closely, noticing things they hadn't seen before, even reading social science literature. Thus, not only may social science be incorporated within the world it describes but it can also undergo an extraordinary shift in valuation. What may previously have been banal or trivial, now becomes – for a moment at least – of great importance. Fields in natural science too of course experience major swings in their popularity according to their immediate political relevance.

6 'Ethics and the nephrologist'. *Lancet*: 1981 gives an excellent example of this amongst physicians.

However, given the greater esteem in which they are generally held, these are not, perhaps, quite so dramatic.

(iii) Social science breaks with commonsense perspectives, not only by considering the unintended results of actions and by studying features to which little conscious attention is normally paid, but also by the very form in which it presents its results. Take, for example, the vexed question of jargon. Social scientists are notorious for their illiterate use of language and for the ugly neologisms which scatter their pages. Medical reviews of social science routinely complain about our language. And yet, though some of this criticism is plainly justified – we could all write better – there is an important sense in which to complain of jargon is to miss the point. To be a science at all, social science must break with lay thought in certain crucial respects. In doing so, it will necessarily devise a language of its own, just as natural science has done. Yet very few members of the laity complain of the jargon of the natural sciences. Just as they expect them to be mysterious, so they expect their language to be strange. Thus the especial closeness of social science to the social world engenders a false set of expectations. (It is in just the same manner, one might add, that social science is particularly vulnerable to complaints about the irrelevancy of its work. Even though it may be jargon ridden it remains fairly intelligible, whereas the very obscurity of natural science renders it safe from politicians aiming to cut 'wasteful' public expenditure.) Finally, the most successful social science jargon enters the public language and there, by some mysterious process, is converted to sense and its links with social science forgotten.

Jargon is not the only instance of a necessary feature of a scientific description or explanation which somehow engenders especial resentment when it is the social world which is being studied. Any individual piece of science necessarily simplifies the world which it describes. Out of all the many complex features in a particular situation, just one or two are selected for detailed study and the rest ignored for present purposes. This engenders no complaint at all in natural science – after all the natural world cannot answer back – but the human world can and does.

Finally, the special form which social scientific work takes can create misunderstanding not just among its subjects but among social scientists themselves. The fact that they have special methods and a special language may conceal from them the fact that, in a limited but highly important sense, everyone is a social scientist. And to ignore this is bad social science. We have already noted the tendency to ignore the work of professional novelists and essayists but the point is far more general than this, for there is much to be learned from the laity themselves.

To take an example from the field of alcoholism. Perhaps the central methodological problem in the epidemiology of alcoholism is the difficulty of defining precisely what constitutes alcoholism. This is a vexed and pretty much an insoluble question, but one for which a variety of *ad hoc* rules are elaborated. Now what is also striking about this is that it is not just a professional's problem. Every heavy drinker who has run into difficulties with their drinking is confronted by exactly the same problem when they ask, as our culture obliges them to do, am I or am I not an alcoholic? Now, it turns out that in answering this question 'problem drinkers' use pretty much the same set of *ad hoc* criteria as professional researchers. The only difference between lay and professional science here being that the latter is written down and somewhat more elaborated. Yet, despite this similarity, some of those who research alcoholism refuse to grant problem drinkers the same intellectual status as their own. The researcher, apparently, faces complex epistemological problems and therefore cannot define alcoholism too well; the problem drinker, however, who is not certain whether or not he is alcoholic merely suffers from a weak will and a deliberate refusal to face up to reality.

(iv) Finally, social science breaks with the lay social world because, even where it is most conformist – and a good deal of it certainly is – it nevertheless challenges the traditional moral and political authority of that world (Coleman 1978). Natural science was once shocking – 'the new philosophy calls all in doubt' – but is now no longer. Social science however will continue to be so. Moreover this is so regardless of the moral and political sympathies of particular researchers. For even if researchers share or confirm the version of social reality held by traditional authority, they nevertheless supply a new, avowedly scientific, basis on which to rest those beliefs. Social science therefore corrodes the ultimate authority, in one sense at least, of all those whom it studies. All modern governments, even British Conservative Party governments, now appeal to social science to warrant their actions – Burke's 'mere experience', however ripe, is no longer enough.

At the same time, this incorporation within the modern political world does not mean that social science, or some of it, thereby ceases to shock, nor that it becomes the new authority to which all must bow. This latter option is precluded, save in totalitarian countries – and then only partially – by the multi-paradigmatic nature of social science and by the powerful tradition of lay analysis. Its capacity still to shock stems from three continuing social science traditions. There is a long and powerful tradition that holds the world to be much nastier than we conventionally like to think it. This tradition, the tradition of Machiavelli, Hobbes, Marx, Pareto, Michels and Goffman, emphasises that *real-politik* and hypocrisy are two of the main factors which make the world go round. Since there are good reasons why human beings often prefer to forget this – reasons that are as much to do with *real-politik* and hypocrisy as with other more charitable well-springs of human behaviour – it seems unlikely that there will come a time when these lessons do not need teaching. Social science therefore is both endlessly incorporated within the world and yet endlessly withdraws from it.

The second and somewhat related reason derives from the centrality within social science of under-doggery. If we can assume that ignorance, *real-politik* and hypocrisy are powerful features of human social life, and there are many compelling reasons to do so, then it follows that conventional versions of how things happened are often likely to omit or repress the views and roles played by the lower orders. The work of many social scientists aims to assert the importance of those whose opinions are rarely heard. We therefore get 'people's history', feminism and so on. This tradition has a major role in the social science of medicine and will continue to surprise and offend the more unimaginative of those in medical authority. Thus, however many reforms are made, studies done from the view-point of the patient, the alcoholic, the mentally ill or, where this is neglected, the doctor, are always likely to be instructive.

Finally, even the most neutral of styles is liable to shock. Researchers in the under-dog tradition tend to wear their hearts on their sleeves and believe in the not inconsiderable virtues of 'commitment'. But even those who claim or aspire to be neutral in their study are still liable to surprise. For since social life is thoroughly moral, to try to be neutral or amoral, is, necessarily, to cause offence to many.

(C)   In concluding our discussion of the intimate relation of social science to social life, one may note how the intricate movement back and forth which social science must make is mirrored by a parallel movement of the social world. On the one hand it borrows freely from social science, seeking out its wares with enthusiasm; but on the other hand there is a long and equally respectable tradition of rejecting what it has to offer. In this tradition; utilitarianism equals the banal horrors of Gradgrind and economics is a truly dismal science. This 'touching tendency to keep a part of the world safe from sociology' (Goffman 1961b), or social science, is unlikely ever to disappear. Even social scientists show a remarkable unwillingness to be analysed in the same terms as they use for their subjects. There is, perhaps, something essentially demeaning to the creative human spirit in viewing oneself as merely the product of social forces. For this reason, also, social science is unlikely ever to gain quite the acceptance that natural science has established for itself.

5. Theoretical Progress in Natural and Social Science in Medicine

(A) Thus far we have approached our problem from four separate angles. We have attempted to do the following things; all fairly crudely it need hardly be said:

(i)   to view social sciences from a medical science perspective, perhaps a rather jaundiced one;

(ii) to summarise those key elements of the ideal scientific programme which, for all their differences, the two sorts of science hold in common;

(iii) to place the human species in evolutionary perspective and thus identify those distinct properties which have given us our particular place in creation;

(iv) to indicate at least some of the problems created for social science by its special intimacy with lay thought.

(B) We conclude – perhaps more, perhaps less jaundiced – with a return to our initial vantage point, the view from medical science. This time, our aim is to compare the conditions for the development and testing of theory in medical and social science. Any social scientist who has glanced at the specialist medical journals will have been impressed by the frequency with which terms such as 'progress' and 'advances' are used. Here is cumulative knowledge apparently, and rapidly accumulating at that; what was thought 10 or 15 years ago is often of little more than historical interest. Considering just how this is possible may throw extra light on the problems of the social sciences.

(i)   Take first the notion of *stability*. We have already stressed the extraordinary flexibility of human behaviour and our consequent rapid and profound cultural evolution. But, although this has enabled the creation of science it renders the application of that science to humankind a most tricky affair. For much of the success of natural science in medicine depends upon the intrinsic stability of the phenomena it describes. There is generally a comprehensible limit to the number of possible influences on a particular phenomenon. The influence on the magnitude of a given electric current in a resistance is strictly limited by its very nature. In the social sciences on the other hand, it is extremely rare to investigate something of consequence for which it is possible even to name all the possible influences, let alone observe more than a small fraction of their possible combinations.

(ii)　Secondly and relatedly, quantification, prediction, and experimentation are as we have seen, all far easier in the natural than in the social sciences. As a consequence, the programme of *reductionism* has been much more successful. In other words advances in physics can be used to generate research in chemistry, and advances in both can be borrowed by biology. The bio-medical scientist thus has a chain of independent yet hierarchically ordered disciplines from which to draw.

(iii)　Whereas many, though not all, of our social accomplishments find no ready parallel in other species, our physical constitution is, mostly, remarkably similar to many other species. We are, for example, genetically closer to chimpanzees than horses are to zebras. This closeness produces some major research advantages for the bio-medical scientist. Extrapolation from animal work provides independent evidence for research problems in human physiology. Moreover, this appeal to what is termed '*biological plausibility*' has great charm since we find it both ethically and practically far easier to experiment on animals than on human beings. Many major difficulties in studying ourselves can be avoided by inflicting the research on other species.

(iv)　As a consequence, *theory,* has a very distinct meaning in the natural science. It is firmly based in empirical research; it is independent of this or that experiment – indeed it may well be drawn from another discipline; it can assume a precisely specified law-like form and one which can normally be mathematically expressed. Finally, and in consequence of all this, there is a well-established division of labour in sciences such as physics between theorists and experimentalists with each contributing, relatively harmoniously, towards the whole. Social scientists sometimes ape the division – mostly with very little justification.

(C)　If we now turn back to social science and consider the development and testing of theory from this viewpoint, we notice immediately that little of the above applies. Many social phenomena are intrinsically unstable and determined by innumerable influences. There is some rough equivalent of biological plausibility via the use of comparative data from other cultures and societies, but the task of comparison is much more formidable, while experimentation at this level is quite impossible. As regards theory, it normally shows few of the special qualities that it has in natural science. It is far less securely based on empirical research; when it assumes a mathematical or else a law-like form, which it does only occasionally, it is tellingly even further from empirical reality than when it does not; and, finally, far from being an independent collaborator in the production of new social knowledge it is often either almost totally removed from empirical research or else far more closely intertwined.

(D) In consequence, the possibilities for the convincing refutation of a hypothesis are far greater in medical science than in social science. The validity of a particular refutation depends first, on the extent to which other plausible influences were held constant; secondly, on the possibility that other influences, known not to be constant, were also having an effect; and, finally on the possibility that quite immeasurable influences were also having an effect. As we can now see, this Popperian model of scientific progress faces two major difficulties in the social sciences. It is typically impossible to hold other matters constant, very hard to define many matters and equally hard to measure their effects. At the same time, precisely because social researchers are themselves human, they normally have a strong emotional investment in their hypotheses, for these are heavily shaped by their personal and political sympathies.

By contrast this model works far more smoothly in the natural sciences. Many false turnings can be quickly dismissed, debates more or less satisfactorily settled and collective scientific effort concentrated on the more promising options. Moreover, the methodology itself advances if refutation relies on a successful critique of a particular method of analysis. And all this remains true despite the important emphasis by recent historians, philosophers and sociologists of science that there is no possibility of completely decisive refutation in natural science that one can always find fault, if one wants, with this or that aspect of method.[7] Likewise, it is still true despite the fact that natural scientists have a considerable personal or career investment in their pet hypothesis.

Both these things must of course be granted. Nevertheless, although there is no decisive break here, although both types of science are clearly on the same continuum – and this, after all, has been one of our principal

7   Of course, within the social sciences there is some variation in this. Social science will be more chastening the more the following are true: The more empirically oriented the tradition, the greater the independence of data and hypothesis: the greater the public availability of data sources and thus the possibility of re-analysis by others; the more that precise sampling and measurement are possible.

arguments – the difference between them is still very wide. Medical science is regularly chastening to those who pursue it in a way in which social science often is not. The difference between them may only be relative, natural science may still have neither absolute certainties, whether of proof or refutation, nor absolute neutralities, yet nevertheless, for most practical scientific purposes consensus can still be achieved and, if not now, then normally in a few years time.

(E)   The difference that this makes is seen most clearly if we return to the topic with which we began, the topic which puzzles medical scientists perhaps more than any other – the bewildering confusion of paradigms and disciplines within the social sciences. For even the weak programme of reductionism[8] has, so far, signally failed to bear much fruit in the social science. The crucial independence of theory and research in the natural sciences stems in large part from quite separate, independent disciplines such as physics and chemistry. The fundamental psychology and ethology of the human species is, however, no more than a dream as things stand at present. They provide no body of empirically elaborated theory from which higher level social science may draw. Moreover, even when such theory is produced it will, as we have argued, necessarily lack the law-like character of some natural science theory but consist simply of statements of typicality. And, obviously, from such statements no immediate and necessary implications may be drawn for higher levels.

Nevertheless, the possession of such a body of generalisations would be a major advance on what we have at present. Of course, there is certainly a discipline called psychology. However, not only is this riven by major internal disputes but it is challenged externally by a variety of other social sciences which, in the absence of anything else, have felt obliged to create their own psychologies to furnish their own particular needs. Thus psychology is a discipline practised separately and often speculatively in anthropology, economics, history, politics and sociology.

The position is even worse as regards human ethology. Not only does every other discipline create its own speculative ethology but there is as yet very little which actually calls itself human ethology. Despite Darwin, the discipline is barely recognised as such. Several issues are compounded here:

(i)   the scientific study of animal social behaviour has been carried out largely without any comparative study of the human species;
(ii)   there is no accepted paradigm for the study of human social behaviour;

---

8   See footnote 3.

(iii) although the notion of comparative study of the social behaviour of animals and man is not new – for the members of human society have always compared themselves in one way or another with other animal species – such comparison as has taken place has usually been crude, non-scientific and put to even cruder social and political purposes. It is therefore still regarded with the gravest suspicion by many social scientists;

(iv) at the same time, and despite such crude comparisons, it seems hard for human beings systematically to compare themselves with other animals, particularly when our own achievements are so spectacular and so many of our former competitors are now obliged to live in zoos.

It is therefore standard practice for social scientists to ignore our animality. Even a self-consciously materialist tradition like Marxism can end up largely presuming that we can transcend the animal realm altogether and become self-determining (Midgley 1980, Timpanaro 1980, Strong 1979).

(F) Not surprisingly, perhaps, given this confusion in the base disciplines of the social sciences, great confusion reigns at higher levels also. Two main problems can be discerned:

(i) First, and not surprisingly perhaps given the confusion at the micro-level, the fundamental nature of macro-systems and their relationship to individuals is still a matter of intense debate: though it must be said that in recent years some measure of consensus has been achieved on basic principles:

> "The most that we can ask of the social scientist is that he keep the principle of methodological individualism firmly in mind as a devoutly-to-be-wished for consummation, an ideal to be approximated as closely as possible. This should at least help assume that nevermore will he dally with suspect group-minds and impersonal "forces" economic or otherwise; nevermore will non-observable properties be attributed to equally non-observable group entities. At the same time, he will not be struck dumb about matters on which there is, no matter how imprecisely a great deal to be said" (Brodbeck *in* Blaug 1980).

(ii) Likewise, there is still vast confusion about the relationship of one discipline to another. In what sense can sociology, history, archaeology and anthropology be seriously treated as independent disciplines'? If we lump these four together, then what is the relationship between this new discipline and disciplines like economics, geography and politics? Plainly there is still a good deal of sorting out to be done before we can achieve a properly ordered social science in and of medicine – nevertheless, just as the debate over macro and micro systems has moved forward, however slowly; just as a serious human ethology is now being created (von Cranach 1979); so too, one can clearly discern at least the beginnings of re-alignment amongst social science disciplines, though advance is likely to be slow.

(G)   Serious theoretical and empirical progress is therefore possible in the social sciences; indeed, though progress is often slow; solid advances have been made, and will continue to be made. However, as we have implied, such advances are, and will remain, of a different form to those made in the natural sciences. For social science is endlessly incorporated in the social world. For theories to have serious effect, they do not have to be correct merely to be taken seriously. Whatever one thinks of the following writers there is an important sense in which we live in a post-Smithian, post-Marxist, post-Keynesian and post-Freudian age. Likewise, and at a rather less exalted level perhaps, Western medicine is now in a post-Ilichian age.

Put another way, the increasing development and dissemination of academic social science continuously heightens the sophistication of that lay world which social scientists are trying to understand. In consequence, however hard they run, they can never say anything truly definitive. Even their greatest achievements entail yet more work for the generations of social scientists who follow after them. Pettit makes the point thus when discussing the future of Goffman's dramaturgic perspective, a perspective which emphasizes that we spend a lot more time carefully managing our public image than we normally like to think:

"And what, in conclusion, is the destiny of such social psychology? It can only be to vanish into common sense as the lessons of the discipline are popularly learned. In those enlightened days there is little saying what will happen, for men will have put themselves in a position to go a reflexive level further, acting out of a concern with being seen (or not being seen) to act out of a concern with being seen (or not being seen) to act out of concern ... Perhaps it will be the time when some new Goffman, his hour come at last, slouches towards Bethlehem to be born" (Pettit 1978: 63).[9]

---

9   One should add in consolation that there will, therefore, always be jobs for social scientists.

Chapter 11

Epidemic Psychology: A Model

Introduction

This essay is a first attempt at a general sociological statement on the striking problems that large, fatal epidemics seem to present to social order; on the waves of fear, panic, stigma, moralising and calls to action that seem to characterise the immediate reaction. Of course, severe epidemics may also present serious threats to both the economy and to welfare. The assault on public order is, in part, moulded by the other ravages made by the epidemic. Singling it out for separate theoretical treatment may, however, lead to important analytic gains. Not only may public order be challenged in a most unusual fashion, but the subjective experience of the first social impact of such epidemics has a compelling, highly dramatic quality (Rosenburg 1989). Societies are caught up in an extraordinary emotional maelstrom which seems, at least for a time, to be beyond anyone's immediate control. Moreover, since this strange state presents such an immediate threat, actual or potential, to public order, it can also powerfully influence the size, timing and shape of the social and political response in many other areas affected by the epidemic.

How can this initial drama be analysed? I shall argue that the early reaction to major fatal epidemics constitutes a distinctive psycho-social form; one which I shall term *epidemic psychology*. Its underlying micro-sociology may well be common to all such diseases – or so I shall hypothesise – but is manifested in its purest shape when a disease is new, unexpected, or particularly devastating. Versions of it may also perhaps be found, mutatis mutandis, in other distinctive but parallel types of dramatic social crisis, in times of war and revolution as well as those of plague. (Hobbes' *Leviathan,* published in 1651, was both the first major analysis of social order and written in a time of civil war.)

The essay itself is in two main parts. The first explores the general nature of epidemic psychology and the special challenge it presents to public order; the second considers some contrasting psychological and sociological explanations. The model has been built in the normal, inevitable but still fairly dubious way, moving back and forth from the particular features of AIDS to more general reflections on the hypothesised wider social form. Not only are inquiries in both fields still highly preliminary, but the general model is heavily informed by the particular instance of AIDS. The paper is not alone in such sins. The first shock of AIDS has already produced several interpretations of the epidemic sensibility, some more global than others (Frankenburg 1988, Rosenburg 1989, Weeks 1989). Each of these differing interpretations has considerable power. Some problems, however, remain. Frankenburg and Weeks, while drawing on sociological theory, are explicitly committed to particular lines of action, for these papers were written at a time when the maelstrom still roared. For all their contribution, their deliberate involvement in efforts to control epidemic psychology means that they are still part of the very process that needs to be described. Rosenberg, who deals with epidemics in general and not just with AIDS, is much the most dispassionate of the three. He too wishes to uncover a standard social form. However, the form he attempts to describe is rather different from that considered here. He focuses on a broad hypothesis concerning the common social trajectory of major epidemics and says relatively little about their initial social impact. (Moreover, despite noting how 'epidemics have always provided occasion for retrospective moral judgement,' (1989: 9) he too falls victim to the same disease on occasion.)

There is, therefore, still plenty of scope for a systematic exploration of the first shock of fatal epidemics. My hope is to provide a general model of epidemic psychology; a model which is, at the same time, directly rooted in some fundamental properties of human society and social action. Through this means, the peculiar features of the first impact of AIDS (and other such related phenomena) can be much more systematically explored. The paper is based on some initial general reading and a pilot round of interviews with some key participants in the early years of the British AIDS story. It forms part of a wider programme of studies funded by the Nuffield Provincial Hospitals Trust into the social history of the impact of AIDS on the UK (Berridge and Strong 1993, Strong and Berridge 1990). The aim of this essay is not to present the data on which these preliminary conclusions are based but simply to sketch out the model.

Epidemic Psychology: Notes on the Model

Epidemic psychology is a phrase with a double meaning. It contains within it a reference, not just to the special micro-sociology or social psychology of epidemics, but to the fact that that psychology has its own epidemic nature, quite separate from the epidemic of disease. Like the disease, it too can spread rapidly from person to person, thereby creating a major collective as well as individual impact. At the same time, however, its spread can take a much wider variety of forms. Epidemic psychology, indeed, seems to involve at least three types of psycho-social epidemic. The first of these is an epidemic of fear. The second is an epidemic of explanation and moralisation and the third is an epidemic of action, or proposed action. Any society gripped by a florid form of epidemic psychology may, therefore, simultaneously experience waves of individual and collective panic, outbursts of interpretation as to why the disease has occurred, rashes of moral controversy, and plagues of competing control strategies, aimed either at containing the disease itself or else at controlling the further epidemics of fear and social dissolution.

The particular features of all three psycho-social epidemics need closer examination. But, before doing this, several qualifications and asides should be made. From a sociological point of view what is interesting about these epidemics of fear, explanation and action is that they have the potential capacity to infect almost everyone in the society. Just as almost everyone can potentially catch certain epidemic diseases, so almost everyone has the capacity to be frightened of such diseases – and, likewise, has the capacity to decide that something must be done and done urgently. All three epidemics, therefore simultaneously possess profound psychological and collective characteristics.

A second comment concerns the status of the overall conceptual schema. This is a paper which deals with ideal types, with necessarily gross simplifications. Its aim is to build a core model of epidemic psychology, of both its characteristic features and its underlying possibilities. It presents some of the sorts of things that may potentially happen. Of course, on any particular occasion, not all of them will. But creating idealised types of social form helps us make patterns out of the chaos of events. Such patterning is an ancient tradition in social science. In this instance, however, it has a further analytic utility. Epidemic psychology may only rarely take the strongest of the forms sketched here but, at the very beginning of a new epidemic when so much is unknown, there is always the prospect that it might. This inherent possibility is itself a powerful determinant of both the crisis and the subsequent response. Fear can feed on itself, just as governments must respond to what might happen as well as to what has already come to pass.

Put another way, although epidemic psychology has not been a conventional subject in modern medical or micro-sociology, it seems to be a clearly recognized possibility in lay thought. It may never be elaborated in the way described here but the potential reality of the phenomenon seems a fundamental given, an all too vivid danger, in human social apprehension. Even if the apocalypse is not now, who knows when the four horsemen may ride? Everyone has deep personal experience of panic. Most of us, moreover, know something of minor social crisis and most of us, more particularly, have been taught something dramatic about bubonic plague. Many commentators have criticised the tabloids' use of the phrase 'gay plague' to describe AIDS. Fewer have noted the extraordinary historical resonance of the Black Death in popular culture. Six hundred years on, it remains one of the most powerful of all European folk memories. Epidemic psychology, then, is not just an analyst's construct but an ideal-type which is in everyday use.

Some comment must also be made on the validity of the distinctions I have just introduced between the different types of psycho-social epidemic. Any sharp separation between different types of epidemic psychology is a dubious business. To distinguish fears from action and morality from strategy seems arbitrary and inaccurate. In actual life, these matters are inseparably intertwined. Different sorts of fear, for example, generate quite different sorts of action. Analytically, however, the distinction has its uses.

Finally, it is worth elaborating a little on the point that the epidemics of fear, interpretation and action seem to be much more severe when the disease is new or strikes in a new way. Once bubonic plague had returned again to Europe in the fourteenth century, major epidemics broke out roughly once every twenty years. After the first horror of the Black Death, these outbreaks were never quite as virulent, except in particular isolated locations, but there was still an overall mortality of perhaps fifteen or twenty per cent in many towns (Open University 1985). However, although the plague was always awful, individuals, towns and cities developed routine, often rapid, ways of responding to it – at least some of the time (Cipolla 1973). Plague, then, became normalised and institutionalised (just as AIDS has begun to become now). In these changed circumstances, plague was still appalling but it was now, at least on some occasions, a familiar condition and could be greeted in a familiar way: 'Oh God, it's plague again, we'll have to shut up the city,' rather than 'Oh my God, what is this, is it the end of the world?'

By contrast, as the instance of the Black Death so vividly illustrates, new forms of fatal, epidemic disease can potentially be much more terrifying and may generate much more extreme reactions and diverse reactions. When routine social responses are unavailable, then a swarm of different theories and strategies may compete for attention.

The Different Psycho-social Epidemics

Consider the different psycho-social epidemics in turn. The epidemic of fear seems to have several striking characteristics, or potential characteristics, all of which will be fairly obvious to the reader, since we have just lived through such an epidemic ourselves. None the less, they are worth listing systematically. First note that the epidemic of fear is also an epidemic of suspicion. There is the fear that I might catch the disease and the suspicion that *you* may already have it and might pass it on to me. A second characteristic of novel, fatal epidemic disease seems to be a widespread fear that the disease may be transmitted through any number of different routes, through sneezing and breathing, through dirt and through doorknobs, through touching anything and anyone. The whole environment, human, animal and inanimate may be rendered potentially infectious. If we do not know what is happening, who knows where the disease might not spring from?

A third striking feature, closely linked to the two above, is the way that fear and suspicion may be wholly separate from the reality of the disease. Just as HIV spread silently for several years before anyone was aware of its presence, so it is possible for great waves of panic and fear to spread among a population even when almost no-one has actually been infected. Japan seems to have experienced such a reaction to just one case of AIDS in 1987 (Ohi *et al* 1988). Likewise, as soon as AIDS became a public crisis in the UK (a process which began in the last week of April 1983, when mass media coverage suddenly erupted) doctors began to see a wave of patients who were obsessed with the fear that they had the disease and could not be persuaded to the contrary (Weber and Goldmeier 1983; see also Jaeger 1988).

Such panic and irrationality can extend even to those who are nominally best informed about the disease. Experienced doctors could still turn hot and cold when they saw their first AIDS patient, or be unable to extend the normal social courtesies to AIDS campaigners. Experienced natural scientists could find themselves unable to treat HIV like any other virus (Strong and Berridge 1990).

Classically associated with this epidemic of irrationality, fear and suspicion, there comes close in its train an epidemic of stigmatisation; the stigmatisation both of those with the disease and of those who belong to what are feared to be the main carrier groups. This can begin with avoidance, segregation and abuse and end – at least potentially – in pogroms. Personal fear may be translated into collective witch-hunts. Moreover, so we should note, such avoidance, segregation and persecution can be quite separate – analytically at least – from actions aimed at containing the epidemic. Such behaviour can occur with all types of stigma, not just with that of epidemic disease. We are dealing here with magic and taboo, not just with quarantine.

Now consider the epidemics of explanation, moralisation and action, epidemics which can be a response both to plague itself and to the plague of fear. Here, too there are several different dimensions. One striking feature of the early days of such epidemics seems to be an exceptionally volatile intellectual state. People may be unable to decide whether a new disease or a new outbreak is trivial or whether it is really something enormously important. They swing backwards and forwards from one state of mind to another. There is, then a collective disorientation. (See Ferlie and Pettigrew 1990, 203.) And if individuals do finally decide that this is something very serious, further unusual psychological states may occur in some people. The process seems rather similar to that of religious conversion. Like St. Paul on the road to Damascus, some people may suddenly find their beliefs and their lives transformed. Some of those whom we have interviewed could remember the precise moment at which they had become converted about AIDS. And some of these, in turn, became messianic – from then on, they rushed out and tried to warn, educate and convert other people.

Thus, when a disease is new and there are no routine collective ways of handling it, a thousand different converts may spring up drawn from every part of society, each possibly with their own plan of action, their own strategy for containing and controlling the disease. Moreover, this epidemic of converts, actions and strategies is matched by an epidemic of interpretation. When an epidemic is novel, a hundred different theories may be produced about the origins of the disease and its potential effects. Many of these are deeply moral in nature. All major epidemics pose fundamental metaphysical questions: how could God – or the government – have allowed it? Who is to blame? What does the impact of the epidemic reveal about our society? The Black Death was a challenge to orthodox Christianity, just as AIDS challenged, at least for a time, the power of biomedical science. Likewise, while some traditionalists have seen AIDS as a terrible judgement on the state of our sexual morality, some liberals have viewed its consequences as an appalling indictment of the state of our health services, or of our attitudes to homosexuality.

The furore and hubbub of intellectual and moral controversy may, in turn, be dramatically increased by the huge rash of control measures now proposed to contain the disease. Many suggestions for limiting the contagion may cut across and threaten our conventional codes and practice. Trade and travel may be disrupted, personal privacy and liberty may be seriously invaded, health education may be enforced on matters that are normally never talked about. Even treatment may be unethical to some. (Brandt's [1987] social history of STDs contains many examples of this latter tendency.)

Finally, because of the disruption and disorientation that such epidemics produce they are also fruitful grounds not just for moral debate and moral challenge but for all kinds of 'moral entrepreneur' (Becker 1963). For

anyone who already has a mission to change the world – or some part
of it an epidemic is a new opportunity for change and conversion. Thus,
cholera gave a platform to both religious revivalists and to those who
wished to clean up Victorian cities. Likewise, AIDS has offered new sorts
of possibility for the religiously conservative, for those who wished to
reform services for STDs and drug addicts, for those gay men who were
unhappy with recent trends in gay sexual expression.

In conclusion, the distinctive social psychology produced by large-
scale epidemic disease can potentially result in a fundamental, if short-
term, collapse of conventional social order. All kinds of disparate but
corrosive effects may occur: friends, family and neighbours may be feared
– and strangers above all; the sick may be left uncared for; those felt to
be carriers may be shunned or persecuted; those without the disease may
nonetheless fear they have got it; fierce moral controversies may sweep
across a society; converts may turn aside from their old daily routines to
preach a new gospel of salvation; governments may panic. For a moment
at least, the world may be turned upside down.

The Origins of Epidemic Psychology

Epidemic psychology is unusual, powerful and extremely disturbing. How
can it best be explained? Why do human beings behave like this? This next
section considers alternative sorts of explanation. The first of these will
be familiar, for it has been the most common interpretation of the crisis
over AIDS, though the argument itself is rarely spelt out. What we have,
instead, is argument by implication. The key terms in this implicit theory
are words like 'panic', and 'hysteria'. The analysis is, thus, essentially
psychological in form.

Epidemic psychology is based, so this story implies, on the primitive,
irrational emotions that are buried within each human being. The
fundamental model of human beings and human society presented here
is essentially Manichean. Humanity, apparently, has a dual nature. A
thin veneer of rationality covers a mass of dark, unpleasant passions. In
ordinary times, most human beings manage to stay more or less rational,
but in a crisis – such as epidemics produce – the unpleasant emotions
dominate. Enter fear, frenzy and the Witch-finder General. In the most
common variant of this tale, there is a sharp separation between the right
minded few who know better (you and me) and the ignorant and atavistic
many who are whipped to a frenzy by cynical politicians and journalists
(in former days the mob, nowadays the readers of the *Sun*).

I want to present, instead, another version based on the American
tradition of micro-sociology (Collins 1985) and, in particular, on the

perspective of two philosophers who have shaped much of that tradition, George Herbert Mead (1956) and Alfred Schutz (1970). Take a broadly Meadian position first. In this, the conventional distinction between the individual and society is abolished. Human social institutions exist in their own right and yet also comprise a myriad encounters between individual human beings. On close examination, for example, both British sexual mores and the British National Health Service splinter into a billion, diverse acts and interactions. Psycho-social matters are, thus, concerned with those properties of individuals and their interactions that have consequences for the societies which they compose – and vice-versa. Their analysis can proceed in at least three directions: staying at the micro-macro interface to examine its precise mechanics; moving down towards the response from or impact upon the individual psyche; or, moving up to consider the interaction with the macro world. This third area of investigation is the collective psycho-social realm – the realm of epidemic psychology as I have defined it here.

That realm, like the other parts of the human micro-social world, has some distinctive features. Certain aspects of human beings and the societies they create are natural phenomena, species characteristics. However, while part of our nature may be fixed, we are the only species to have escaped from a conventional ecological niche. The unique human capacity for language moulds our individual and collective social being in radically different ways from any other part of creation. Language creates the possibility of uniform, sometimes coordinated action involving two, three, tens, hundreds, thousands, even millions of human beings. But language also creates the prospect of alternative programmes, of innovation as well as stability, of revolt as well as obedience, of sectarian as well as communal goals. Unlike their animal counterparts, human societies are, thus, enormously diverse, far more complex and, though elaborately organised, still potentially subject to fundamental change, simultaneously massively ordered and extraordinarily fragile. Of course, most of the time, in the dull grind of our daily lives, our dominant perception is of order. But every now and then chaos erupts in a wholly unexpected and spectacular fashion: epidemics and revolutions erupt, empires suddenly rise or fall, stock markets crash. The world appears brittle, flimsy and open, at least for a moment.

Since the macro sphere is, in key part, constructed through the micro-social world, a similar balance of solidity and fragility can be found at the micro as well as the macro-social level, as Goffman has elegantly shown (Goffman 1961b, 1971; Strong 1988). Social occasions are little social systems, each possessing distinct sets of conventional identities whose scripts have been constructed over the years. Of course, since human beings are ingenious creatures, these identities are not simply allocated, internalised and possessed, they are also displayed, denied and negotiated. The micro-social world is thus (like its macro-social counterpart) simultaneously highly ordered and extremely fragile, exerting massive pressure on the individual actor and yet endlessly redefined and repaired.

With the work of Schutz, we can take the analysis of the micro-social world further still. The popular theory of epidemic psychology rests on a contrast between the surface rationality of everyday life and the raw emotions that lurk beneath. Schutz saw everyday life rather differently. For him it was a matter neither of rationality nor irrationality, but of routine. On his account, the ordinary daily life of individuals and societies is a matter of recipe – endless, humdrum work using taken-for-granted solutions to the thousand and one minor tasks which life constantly presents. These routines and recipes are individually learnt but mostly social in origin. Indeed, they form much the most important part of our collective social consciousness.

This daily work has one further important characteristic. We do many things simultaneously but, in the nature of human consciousness, our immediate attention can be given to only one of those things at a time. All our other, innumerable tasks are, meanwhile, conducted on auto-pilot. If we are worried or well-organised, they may occasionally be monitored to check whether problems have arisen. Otherwise, they are simply processed as before. Most of our actions are habitual and unthinking. (We rarely examine, for example, just which people we touch and how.) Much of our collective consciousness is therefore assumed and unexamined.

Unusual but persistent trends or events can, however, force themselves upon our consciousness, upsetting some or many of the mundane ways in which we are geared into the everyday world. Wholly new sets of recipes must be devised, novel ways of coping with new sorts of problem. Such adjustment is a permanent process. Very few parts of our lives are wholly stable. A few events, however, stand quite outside this process of routine evolution, for some present immediate challenges to our whole way of life, or to life itself. In this situation, two polar responses may be singled out. At one extreme, major threats may be handled in a coordinated fashion, with a cool, sustained focus on the problem at hand, a shunting aside of many other issues, a sustained mobilisation of programmes, recipes and resources. But there may also be a very different reaction, a distinctive epidemic psychology in which contagious waves of panic rip unpredictably through both individuals and the body politic, disrupting all manner of everyday practices, undermining faith in conventional authority, feeding on themselves to produce further, more intense panic and collapse. Different phases of the French Revolution illustrate both reactions. (See

Lefebvre 1932, tr. 1973; Schama 1989.) So, also, does large-scale, fatal, epidemic disease.

Language's fundamental role in the construction of human society can, therefore, explain much of the societal potential for epidemic psychology. The first form of that psychology, the epidemic of fear and suspicion is, at bottom, an unusually powerful pathology of social interaction. No social order can last long when basic assumptions about interaction are disrupted, when every participant fears the other, or suspects that the other may fear them. Fatal epidemics have the potential, in theory at least, to create a medical version of the Hobbesian nightmare: the war of all against all. Moreover, not only does contagious disease strike directly at the micro-processes through which society is constructed, but the human possession of language means that the fear of such disease can be rapidly, even instantly transmitted (as through television) across millions of people and from one society to another.

The plagues of competing moralities and control strategies also have their origins in language. Deviance, for example, is a collective product. We are moralising and typifying animals. The human capacity for language generates the possibility of evaluation and every aspect of our lives is shot through with such judgements. The boundaries of the good cannot be established save through the identification of the wicked. The boundaries of the normal are defined by the abnormal. Stigma is, thus, a human universal (Goffman 1968) not an aberrant unpleasantness which could be banished if only we were all nice to one another. Routinised stigma will always be with us and social crises, such as plague, create the potential for major outbreaks of new or more intense forms of stigmatisation. As for strategies to control both plague itself and the psychology it produces, language creates the possibility of science and technology – both natural and social – and also of religion and magic. It thus shapes both the means through which we can respond to epidemics and the huge potential diversity of such means.

In summary, the human origin of epidemic psychology lies not so much in our unruly passions as in the threat of epidemic disease to our everyday assumptions, in the potential fragility of human social structure and interaction, and in the huge diversity and elaboration of human thought, morality and technology; based as all of these are upon words rather than genes. Epidemic psychology can, thus, only be conquered when new routines and assumptions which deal directly with the epidemic are firmly in place, a process which requires collective as well as individual action. Such reactions are likely to be a little more varied than the matters discussed in this essay. Epidemic psychology would seem, on the face of it at least, to be a human universal. But in dealing with the threat to public order that it poses, different societies may have very different sets of preferences, very different types of structure and very different means at their disposal.

Chapter 12

One Branch of Moral Science: An Early Modern Approach to Public Policy[1]

Introduction

Unlike our immediate ancestors, or some of our colleagues in other disciplines, or indeed (for those of us who are middle-aged) some of our earlier selves, sociologists – qualitative or quantitative alike – work in an ethically incoherent world in which there is no clear disciplinary morality which connects our research to public policy. To say this is not to yearn for some lost golden age, or to assume that there ever was or ever could be a completely coherent disciplinary ethic on which all could agree. It is merely to note that modern sociology now mostly lacks what it has had on some occasions in the past: a powerful sense of moral purpose and commitment to public policy. We commonly feel and are now often treated as marginal.

This feeling is not just a matter of which political party is in power but a sense of the times; that either they are out of joint or, worse, that we ourselves are. Not only are we often critics from the side-lines rather than players in the main debates but, more revealingly, many of us aspire to no higher status. Indeed, the very term policy has long seemed squalid

---

1 [Editor's note: The editors of the volume which originally carried this posthumously published chapter added the following note.]

'Philip Strong died on 11 July 1995 while this manuscript was still in advanced draft. Following discussions with his partner and literary executor, Anne Murcott, it was agreed that the text was substantially that which he would have wished to see published and that his main further addition would have been to provide a bibliography. Rather than guess at his intentions in this respect, and possibly misdirect the reader, we have chosen to publish the text exactly as it was left in a computer file dated 16 April 1995 (the manuscript carried the date of 19 March 1995). This also has the advantage of emphasizing his gifts as an essayist for whom the sweep of the argument was sometimes more important than the detail' (Miller and Dingwall 1997: 195).

and second-rate in some prestigious sociological circles, for it implies a commitment to a world which some of us do not really like and wish we could do without; a world which we can, perhaps, intellectually understand – or so we may think – but to which we cannot join ourselves in any ethically comfortable fashion.

This essay tries to resolve such problems: first, by providing a model of the contemporary policy arena in liberal societies, so that we can see how our own experiences are matched by many others; then, by sketching out the foundations of a new disciplinary public ethic; a liberal metaphysics which may not appeal to all, but is a good deal more effective and more durable than the alternatives currently on offer. Of course, not all the dilemmas that face modern sociologists when they consider public policy can be settled in an essay. As in all branches of human action, there are inherent controversies and conflicts of interest in the policy arena; some must be left to the skill, judgement and conscience of the individual actor; others can only be managed rather than permanently resolved. Nonetheless, some of the problems that cause us the most public agony do seem capable of resolution; are not, in fact, as difficult as they might at first appear.

To say this is not to diminish the solution that I shall propose. It is, instead, merely to be humble; to acknowledge that my solution is not really mine at all, that the approach of early modern moral science whose cause I shall advocate, is now several hundred years old, has found wide acceptance in some other disciplines, and is, indeed, part of our own genealogy, even if it has long passed from our collective memory; for to understand, feel at ease, and act effectively in a modern, liberal society, sociology needs to appreciate liberalism in a much deeper fashion than has been conventional for several generations.

Such an ethical realignment does not mean rejecting the sociological tradition. This is, and will continue to be, a valuable and distinctive source of insight into the human condition. But it does mean abandoning the relatively recent idea that if the heroic sociological morality fashionable for most of this century has failed, then we are doomed, or even honoured, to be the permanent member of the awkward squad; to be a discipline whose unique contribution is not to join in but to stand on the sidelines and sneer. It also means abandoning the arrogant notion, more common perhaps amongst grand theorists than amongst empirical researchers, that modern sociology, by itself, can provide the explanation for most human social problems.

To see where we might go and what we might learn from liberalism, we need to stand back and view ourselves in much broader and much longer perspectives than we are currently prone to do. This essay summarizes two such prospects. The first examines our relationship with the contemporary policy process in liberal societies, drawing not just on sociology, but also on the vision of these matters in parts of policy history, political science and political philosophy; disciplines which have made a much deeper study of some aspects of the science–policy relationship and have rather better resources for grasping the essentials of the modern liberal world.

Relocating our place in the historical tradition of liberal thought, the task of the essay's second section, requires a bigger imaginative leap. A core part of my argument here consists of a brief sketch of the new moral science produced in the early modern period of European history; the period from the sixteenth to the eighteenth centuries which saw the birth of the modern world. This vital era has been seriously neglected by modern sociological thinkers, for both the name 'sociology' and the academic discipline itself date from the nineteenth century, and this late academic origin has had a peculiarly distorting effect upon our self-understanding. Far too many sociological theoreticians, even those like Alexander, Giddens and Turner who proclaim that the subject of sociology is modernity, go back no further than the theorists of the nineteenth century who, great though they undoubtedly were, were also, as we are too, latecomers to the modern world. For that world began, not with the Industrial or French Revolutions, but two hundred years earlier and it is to the first great theorists of the modern world, to Machiavelli, Montaigne, Hobbes, Montesquieu, Smith and the like, that we must also look if we wish to fully comprehend the world in which we live.

This new appreciation also means a new course of reading. For the absence of any serious appreciation of early modern thought has been massively reinforced by the way in which we, like most other occupations, depend on home-grown, amateur histories of our discipline; presentist, 'Whig' affairs, which, in our case as in psychology's, rarely look further back than the nineteenth century, often fail to place even nineteenth century writers in any adequate historical context and, thus, have fundamentally misleading effects upon the theory we produce and the moral and political judgements we make. Instead, to understand our past properly, we must study, not just the classical early modern texts themselves, but the professional, not the amateur, historians of ideas; and we must study them, not just out of whimsical, antiquarian curiosity, but for a much deeper understanding of the liberal world in which we still live. For the version of liberalism we are taught as sociologists, though it has powerful, critical points to make, is the product of a later, oppositional, somewhat deviant branch of the mainstream tradition; a branch which needs to understand the tree from which it has grown.[2]

---

2   A nice example of this systematic neglect of the early modern tradition is the way in which the debate over 'the Hobbesian problem of order' – one of sociology's more fundamental concerns – proceeds with little or no attention to what Hobbes actually said, or to the great wealth of modern Hobbes' scholarship.

Scientific Research and the Policy Process

Let us begin, however, by considering the contemporary relationship between policy and scientific research. Like most human beings, qualitative sociological researchers exaggerate both their problems and their unique qualities. In fact, we share a good deal in common, not just with quantitative colleagues in our own discipline but with all other scientific researchers in liberal society. First, in common with almost all other scientists, we share three fundamental beliefs which stem from the scientific revolution of the early seventeenth century: a secular materialism which excludes supernatural causation; a vision of science as a collective, public endeavour; and a post-sceptical epistemology which asserts that, though much may be doubted, there is still sufficient certainty in our perception of the world on which to base a science.

Secondly, however, neither materialism, nor collective endeavour, nor scientific method guarantee complete certainty or certain public approval, either within or outwith science. As a result, we also share a common policy dilemma. There is no direct process by which research necessarily informs or transforms policy in any dramatic, rational or linear fashion. Instead, the relationship is, for the most part, little different from any other form of human social relationship and is shaped by the same contrary mix of reason, emotion, interest, exchange, altruism, representation and low cunning. Thus, it would seem that in every shade of government, powerful interests may block, distort or ignore, well established scientific findings so far as it suits them to do so. Moreover, insofar as research does affect policy, this is normally due to a slow process of diffusion, commonly, if perhaps optimistically, described by modern commentators as 'enlightenment'. Most often, a slow crab-like process of increasing influence is the norm, not dramatic, Pauline mass conversion. Moreover, as Kuhn and his successors have shown, similar processes seems to take place within science itself. Even here there seems relatively little room for purely 'rational' debate.

Thirdly, in such diffusion, networks are fundamental. At both a national and local level, the key policy worlds are often backstage arenas where a small number of key players represent different interests. Many policy shifts commonly occur primarily through a slow transformation of opinion within these and national attempts to transform local policy are often best conducted through targeting influential figures within the local policy arenas, rather than through general campaigns. Moreover, diffusion through such networks is often shaped by imitation and fashion rather than by any more rational assessment – 'if others are doing it we must not be left behind' – and, equally, through powerful currents of collective emotion in which 'science' and its 'findings' take on a decidedly religious air.

The behaviour of network members is also powerfully influenced by the constraints and opportunities in their environment. Key players, whether politicians, managers or research entrepreneurs use research in a way that often appears self-interested, cynical and imperialistic to others, though it may sometimes be viewed rather differently by the actors themselves.

Fourthly, the representation of our science to outsiders, whether it be qualitative sociology or quantum physics, and whether that representation occurs in public or private debate, also has its own characteristic forms; forms which are heavily determined by the occasions of scientific utterance and the means and needs of communication and not simply by scientific theory and data. Thus, not only is there a distinctive rhetoric of science within academic publications, but the mass media representation of science is fundamentally shaped by journalistic genres; by internal press criteria of what constitutes a tellable story to a mass audience. Likewise, the diffusion of scientific doctrines through private policy networks depends heavily on soundbites and on dogma; on readily intelligible, and thus repeatable, slogans and stories as much on scientific adequacy.

At the same time, if the basic tenets of science – and much of the policy process – are common to all of its forms, there are still important differences between the social and the natural sciences; differences which produce distinctive relationships to public policy. These differences take a contrary form. On the one hand, the social world is, by and large, a far more complex field of determination, prediction and intervention than is true of most natural science arenas. In consequence, professional social scientists, quantitative and qualitative alike, possess less epistemic authority as a social class and play, at least at the technical level, a smaller part in relevant debate than their natural science colleagues. Individual gurus and sometimes particular disciplines and sub-disciplines may, of course, exert considerable influence in particular historical periods but, overall, lay theory and perception is more powerful here than is now normally true of the natural sciences. As a result, 'critique' is an intrinsic feature of all social science and not just the property of a special school within it.

This important bunch of properties is, however, mediated by an opposite and equally important set. Although the laity may claim much greater understanding of the social than of the natural world, the understandings they do claim are powerfully shaped, though not wholly determined, by social science traditions; traditions which, of course, reach them through the distorting mirrors of representation discussed earlier. Moreover, unlike modern natural science, social science remains an integral branch of politics and of ethics. Social science began as, and in fundamental respects continues to be, a 'moral science'; an attempt to create an ethically justifiable public policy on a secular and materialist basis. Thus, although all science can potentially be used by power, social science has a special

240 *Sociology and Medicine*

relationship to it. It began as advice to the powerful, (Machiavelli's *The Prince* is the paradigm case), and has, for the most part, been closely linked to power ever since (as rationalization, discipline or the civilizing process according to taste). And, even where social science is in opposition, it still continues to make a powerful, if implicit claim to power.

Finally, there are, therefore, many good grounds for doubting whether the Millian and Habermasian ideal of a rational critical sphere comprising both systematic private deliberation and rigorous, informed and public debate can ever be fully realised. The world is not a seminar, and even seminars do not have the properties that they were once ideally ascribed. But having said this, we must also recognize – and this is my first fundamental, liberal point – that there is still a crucial difference between policy formation in liberal and authoritarian societies. Mill and Habermas do have a powerful point. The human social world is not and never can be constructed solely through collective reason. But societies which offer serious and methodical scope for the expression of collective reason, societies, that is, with a liberal public sphere, do offer the opportunity for critical debate and, with all its interests and intrinsic irrationalities, this demonstrably can and does make a difference on some crucially important occasions, even if it does not do so on others. There are clear and systematic differences in societies with and without a liberal public sphere, including, of course, the very existence of most forms of critical social science.

The Moral Science Tradition and Our Place Within It

So far, I have suggested that the problems faced by qualitative researchers in relationship to policy are far from unique; that though we may sometimes feel that our case is not heard and that others discriminate against us or distort what we have to say, such feelings are common right across the sciences; are, in fact, the everyday product of intrinsic features of policy formation.[3] I have also made two further, perhaps more important points: on the one hand, that though the policy process may be far from perfect, perfection is not to be looked for in this life – that policy formation is constructed from the same fallible human materials as every other social process; and, on the other hand, that despite these fallibilities, the liberal version of the policy process offers more space for the operation of

---

3   Moreover, although it may be the case that some are more discriminated against than others, and that qualitative researchers are sometimes at the bottom of the heap, we need to remember, not only that some qualitative sociologists such have had a very significant policy influence, but that in other areas such as history, management and political science, qualitative researchers have very considerable prestige.

collective reason than any other.[4] What I now want to show is that these last two claims are intimately connected; that the liberal tradition is premised on human fallibility, recognizes that we can never transcend it, but tries instead to make the best of what we have got.

This position lies at the heart of the public ethic which modern sociology now needs to embrace. To fully grasp what that ethic is and where we currently stand in relationship to it, I need to say more about the early modern period when that ethic was first pronounced. The new moral science proposed by writers such as Hobbes, was based on a novel approach to the public realm. This was a secular, chastened, pluralist, materialist and experimental morality which, breaking with the dominant classical and medieval ideals of consensus and virtue, set its sights a good deal lower. Drawing on other aspects of their intellectual inheritance, in particular, on the disenchanted historical analysis and collective psychology of Thucydides and Tacitus, on the pessimistic Stoical tradition of post-republican Rome and on the sinful view of fallen humanity found in Stoicism's Christian successors, the moral scientists of the early modern period argued that this much more glum approach to human behaviour was not only more realistic, but could also – and this was their real innovation – be systematically used in ways that its original inventors had never imagined; could be used, in fact, on Baconian lines, for systematic, secular, human amelioration. Through sustained investigation and experiment, human ingenuity could learn to exploit the worst as well as the best aspects of human behaviour to our mutual, collective advantage. For, once we knew and recognized what the worst was, then it became possible to base realistic, practical, effective public policy upon it.

By contrast, it was ethically irresponsible and socially unproductive to collectively aspire to the moral heights. This was a reasonable pursuit for saints, but not for societies, for such attempts inevitably failed, sometimes with catastrophic consequences. We should aim, instead, for much lower and more achievable targets; targets on which it was possible to establish, if not unanimity, then at least a fair measure of collective agreement. Our public policy goal should therefore be, not the '*summum bonum*', the greatest good, but the more pragmatic avoidance of the '*summum malum*', the systematic circumvention of the greatest human evils such as tyranny, famine and civil war. The provision of liberty, food and security might not

---

4 For the detailed arguments as to why this is so, see the classic statements by Mill and Habermas. As most commentators have noted, Habermas' analysis of the properties of the liberal public sphere is seriously historically flawed. His ideal model, however, does represent an important addition to Mill. Both perhaps need supplementing by Dahl's powerful summary of the virtues of democracy and Oakeshott's subtle substitution of the term 'conversation' for that of 'debate'.

be everything but this was, still, a fundamental framework within which many other things might flourish. Moreover, once such a framework had been established within a society, its members could and should be left to do pretty much as they pleased. There was little possibility of reaching any more tightly focused consensus on the good life and a great deal of danger in attempting to do so.

This fundamental ethical and governmental innovation was associated with two further radical intellectual breaks. The dominant traditions in classical and medieval thought had stressed the ethical and social priority of the polis, or community, of a single authoritative, collective standard. But the new *summum malum* doctrine minimized any such collective agreement and substituted, instead, the ethics of effectiveness and of the lowest common denominator. For in its stress on the need to deal realistically with egoism, the new ethic placed the individual, not the collectivity, at the heart of social arrangements and moral standards. The community now became what you could get individuals to agree on and actually carry out, not an ultimate source of good, while the state was a backstop which supplied the necessary framework for the individual pursuit of life, liberty and happiness; a 'mortal God', certainly, at those times when it was necessary to awe an unruly populace into the ways of peace, but not a sovereign moral and intellectual authority.

Theorizing about the fundamental constitution of the social world was also radically transformed. In the new secular, materialist vision, both individuals and the communities in which they lived were simply machines. Human social life, in fact, was a matter of artifice – or, in more modern terminology, of social construction – not a product of some divine order. The polis or community did not fulfil a transcendent end or *telos*, as it had done for Plato, Aristotle and St Augustine, rather it should be made to serve the ends that its members wished it to serve, and should be re-arranged, where mechanically possible, to further those individual needs and purposes.

In breaking so fundamentally with the classical and medieval *summum bonum* tradition, the new seventeenth century moral science was, thus, mechanical, rational, egoistic, individualistic and egalitarian in its orientation. But this extreme form of the reaction against the Platonic, Aristotelian and Catholic past, did not last long. By the eighteenth century, many leading moral scientists began to stress the need for organic and collective perspectives to complement the seventeenth century's vision. In Scotland, the heart of Enlightenment liberal moral science, a new synthesis began to be created, one which was still firmly premised on the *summum malum* position invented a century before, but which recognized that a purely mechanical, individualistic and egoistic model of human behaviour, though enormously powerful, needed serious qualification. Human society was a natural phenomenon as well as an artificial one; there was a role for sympathy as well as self-interest; the stress on egalitarianism needed to be complemented by noting the stratification which also accompanied most human activities.

This synthesis of old and new was in its turn, however, rapidly upset. The French and Industrial Revolutions, the associated rise of a far more powerful state than early modern liberalism had ever envisaged and the development by the late nineteenth century of a remodelled university system with massively increased academic specialization, fragmented the older versions of moral science into new, isolated, self-enclosed disciplines. 'Economics' grew out of the seventeenth century vision; 'sociology' was born from the revived emphasis on the collective aspects of social life, and came to specialize almost solely in these. This separate, collective focus had three powerful effects on the discipline we now inhabit:

1   We possess a much more comprehensive account of the effects of social structure and of culture: 'society', a radically new notion in the seventeenth century, has been made visible in myriad ways.

2   At the same time, the middle-class radicals' rejection of the aristocratic interest in etiquette and micro-social behaviour and the new awareness of the properties of the collectivity – both consequences of the Industrial and French Revolutions – produced a fundamental split between micro and macro theory; a split which would have been incomprehensible to theorists of the seventeenth or eighteenth century who drew automatically on both; a split which we are only now trying to start to mend in any systematic fashion.

3   Finally, the separate, collective focus has had powerful but temporally variable consequences for the discipline's relationship to public ethics and policy. At first, with Hegel, Marxism, normative functionalism and the revival of Plato (the dominant theorist in early twentieth century British sociology), *summum bonum* morality made a highly successful return. Here, so it seemed, was a public ethic which provided a solid basis for sociological involvement in matters of policy: an ethic which had a powerful appeal to many liberal – and other – governments in the latter half of the nineteenth and the first half of this century as they struggled with the potentially frightening implications of industrialization, mass society, militarization and the new world of nation-states.

However, with the massive post-war success and stability of liberal government, the nineteenth century forms of *summum bonum* morality have lost much of their appeal both in and outside the discipline. And, with this faith gone, the alternative ethical vision in sociology, the Nietzschean strand represented by Weber and Foucault, has come to dominate most of the more fashionable forms of sociological theory.[5] This particular vision bears some striking resemblances to the sceptical and post-sceptical morality of the early modern period.[6] It too argues that there is no *summum bonum*; it too recognizes the enormous variety of formal moral belief even within any one society; and it too stresses the fundamental role of power and self-interest in human life. There is, however, a crucial difference. Unlike their early modern ancestors, the Nietzschean strand in modern sociology sees these features of our existence as largely inevitable; not as things which can potentially be turned to public advantage. In this bleak, structuralist vision, all of us are used by an impersonal and decentred system; a machine world, an iron cage whose disciplining bands bind ever tighter; not a mechanism which presents a challenge to human ingenuity.[7] Such nihilism offers little place for a public ethic for research practice; room for critique but not for constructive comment or collaboration. Thus it is that theoretical sociology, once a flourishing part of moral science, is now in some danger of becoming a largely amoral tradition.

Of course, quite regardless of these shifts in metaphysical fashion, empirical sociologists have continued to conduct research in a vast range of areas relevant to public policy. This is where most of the research money is and getting research money drives most modern academic departments, at least in the more elite parts of higher education. So public policy research continues for quantitative and qualitative sociologists alike. But it does so in ways which often lack any real sense of disciplinary mission and which are constantly and often savagely internally critiqued, both by the

---

5   The extent to which Foucault was wholly Nietzschean can be disputed. He showed a good deal of interest in liberalism in his later, mostly unpublished lectures. Nietzsche himself might have argued that sociological Nietzscheanism represents, merely, the profoundly frustrated theological aspirations of the discipline: the children of the 1960s have seen both Parsons and Marx dethroned and now fear that ethical meaning has gone out of human life; indeed may never have been there to begin with. This would explain why writers such as Giddens and Turner combine a dominant Nietzschean motif with a strain of wistful *summum bonum* yearning; a yearning which Nietzsche would surely have condemned as weakness.

6   Not surprisingly, perhaps, since Nietzsche's precursor, Schopenhauer, drew directly on the early modern tradition.

7   This moral pessimism may also stem from the distinctive national traditions on which modern sociology has rested. Liberalism, with its base in Anglo-American society, has been a largely optimistic vision. The Nietzschean perspective has been based on the much more pessimistic German experience of modernity.

Nietzschean members of the community and by the radicals of varying kinds who cling to the fragments of the more millenarian versions of the *summum bonum* tradition. As a result, there is considerable unease amongst some sociologists about many forms of policy research, and a profound sense of estrangement from the main discipline amongst many of those who do conduct such enquiry.[8]

Conclusion

What should be done? Perhaps nothing should be. Moral nihilism has an important ethic of its own. Standing aside and doubting is and will remain a valuable part of social science. It cannot, however, provide a satisfactory moral and practical foundation for many of the forms of research which sociologists do and should undertake. As a result, there has been a growing demand for a new sociological morality and a seemingly wide range of suggestions has been made over the past two decades. But, on close inspection, almost all still cling to the *summum bonum* past, exhuming ancient variants of the tradition to see if this or that version might offer some present help. A variety of such warmed-up remains are now on offer, most with their more unattractive elements cosmetically treated or discreetly removed. Neo-functionalism, a much weaker form of normative functionalism has attracted some adherents. Others have followed Taylor in an attempt to create a new communitarianism. Yet other communitarians have turned with Macintyre and Bauman (the latter in a nominally post-modernist ethics) to an essentially religious faith. None of these, however, seem a particularly plausible candidate for a revived public ethic. At first sight, the American pragmatist tradition, as revived by Selznick, looks a more likely bet, since it has always rejected *summum bonum* foundations. However, it still suffers, even in its new form, from inadequate attention to the problem of human evil; a problem that liberal moral science puts at the very heart of its programme.

My own belief is that none of these moves will prove particularly effective. They have been tried before and failed. If sociology is to regain and hold onto its formerly prominent place on the public stage, we must look beyond faith and beyond the nineteenth century and start to place our trust, once again, in the *summum malum* tradition; a tradition with which we once broke, but with which we must now learn to be reconciled. For, if the *summum bonum* tradition has floundered, the *summum malum* tradition

---

8 Many such sociologists belong, instead, to a 'virtual' discipline; the imagined ideal sociology with which they would like to associate but can never actually find.

has not. Following in the footsteps of Machiavelli and Bacon, the great early modern theorists searched for social mechanisms that would enable us to outride Fortuna, that would lessen, even if they could never abolish, the many evils that beset the human condition; that would provide a robust, durable framework inside which humanity, in all its different forms, might flourish. The aim of liberalism is merely to do better, not to be the best. It has favoured, instead, the incremental and the controlled, cautious experiment. That hope has, by and large, been granted. Liberalism has proved durable and those who have been fortunate enough to live inside liberal societies have prospered in comparison with both their ancestors and their contemporaries in other forms of society.

Such an observation, though common enough, is often seen as smug by the many critics of liberalism in the sociological tradition. However, when we rightly observe that liberal society had and still has many obvious and glaring faults, we should not forget that it itself is an open and experimental doctrine that encourages both criticism and invention in order to do better next time. And, when we respond that some of its evils are essential and inbuilt, we must also remember that its more fundamental faults were wryly foreseen by its key early theoreticians. Liberalism is a worldly, unheroic doctrine. Hobbes, the founder of modern liberalism, saw only too well that the state of nature would continue to thrive between nation states and that even within them, though its very worst excesses might be abolished, a low-level, insidious state of nature would continue to inform a great deal of individual human action.[9] Ferguson and Smith both recognized that the liberal, commercial society, while it had many advantages over the old heroic, aristocratic society, was also 'a society of strangers'; that there were and would continue to be important losses as well as gains.

Of course, some liberal thinkers can and do become complacent.[10] We should remember, instead, what the great early modern theorists of the *summum malum* tradition still have to tell us. Modern science, the modern state and their associated welfare order have removed some important elements of the uncertainty and tragedy that so powerfully shaped every human life until relatively recently, but such success is only a thin veneer. Tragedy and evil are and will always remain part of the human condition and only a systematic *summum malum* public ethic pays serious attention to the hard thought and hard choices that the human condition inevitably requires.

---

9 Consider, for example, the unpleasant truths contained in the following eloquent and profound passage: 'The comparison of the life of man to a race, though it holdeth not in every point, yet it holdeth so well for this our purpose that we may thereby both see and remember almost all of the passions [which Hobbes has just discussed]. But this race we must suppose to have no other goal, nor no other garland, but being foremost. And in it: to endeavour is appetite; to be remiss

A reconciliation between sociology and the *summum malum* tradition would give us a firm basis on which to face up to such facts; a firm ethical base on which we might stand without falling prey to either the despair of the Nietzschean tradition, or the utopianism of the Platonic and Socialist dream; would provide a clear and coherent purpose to our current involvement in public policy. It would, moreover, teach us to pay systematic attention to effectiveness and efficiency, as well as to humanity and equity, and require us, also, to think of invention as well as description. All this could be done without abandoning the many things we have learned from the collective vision of the last century and a half. Though some sociologists, such as Coleman, have sought to look outside sociology and refound it solely on the rational, egoistic tradition, such a move is both unnecessary and profligate, for it abandons the many important lessons that the collective tradition still has to teach. If we seek a model, we must look instead to the eighteenth century Scottish synthesis and try to build along the lines suggested there. Though it obviously contains much with which any of us would now quarrel, its broad outline is a most valuable template. It makes room for the micro as well as the macro; gives space for the individual, rational and mechanical as well as the organic, collective and emotional aspects of social life; and, above all, pays more attention to *summum malum* than to *summum bonum* arguments; as indeed any public ethic must do which wishes to engage systematically with policy in a modern liberal society.[11]

---

is sensuality; to consider them behind is glory; to consider them before is humility; to lose ground with looking back, vain glory; to be holden, hatred; to turn back, repentance; to be in breath, hope; to be weary, despair; to endeavour to overtake the next, emulation; to supplant or overthrow, envy; to resolve to break through a stop forseen, courage; to break through a sudden stop, anger; to break through with ease, magnanimity; to lose ground by little hindrances, pusillanimity; to fall on the sudden is disposition to weep; to see another fall, disposition to laugh; to see one out-gone whom we would not is pity; to see one out-go we would not is indignation; to hold fast by another is to love; to carry him on that so holdeth is love; to hurt oneself for haste is shame; to continually to be outgone is misery; continually to outgo the next before is felicity; and to forsake the course is to die.' (Hobbes *Human Nature* 1994: 59–60.)

10 See Hampshire for a powerful critique of contemporary forms of liberal complacency from a *summum malum* position. Hampshire, it might be noted, was in charge of the Gestapo section in British counter-intelligence during the Second World War.

11 Although we are obviously still a long way from such a modern synthesis, those of us in the qualitative tradition have a head start over some of our more quantitative colleagues. For in Erving Goffman, we possess a scholar who successfully combined both the Durkheimian and the Hobbesian traditions.

Acknowledgements

This paper has grown out of a study of the British public debate over AIDS policy and what that, in turn, reveals about policy formation in a liberal society. I would like to thank the Nuffield Provincial Hospitals Trust [now the Nuffield Trust] both for their generous funding of the study and for the intellectual openness which has given me the opportunity to engage in these more general reflections. I must also thank Nick Black, Virginia Berridge and Gill Walt, my colleagues in other policy disciplines, for what I have learnt from them; and my partner, Anne Murcott, who has tolerated, listened to, and sometimes commented sharply upon, innumerable verbal formulations of some of the ideas in this paper. I must also thank Nick Black for his patient support in his other capacity as grantholder. My greatest intellectual debt is to Graham Burchell, from whom I have no doubt pinched even more than I am currently aware of and distorted that which I think I have understood.

A Bibliography of the Work of Philip M. Strong

Books

1979 *The Ceremonial Order of the Clinic: Parents, Doctors and Medical Bureaucracies* London: Routledge & Kegan Paul.

1985 Joint academic editor (with Steven Rose) and one of the principal authors of *Health and Disease*, an eight-volume series: *Studying Health and Disease; Medical Knowledge: Doubt and Certainty; The Health of Nations; The Biology of Health and Disease; Birth to Old Age: Health in Transition; Experiencing and Explaining Disease; Caring for Health: History and Diversity; Caring for Health: Dilemmas and Prospects* Milton Keynes: The Open University Press.

1990 *The NHS – Under New Management* (with Jane Robinson) Buckingham: Open University Press.

1993 *AIDS and Contemporary History* (edited with Virginia Berridge) Cambridge: Cambridge University Press.

Articles

1976 'The management of a therapeutic encounter with young children' (with Alan Davis) *in* M. Wadsworth and D. Robinson (eds) *Studies in Everyday Medical Life* London: Martin Robertson.

1976 '"Aren't children wonderful?": a study of the allocation of identity in developmental assessment' (with A.G. Davis) *in* M. Stacey (ed) *The Sociology of the NHS* Sociological Review Monograph 22. Keele, Staffs.: University of Keele.

1977 'Working without a net: the bachelor as a social problem' (with Alan G. Davis) *The Sociological Review*, 25(1), 109–29.

1977 'Roles, role formats and medical encounters: a cross–cultural analysis of staff–client relationships in children's clinics' (with A.G. Davis) *The Sociological Review*, 25(4), 775–800.

1977 'Medical errands: a discussion of routine patient work' *in* G. Horobin and A.G. Davis (eds) *Medical Encounters* London: Croom Helm.

1978 'Who's who in paediatric encounters: morality, expertise and the generation of identity and action in medical settings' (with Alan Davis) *in* Alan G. Davis (ed) *Relationships Between Doctors and Patients* London: Saxon House.

1979 'Sociological imperialism and the profession of medicine – a critical examination of the thesis of medical imperialism' *Social Science and Medicine*, 13A, 199–215.

1979 'Materialism and medical interaction: a critique of "Medicine, Superstructure and Micropolitics" *Social Science and Medicine*, 13A, 613–19.

1980 'Doctors and dirty work – the case of alcoholism' *Sociology of Health and Illness*, 2(1), 24–46.

1980 'On "Method of Payment for Medical Care and Public Attitudes Toward Physician Authority"' *Journal of Health and Social Behaviour*, 21(2), 195–7.

1980 'Childhood as an estate' (with David May) *in* R.G. Mitchell (ed) *Child Health in the Community* Edinburgh: Churchill Livingstone, 2nd edition.

1981 'Regional variations in the use of common surgical procedures: within and between England and Wales, Canada and the United States of America' (with K. McPherson, A. Epstein and L. Jones) *Social Science and Medicine*, 15A, 273–88.

1982 'Natural science and medicine, social science and medicine: some methodological controversies' (with K. McPherson) *Social Science and Medicine*, 16, 643–57.

1982 'Prevention: who needs it?' (with Nick Black) *British Medical Journal*, 285, 1543–4.

1982 'Materialism and microsociology – a reply to Michele Barratt' *Sociology of Health and Illness*, 4(1), 98–101.

1983 'The Rivals: an essay on the sociological trades' *in* R. Dingwall and P. Lewis (eds) *The Sociology of the Professions: Lawyers, Doctors and Others* London: Macmillan.

1983 'The limits of negotiation in formal organizations' (with R.W.J. Dingwall) *in* G.N. Gilbert and P. Abell (eds) *Accounts and Action* Aldershot, Hants.: Gower.

1983 'The importance of being Erving: Erving Goffman, 1922–1982' *Sociology of Health and Illness*, 5(3), 345–55.

1984 'Viewpoint: the academic encirclement of medicine?' *Sociology of Health and Illness*, 6(3), 339–58.

1985 'Do cholecystectomy rates correlate with geographical variations in the prevalence of gallstones?' (with K. McPherson, L. Jones and B.J. Britton) *Journal of Epidemiology and Community Health*, 39(2), 179–82.

1985 'The interactional study of organizations: a critique and reformulation' (with R. Dingwall) *Urban Life*, 14(2), 205–31.

1986 'A new-modelled medicine? Comments on the WHO's Regional Strategy for Europe', *Social Science and Medicine*, 22(2), 193–9.

1988 'Minor courtesies and macro structures' *in* P. Drew and A. Wootton (eds) *Erving Goffman: Exploring the Interaction Order* Cambridge: Polity Press.

1988 'Qualitative sociology in the UK' *Qualitative Sociology* 11(1–2), 13–28.

1989 'Romantics and stoics' (with R. Dingwall) *in* J.F. Gubrium and D. Silverman (eds) *The Politics of Field Research: Sociology beyond Enlightenment* London: Sage.

1990 'No one knew anything: some issues in British AIDS policy' (with Virginia Berridge) *in* P. Aggleton, P. Davies and G. Hart (eds) *AIDS: Individual, Cultural and Policy Dimensions* London: The Falmer Press.

1990 'Epidemic psychology: a model' *Sociology of Health and Illness*, 12(3), 249–59.

1990 'The collective psycho-social impact of sexually transmitted diseases' *in* N. Job-Spira, B. Spencer, J.P. Moaltti, E. Bouvet (eds) *Santé Publique et Maladies à Transmission Sexuelle* Paris: John Libbey, Eurotext.

1990 'Black on class and mortality: theory, method and historical context – a critique' *Journal of Public Health Medicine*, 12(3/4), 168–80.

1991 'Psychologie épidemique et micro-sociologie: pour comprendre l'impact social des grandes épidémies' *La Nouvelle Gazette de la Transfusion Sanguine*, 65–66, 8–9.

1991 'AIDS and the relevance of history' (with Virginia Berridge) *Social History of Medicine*, 4(1), 129–38.

1991 'AIDS in the UK: contemporary history and the study of policy' (with Virginia Berridge) *Twentieth Century British History*, 2(2), 150–74.

1991 'Strong on Black on class and health – a rejoinder to Townsend, Davey Smith, Bartley and Blane' *Journal of Public Health Medicine*, 13(4), 357–9.

1992 'AIDS Policies in the UK: a preliminary analysis' (with Virginia Berridge) in E. Fee and D.M. Fox (eds) *AIDS: The Making of a Chronic Disease* Berkeley, C.A.: University of California Press.

1992 'The case for qualitative research' *The International Journal of Pharmacy Practice*, 1(4), 185–6.

1993 'Are academic institutions corrupt?' (with P. Garner) *The Lancet*, 342, 8867, 314–15.

1994 'Two types of Ceremonial Order' *in* S.O. Lauritzen and L. Sachs (eds) *Health Care Encounters and Culture: Interdisciplinary Perspectives* Botkyrka, Sweden: Multicultural Centre.

1995 'Leap of faith over the data-tap' (with M. McKee and P. Garner) *The Lancet*, 345, 8963, 1449–51.

1996 'One branch of moral science: an early modern approach to public policy' *in* G. Miller and R. Dingwall (eds) *Strategic qualitative research* London: Sage.

1998 'The pestilential apocalypse: modern, postmodern and early modern observations' *in* Rosaline S. Barbour and Guro Huby (eds) *Meddling with Mythology: AIDS and the social construction of knowledge* London: Routledge.

Selected reviews, reports etc

1970 Review of 'Harry Kidd *The Trouble at L.S.E., 1966–1967*', *Aberdeen University Review*, XLIII(3), 304–5.

1979 Review of 'Anselm Strauss *Mirrors and Masks: the Search for Identity*' and 'Anselm Strauss and Barney Glaser *Anguish: a Case History of a Dying Trajectory*', *Sociology of Health and Illness*, 1(1), 125–7.

1981 Review of 'David Hall and Margaret Stacey eds. *Beyond Separation: Further Studies of Children in Hospital*', *Sociology of Health and Illness*, 3(1), 122–4.

1982 Review of 'Erving Goffman *Forms of Talk*', *Sociology*, 16, 453–5.

1984 'Commentary': on Qualitative Methods and Leadership Research *in* J.G. Hunt, D-A. Hosking, C.A. Schriesheim, R. Stewart (eds) *Leaders and Managers: International Perspectives on Managerial Behavior and Leadership* New York: Pergamon.

1984 'Do cholecystectomy rates correlate with geographic variations in prevalence of gallstones?' (with K. McPherson, L. Jones and B.J. Britton) *The Lancet*, (letter) 1092–3.

1985 'Review essay: medicine, ethics and medical sociology' *Medical Sociology News*, 11, 38–43.

1985 Review of 'J.W. Meyer and W.R. Scott (with B. Rowan and T.E. Deal) *Organizational Environments: Ritual and Rationality*', *Sociology of Health and Illness*, 7(3) 456–7.

1985 'The economists' contribution to health policy: the view from another social science' *Radical Community Medicine*, 24, 7–10.

1987 'Professional nursing advice after Griffiths – an interim report' (with Jane Robinson) Nursing Policy Studies Centre, University of Warwick, i–50 pp.

1988   'The impact of general management on the NHS' *Radical Community Medicine*, 34, 51–3.

1988   'New model management: Griffiths and the NHS' (with Jane Robinson) Nursing Policy Studies Centre, University of Warwick, iii–164 pp.

1988   'Warts and all' (with Jane Robinson) *Nursing Times*, September 28, 84(39), 53–5.

1988   'Griffiths and the NHS (with Jane Robinson) *Health Visitor*, 61, September, 283.

1989   Review of 'K. Melia, *Learning and Working: the occupational socialization of nurses' Sociology of Health and Illness*, 11(1) 94–5.

1989   'Griffiths and the nurses: a national survey of CNAs' (with Jane Robinson and Ruth Elkan) Nursing Policy Studies Centre, University of Warwick, i–130 pp.

1990   Review of 'Christopher Pollitt, *Managerialism and the Public Services: the Anglo-American Experience*', *International Journal of Sociology and Social Policy*, 10(8), 88–9.

1991   'Health service researchers' perspective', *Action in Practice Research*, Pharmacy Practice Research: Conference 1991, Conference proceedings, 27.

1991   Review of 'S. Harrison, D.J. Hunter and C. Pollitt *The Dynamics of British Health Policy*', *Sociology of Health and Illness*, 13(3) 432–3.

1993   Review of 'Charlotte Williamson, *Whose Standards? Consumer and professional standards in health services*', *European Journal of Public Health*, 3(4) 229.

References

Abel P. (1981) 'Whither sociological methodology' in P. Abrams *et al*
(eds) *Practice and Progress: British Sociology 1950–1980* London:
Allen & Unwin.

Abrams, P. (1968) *The Origins of British Sociology 1834–1914* Chicago:
University of Chicago Press.

Acheson, R. (1980) 'Community Medicine: Discipline or Topic? Profession
or Endeavour?' *Community Medicine* 2, 2–6.

Anderson, D. and Sharrock, W. (1979) 'Biasing the News: Technical
Issues in Media Studies' *Sociology* 13, 361–85.

Armstrong, D. (1982) 'The doctor–patient relationship 1930–1980' in
A. Treacher and P. Wright (eds) *The Problem of Medical Knowledge:
Towards a Social Constructivist View of Medicine* Edinburgh:
Edinburgh University Press.

Ashby, E. (1977) *Reconciling Man With The Environment* Oxford: Oxford
University Press.

Atkinson, P. (1990) *The Ethnographic Imagination* London: Routledge.

Avery-Jones, F. (ed) (1970) *Richard Asher Talking Sense* London: Pitman
Medical.

Baumann, Z. (1976) *Socialism: The Active Utopia* London: Allen and
Unwin.

Becker, H. (1963) *Outsiders: Studies in the Sociology of Deviance* New
York: Free Press.

Becker, H.S. (1969a) 'Social Observation and Case Studies' in H.S. Becker
Sociological Work Chicago: Aldine.

Becker, H.S. (1969b) 'Fieldwork Evidence' in H.S. Becker *Sociological
Work* Chicago: Aldine.

Beeson P.B. Godber G.E. Holland N. Tudor Hart J. and Green R.M. (1977)
Review symposium on 'The role of medicine' *Health Society* 55, 361.

Bengmark S. (1975) 'Surgical management of portal hypertension' *Clinics
in Gastroenterology* 4, 439–460.

Berger, P. (1967) *The Social Reality of Religion* London: Faber & Faber.

Berridge, V. and Strong, P. (1990) 'AIDS policies in the UK: a preliminary
analysis' in E. Fee and D. Fox (eds) *AIDS: Contemporary History*
Princeton, N.J.: Princeton University Press.

Berridge, V. and Strong, P (eds) (1993) *AIDS and Contemporary History* Cambridge: Cambridge University Press.

Bigus, O. (1972) 'The Milkman and His Customer: A Cultivated Relationship', *Urban Life and Culture*, vol.1, pp.131–65.

Birtley, J. (1980) 'Thought on Flowers' *The Lancet* I, 587–8.

Bittner, E. (1963) 'Radicalism and the Organisation of Radical Movements' *American Sociological Review* 28, 928–40.

Bittner, E. (1965) 'The Concept of Organisation' *Social Research* 32, 239–255.

Bittner, E. (1968) 'The structure of psychiatric influence' *Mental Hygiene* 52, 424.

Blaug, M. (1980) *The Methodology of Economics* Cambridge: Cambridge University Press.

Bloom, S. (1978) 'The Profession of Medical Sociologist in the Future' in Y. Nuyens and J. Vansteenkiste (eds) *Teaching Medical Sociology* Leiden: Martinus Nijhoff.

Bloor, M. (1976a) 'Professional autonomy and client exclusion: a study in ENT clinics' in M. Wadsworth and D. Robinson (eds) *Studies in Everyday Medical Life* London: Martin Robertson.

Bloor, M. (1976b) 'Bishop Berkeley and the Adeno-Tonsillectomy Enigma' *Sociology* 10, 43–61.

Bloor, M. (1978) 'On the analysis of observational data: discussion of the worth and uses of inductive techniques and respondent validation' *Sociology* 12, 545–52.

Bloor, M. (1996) 'Review essay: Philip Strong (1945–1995) an appreciation of an essayist' *Sociology of Health & Illness* 18(4), 551–64.

Booth, C.C. (1980) 'Clinical Science in the 1980s' *The Lancet* Oct. 25, 904–7.

Bott, E. (1976) 'Hospital and society' *British Journal of Medical Psychology* 49(2), 97–140.

Brandt, A. (1987) *No Magic Bullet* Oxford: Oxford University Press.

Bridges, R. (1878) 'An account of the casualty department' *St. Bartholomew's Hospital Reports* XIV 167–82.

British Medical Journal Editorial (1978) 'The other crisis of health care' *British Medical Journal* 939.

British Medical Journal Editorial (1980) 'More Anthropology and Less Sleep for Medical Students' *British Medical Journal* 20 Dec. 662.

Brody, D.S. (1982) 'The Lie That Heals' *Annals of Internal Medicine* 97, 112–18.

Bucher, R. and Strauss, A. (1961) 'Professions in process' *American Journal of Sociology* 66, 325–34.

Bulgakov, M. (1976) *A Country-Doctor's Notebook* London: Fontana.

References 257

Bunker, J. *et al.* (1978) 'Surgical Innovation and its Evaluation' *Science* 200, 26 May, 937–41.

Burchell, G. (1991) 'Peculiar interests: civil society and governing the system of natural liberty' in G. Burchell, C. Gordon and P. Miller (eds) *The Foucault Effect: Studies in Governmentality* Hemel Hempstead: Harvester Wheatsheaf.

Burgess, R.G. and Murcott, A. (eds) *Developments in Sociology: where are we now?* London: Pearson.

Burns, T. (1979) 'Sociology as a Discipline: A Retrospective View' (mimeo) Paper given at the BSA Annual Conference Lancaster.

Burns, T. (1992) *Erving Goffman* London: Routledge.

Byrne P.S. and Long B.E.L. (1976) *Doctors Talking to Patients* London: Her Majesty's Stationery Office.

Campbell, C.M. and Wiles, P. (1976) 'The Study of Law and Society in Britain' *Law and Society* Summer, 547–78.

Christie, R.J. (1969) 'Medical Education and the State' (Harveian Oration) *British Medical Journal,* iv, 15 Nov, 385.

Cicourel, A. (1964) *Method and Measurement in Sociology* New York: Free Press.

Cicourel, A. (1973) *Cognitive Sociology* Harmondsworth: Penguin.

Cipolla, C. (1973) *Cristofano and the Plague: A Study in the History of Public Health in the Age of Galileo* London: Collins.

Clifford, J. and Marcus, G.E. (eds) (1986) *Writing Culture* Berkley, CA: University of California Press.

Cochrane, A.L. (1972) *Effectiveness and Efficiency: Random Reflections on Health Services* London: Nuffield Provincial Hospitals Trust.

Cohen, D. (1978) 'Psychiatry at home' *New Society* 486.

Coleman, J. (1978) 'Sociological analysis and social policy' in T. Bottomore and R. Nisbet (eds) *A History of Sociological Analysis* London: Heinemann.

Collins, R. (1975) *Conflict Sociology* Oxford: Oxford University Press.

Collins, R. (1981) 'On the microfoundations of macrosociology' *American Journal of Sociology* 86, 984–1014.

Collins, R. (1985) *Three Sociological Traditions* Oxford: Oxford University Press.

Comroe, J. and Dripps, R. (1976) 'The Scientific Basis for the Support of Biomedical Science' *Science,* 192, 105–11.

Conrad, P. (1975) 'The discovery of hyperkinesis: notes on the medicalisation of deviant behaviour' *Social Problems* 23(1), 12–21.

Coombs, R.H. and Goldman, L.J. (1973) 'Maintenance and Discontinuity of Coping Mechanisms in an Intensive Care Unit' *Social Problems* 20, 342–54.

Cressey, D. (1971) *Other People's Money: A Study in the Social Psychology of Embezzlement* Belmont, CA: Wadsworth.

Crouse, T. (1974) *The Boys on the Bus* New York: Ballantine.

Davies, M.L. (ed) (1978) *Maternity: Letters from Working Women* London: Virago.

Davis, A. (1982) *Children in Clinics* London: Tavistock.

Davis, A. and Horobin, G. (eds) (1977) *Medical Encounters* London: Croom Helm.

Davis, F. (1963) *Passage through Crisis* Bobbs-Merrill: New York.

Denzin, N. and Keller, C. (1981) 'Frame Analysis reconsidered' *Contemporary Sociology* 10, 52–60.

Department of Health & Social Security (DHSS) (1980) *Inequalities in Health: Report of a Research Working Party,* London: DHSS.

Detels, R. (1979) 'The Need for Epidemiologists' *Journal of the American Medical Association* 242, 12 Oct, 1644–6.

Dingwall, R. and Strong, P. (1985) 'The interactional study of organizations: a critique and reformulation' *Urban Life* 14, 205–31.

Dingwall, R. Eekelaar, J. and Murray, T. (1983) *The Protection of Children: State Intervention and Family Life* Oxford: Basil Blackwell.

Dingwall, R. Payne, G. and Payne, J. (1980) 'The Development of Ethnography in Britain' paper presented at the 1980 BSA Annual Conference, published as Centre for Socio-Legal Studies Occasional Paper, Oxford.

Dingwall, R. Rafferty, A-M, and Webster, C. (1988) *An Introduction to the History of Nursing* London: Routledge and Kegan Paul.

Ditton, J. (ed) (1980) *The View from Goffman* London: Macmillan.

Douglas, C. (1977) *The Houseman's Tale* London: Fontana.

Douglas, C. (1980a) *The Greatest Breakthrough since Lunchtime* London: Fontana.

Douglas, C. (1980b) *Bleeders Come First* London: Fontana.

Douglas, J.D. (1971) 'Introduction' in J.D. Douglas (ed) *Understanding Everyday Life* London: Routledge & Kegan Paul.

Draper, P. and Smart, T. (1974) 'Social science and health policy in the United Kingdom: some contributions of the social sciences to the bureaucratization of the National Health Service' *International Journal of Health Services* 4(3), 453–470.

Drew, P. and Wootton, A. (eds) (1988) *Erving Goffman: Exploring the Interaction Order* Oxford: Polity Press.

Ehrenreich, B. and Ehrenreich, J. (1971) *The American Health Empire* New York: Vintage Books.

Ehrenreich, B. and Ehrenreich, J. (1975) 'Medicine and social control' in B.R. Mandell (ed) *Welfare in America–Controlling the Dangerous Classes* Englewood Cliffs, N.J.: Prentice-Hall.

Elton, G. (1969) *The Practice of History* London: Fontana.

Emerson, R. (1969) *Judging Delinquents* Aldine: Chicago.

Engelhardt, H. Jr. (1974) 'The disease of masturbation: values and the concept of disease' *Bulletin of the History of Medicine* 48, 234–48.

Engleman, S. (1980) 'Health Economics, Health Economists and the NHS' *Community Medicine* 2, 126–34.

Ferlie, E. and Pettigrew, A. (1990) 'Coping with change in the NHS: a frontline district's response to AIDS' *Journal of Social Policy* 19(2) 191–220.

Ferris, P. (1967) *The Doctors* Harmondsworth: Penguin.

Fingarette, H. (1968) *Self-Deception* London: Routledge & Kegan Paul.

Frankenberg, R. (1974) 'Functionalism and after? Theory and developments in social science as applied to the health field' *International Journal of Health Services* 4, 411.

Frankenberg, R. (1988) 'Social and cultural aspects of the prevention of the three epidemics (HIV infection, AIDS and counterproductive societal reaction to them)' in A. Fleming A. *et al* (eds) *The Global Impact of AIDS* New York: Alan R. Liss Inc.

Frederickson, D.S. (1981) 'Bio-medical Research in the 1980s' *New England Journal of Medicine* 304.

Freidson, E. (1970) *Professional Dominance* Atherton: New York.

Freidson, E. (1972) 'Disability as Social Deviance' in E. Freidson and J. Lorber (eds) *Medical Men and their Work* Aldine: Chicago.

Freidson, E. (ed) (1973) *The Professions and Their Prospects* New York: Sage.

Freidson, E. *Profession of Medicine* (1970) New York: Dodd, Mead.

Fuller, R.G. and Myers R.R. (1941) 'The natural history of a social problem' *American Sociological Review* 6(3), 320–29.

Garfinkel, H. (1956) 'Some sociological concepts and methods for psychiatrists' *Psychiatric Research Reports* 6, 181–95.

Garfinkel, H. (1967) 'Studies of the routine grounds of everyday activities' *Social Problems* 11, 225–250.

Gay, P. (1970) *Weimar Culture: the Outsider as Insider* New York: Harper and Row.

Gellner, E. (1974) *Legitimation of Belief* Cambridge: Cambridge University Press.

Glaser, B. (1964) 'The Constant Comparative Method of Qualitative Analysis' *Social Problems* 12, 436–445.

Glaser, B.G. (1992) *Basics of Grounded Theory Analysis: Emergence vs Forcing* Mill Valley, CA: The Sociology Press.

Goffman, E. (1959) *The Presentation of Self in Everyday Life* New York: Doubleday Anchor.

Goffman, E. (1961a) *Asylums* New York: Doubleday Anchor.

Goffman, E. (1961b) *Encounters* New York: Bobbs Merrill.

Goffman, E. (1967) *Interaction Ritual: Essays on Face-to-Face Behavior* New York: Doubleday Anchor.

Goffman, E. (1968) *Stigma* Harmondsworth: Penguin.

Goffman, E. (1971) *Relations in Public: Microstudies of the Public Order* New York: Harper and Row.

Goffman, E. (1972) *Interaction Ritual* Harmondsworth: Penguin.

Goffman, E. (1974) *Frame Analysis: An Essay an the Organization of Experience* New York: Harper and Row.

Goffman, E. (1976) *Gender Advertisements* Harmondsworth: Penguin.

Goffman, E. (1981a) 'A reply to Denzin and Keller' *Contemporary Sociology*, 10, 60–68.

Goffman, E (1981b) *Forms of Talk* Oxford: Blackwell.

Goffman, E. (1983) 'The interaction order' *American Sociological Review* 48, 1–17.

Gold, M. (1977) 'A crisis of identity: the case of medical sociology' *Journal of Health & Social Behavior* 18(2), 160–68.

Goode, W.J. (1960) 'Encroachment. charlatanism and the emerging profession: Psychology, Sociology and Medicine' *American Sociological Review* 25, 902–14.

Gouldner, A. (1970) *The Coming Crisis of Western Sociology* New York: Basic Books.

Greenberg, D. (1969) *The Politics of American Science* Harmondsworth: Penguin.

Greenberg, D.S. (1980) 'Washington and Wall Street Report' *New England Journal of Medicine* 302, April, 978–80.

Gronos, G. (1977) '"Situation" *versus* "Frame": the "Interactionist" and the "Structuralist" analyses of everyday life' *American Sociological Review* 42, 854–67.

Gusfield, J. (1976) 'The Literary Rhetoric of Science, Comedy and Pathos in Drinking Driver Research' *American Sociological Review* 41, 165–34.

Haller, J.S. (1971) 'Neurasthenia: the medical profession and the "New Woman" of the late 19th Century' *New York State Journal of Medicine* 71, 475.

Halmos, P. (1966) *The Faith of the Counsellors* London: Constable

Halmos, P. (1970) *The Personal Service Society* London: Constable.

Halmos, P. (1973) 'Sociology and the personal service professions' in E. Freidson (ed) *The Professions and Their Prospects* New York: Sage.

Hammersley, M. (1992) *What's Wrong with Ethnography?* London: Tavistock.

Hawthorn, G. (1976) *Enlightenment and Despair: A History of Sociology* Cambridge: Cambridge University Press.

Healey, M. (1978) 'Is Statistics a Science?' Mimeo. (Chairman's address to the Medical Section of the Royal Statistical Society, 31 Jan.)

Helmer, J. (1970) 'The face of the man without qualities' *Social Research* 37, 547.

Hobsbawm, E. (1977) *Revolutionaries* London: Quartet.

Hofstadter, R. (1963) *Anti-Intellectualism in American Life* New York: Knopf.

Horobin, G. and Bloor, M.J. (1975) 'Role-taking in illness' in C. Cox and A. Mead (eds) *The Sociology of Medical Practice* London: Macmillan.

Hughes, E.C. (1945) 'Dilemmas and Contradictions of Status' *American Journal of Sociology,* 50 (March), 353–59.

Hughes, E.C. (1958) *Men and Their Work* Free Press of Glencoe.

Hughes, E.C. (1971) *The Sociological Eye: Selected Papers* Chicago: Aldine Atherton.

Illich I. (1975) *Medical Nemesis: The Expropriation of Health* London: Calder & Boyars.

Illich, I. (ed) (1977) *Disabling Professions* London: Marion Boyars.

Illsley, R. (1975) 'Promotion to observer status' *Social Science & Medicine* 9, 63–67.

Jaeger, H. (ed) (1988) *AIDS Phobia: Disease Pattern and Possibilities of Treatment* Chichester: Ellis Horwood.

Jamous, H. and Peloille, B. (1970) 'Profession or Self-Perpetuating Systems? Changes in the French University-Hospital System' in J.A. Jackson (ed) *Professions and Professionalization* Cambridge: Cambridge University Press.

Jefferys M. (1974) 'Social science and medical education in Britain: a sociologic analysis of their relationship' *International Journal of Health Services* 4, 557.

Johnson, M.L. (1975) 'Medical sociology and sociological theory' *Social Science & Medicine* 9, 227–32.

Johnson, T. (1972) *Professions and Power* London: Macmillan.

Jones, R.W. and Helrich, A.R. (1977) 'Treatment of alcoholism by physicians in private practice: a national survey' *Q. Jl Stud. Alcohol.* 33, 117.

Kakutani, M. (1980) 'Do Facts and Fiction Mix?' *New York Times Book Review* 27 Jan, 28–9.

Keating, P. (ed) (1976) *Into Unknown England 1866–1913: a Selection from the Social Explorers* London: Fontana.

Kendis, J.B. (1967) 'The effect of attitudes in the therapy of the alcoholic' *British Journal of Addiction* 62, 307.

Kennedy, I. (1980) 'Consumerism in the Doctor-Patient Relationship' *The Listener,* 11 Dec., 778–9.

Kissin, B. (1977) 'Comments on alcoholism: a controlled trial of "treatment" and "advice" 1. *Stud. Alcohol* 38, 1804.

Korn, R. (1964) 'The private citizen, the social expert and the social problem: an excursion through an unacknowledged Utopia' in B. Rosenberg B. *et al* (eds) *Mass Society in Crisis: Social Problems and Social Psychology* New York: Macmillan.

Kosa, J. (1970) 'Entrepreneurship and Charisma in the Medical Profession' *Social Science and Medicine* 4, 25–40.

Krause, E.A. (1977) *Power and Illness: The Political Sociology of Health and Medical Care.* New York: Elsevier.

Kuhn, T.S. (1961) 'The function of measurement in modern physical science' in H. Woolf (ed) *Quantification: A History of the Meaning of Measurement in the Natural and Social Sciences* Indianapolis: Bobbs-Merrill.

Kuhn, T.S. (1962) *The Structure of Scientific Revolutions* Chicago: University of Chicago Press.

Kumar, K. (1978) *Prophecy and Progress: the Sociology of Industrial and Post-Industrial Society* Harmondsworth: Penguin.

Lahr, J. (1980) *Prick Up Your Ears: the Biography of Joe Orton* Harmondsworth: Penguin.

Lancet Editorial (1975) 'Clinical Decision by Numbers' *The Lancet* 10 May, 1077.

Lancet Editorial (1979) 'Academic Medicine – Threatened Institution' *The Lancet,* 29 Sep., 677–8.

Lancet Editorial (1980) 'Clinical Competence and Research' *The Lancet,* 22 March, 637.

Lancet Editorial (1980) 'Professionalism and the Royal College' *The Lancet,* 5 April, 749.

Lefebvre, G. (1970) *The Great Fear of 1789: Rural Panic in Revolutionary France* London: New Left Books.

Lemert, E. (1967) *Human Deviance, Social Problems and Social Control* New Jersey: Prentice-Hall.

Lever, A.F. (1977) 'Medicine under challenge' *The Lancet* 352.

Lewis, L.S. (1973) 'The universities and the professional model: amplification on a magnification' in E. Freidson (ed) *The Professions and Their Prospects* New York: Sage.

Leys, S. (1978) *Chinese Shadows* Harmondsworth: Penguin.

Lilienfeld, A. (1980) 'The American College of Epidemiology' *American Journal of Epidemiology* 111, 380–82.

Lorber, J. (1972) 'Deviance as Performance' in E. Freidson and J. Lorber (eds) *Medical Men and their Work* Aldine: Chicago.

Loudon, I. (1978) 'Historical importance of outpatients' *British Medical Journal* 974.

MacDonald, E.B. and Patel, A.R. (1975) 'Attitudes towards alcoholism' *British Medical Journal* 430.

Macintyre, A. (1967) *A Short History of Ethics* London: Routledge & Kegan Paul.

Macintyre, A. (1971) 'Is a science of comparative politics possible?' *Against the Self-Images of the Age* London: Duckworth.

Macintyre, A. (1981) *After Virtue* London: Duckworth.

Macintyre S. (1977a) 'Childbirth: the myth of the Golden Age' *World Medicine* 12, 17.

Macintyre S. (1977b) 'Old age as a social problem: historical notes on the English experience' in R. Dingwall *et al* (eds) *Health Care and Health Knowledge* London: Croom Helm.

Macintyre, S. (1977c) *Single and Pregnant* London: Croom Helm.

Martin, J.P. (1984) *Hospitals in Trouble* Oxford: Basil Blackwell.

McCaghy, C. (1963) 'Drinking and Deviance Disavowal: the case of child molesters' *Social Problems* 16, 43–49.

McKeown, T. (1976) *The Role of Medicine: Dream, Mirage or Nemesis?* London: Nuffield Provincial Hospitals Trust.

McNeill, W.H. (1979) *A World History* Oxford: Oxford University Press (3rd edition).

McPherson, K. (1972) 'Scientific Collaboration – Fact or Fiction?' *The Wick* (Journal of the MRC Unit, Northwick Park) 5 Sep.

Mead, G. (1956) *George Herbert Mead on Social Psychology* Chicago: University of Chicago Press.

Mead, G.H. (1934) *Mind, Self and Society* Chicago: Chicago University Press.

Melia, K. (1996) 'Rediscovering Glaser' *Qualitative Health Research* 6(3) 368–78

Mick, S. (1978) 'Understanding the Persistence of Resource Problems in Health' *Health and Society* 56, 463–99.

Midgley, M. (1980) *Beast and Man: The Roots of Human Nature* London: Methuen.

Miller, D.L. (1973) *George Herbert Mead: Self, Language and The World* Chicago: University of Chicago Press.

Moll, J.K. and Narin, F (1977) 'Characterization of the alcohol research literature' *J. Stud. Alcohol* 38, 2165.

Mooney, G.H. and Drummond, M.F. (1982–1983) 'Essentials of Health Economics' *British Medical Journal* (in 12 parts) 2 Oct 1982 to 1 Jan. 1983.

Mulkay, M. (1979) *Science and the Sociology of Knowledge* London: Allen and Unwin.

Sociology and Medicine

Murcott, A. (1998) 'An Introduction to Philip Strong's "The Pestilential Apocalypse: Modern, Post-modern and Early Modern Observations"' in R.S. Barbour & G. Huby (eds) *Meddling with Mythology: AIDS and the Social Construction of Knowledge* London: Routledge

Murcott, A. (2001) 'Sociology and health: creating the agenda' in R.G. Burgess, and A. Murcott, (eds) *Developments in Sociology: where are we now?* London: Pearson.

Murphy, E. and Dingwall, R. (2003) *Qualitative Methods and Health Policy Research* New York: Aldine.

Navarro, V. (1977) *Medicine under Capitalism* London: Croom Helm.

Nicolaus, M. (1973) The professional organization of sociology: a view from below' in R. Blackburn (ed) *Ideology in Social Science* New York: Vintage.

O'Brien, C.C. (1968) *Reflections on the Revolution in France* London: Penguin.

Office of Population Censuses and Surveys (O.P.C.S.) (1978) *General Household Survey 1976* London: Her Majesty's Stationery Office.

Office of Technology Assessment (1978) *Assessing the Efficacy and Safety of Medical Technologies* Congress of the United States.

Ohi, G. *et al* (1988) 'Cost-benefit analysis of AIDS prevention programmes: its limitation in policy-making' in A. Fleming *et al* (eds) *The Global Impact of AIDS* New York: Alan R. Liss Inc.

Olesen, V. (1975) 'Convergences and divergences: anthropology and sociology in health care' *Social Science & Medicine* 9, 421–5.

Open University (1985) *Medical Knowledge: Doubt and Certainty* Milton Keynes: Open University Press.

Opie, I. and Opie, P. (1967) *The Lore and Language of Schoolchildren* Oxford: Oxford University Press.

Opie, I. and Opie, P. (1970) *Games Children Play* Oxford: Oxford University Press.

Orchard, T.J. (1980) 'Epidemiology in the 1980s – Need for Change?' *The Lancet,* 18 Oct., 845–6.

Orford, J. and Edwards G. (1977) *Alcoholism. A Comparison of Treatment and Advice with a Study of the Influence of Marriage* Oxford: Oxford University Press.

Parr, D. (1957) 'Alcoholism in General Practice' *British Journal of Addiction* 54, 25–39.

Parsons, T. (1951) *The Social System* London: Routledge & Kegan Paul.

Parsons, T. (1964) *Social Structure and Personality* Glencoe, Ill.: Free Press.

Payne, G. and Williams, M. (2005) 'Generalization in Qualitative Research' *Sociology* 39(2), 295–314

Payne, J.P. and Stafford, T.J. (1980) 'Computers and the Clinician' *The Lancet,* I Nov., 977.

Pearse, I.H. and Crocker, L.H. (1949) *The Peckham Experiment* London: Allen & Unwin.

Petersdorf, E.G. (1980) 'The Evolution of Departments of Medicine' *New England Journal of Medicine* 303, 489–96.

Pettit, P. (1978) 'Rational man theory' C. Hookway and P. Pettit (eds) *Action and Interpretation: Studies in the Philosophy of the Social Sciences* Cambridge: Cambridge University Press.

Pflanz, M. (1975) 'Relations between social scientists, physicians and medical organizations in health research' *Social Science & Medicine* 9, 7–13.

Pfohl, S.J. (1977) 'The "discovery" of child abuse' *Social Problems* 24(3), 310–23.

Phillips, D. (1973) 'Sociologists and their knowledge: some critical remarks on a profession' in E. Freidson (ed) *The Professions and Their Prospects* New York: Sage.

Phillips, D.L. (1971) *Knowledge from What – Methods in Social Research* Chicago: Rand McNally.

Platt, Lord (1967) 'Medical Science: Master or Servant' (The Harveian Oration) *British Medical Journal* 28 Nov.

Powles, J. (1973) 'On the limitations of modern medicine' *Sci. Med. Man* 1(1), 1–30.

Rabin, D. and Bush, P. (1974) 'The use of medicine: historical trends and international comparisons' *International Journal of Health Services* 4, 61.

Rathod, N.H. (1967) 'An enquiry into general practitioners' opinions about alcoholism' *British Journal of Addiction* 62, 103.

Ravetz, I.R. (1971) *Scientific Knowledge and Its Social Problems* Oxford: Oxford University Press.

Reck, A. (1964) *Recent American Philosophy: Studies of Representative Thinkers* New York: Pantheon.

Renaud, M. (1975) 'On the constraints to state intervention in health' *International Journal of Health Services* 5, 559.

Ries, J.K. (1977) 'Public acceptance of the disease concept of alcoholism' *Journal of Health & Social Behavior* 18, 338.

Robinson, D. (1973) *Patients, Practitioners and Medical Care* London: Heinemann.

Robinson, D. (1976) *From Drink to Alcoholism: A Sociological Commentary* London: Wiley.

Robinson, J. Strong, P. and Elkan, R. (1989) *Griffiths and the Nurses: a National Survey of CNAs* Warwick: Nursing Policy Studies 4, Nursing Policy Studies Centre, University of Warwick.

266   *Sociology and Medicine*

Robinson, W. (1951) 'The logical structure of analytic induction' *American Sociological Review* 16, 812–18.

Robinson, W. (1951) 'The Logical Structure of Analytical Induction' *American Sociological Review* 16, 812–18.

Rock, P. (1973) *Deviant Behaviour* London: Hutchinson.

Rogers, D. and Blendon, R. (1978) 'The Academic Medical Center: A Stressed American Institution' *New England Journal of Medicine* 298(27 Apr), 940–50.

Rogers, M. (1980) 'Goffman on power, hierarchy and status' in J. Ditton (ed) *The View from Goffman* London: Macmillan.

Rosenberg, C. (1989) 'What is an epidemic? AIDS in historical perspective' *Daedalus* 118(2), 1–18.

Roth, J. (1969) Letter *American Sociologist* 4, 159.

Roth, J.A (1977) 'A Yank in the NHS' in A. Davis and G. Horobin (eds) *Medical Encounters* London: Croom Helm.

Rubington, E. and Weinberg, M. (eds) (1968) *Deviance – the Interactionist Perspective* New York: Macmillan.

Runciman, W.G. (1970) *Sociology In Its Place and Other Essays* Cambridge: Cambridge University Press.

Rushing, W. (1964) *The Psychiatric Professions* Chapel Hill: University of North Carolina.

Rustin, M. (1976) *Sociology as a Profession.* Sociologists in Polytechnics Series of Occasional Papers, No. 1. Hatfield: Hatfield Polytechnic.

Ryan, A. (1970) *The Philosophy of the Social Science* London: McMillan.

Sahlins, M. (1979) *New York Review of Books* 22 March, 47.

Schama, S. (1989) *Citizens* London: Viking.

Scheff, T. (1968) 'Negotiating reality: notes on power in the assessment of responsibility' *Social Problems* 16, 3–17.

Schegloff, E. 'Goffman and the analysis of conversation' in P. Drew and A. Wootton (eds) (1988) *Erving Goffman: Exploring the Interaction Order.* Oxford: Polity Press.

Schutz, A. (1970) *Alfred Schutz on Phenomenology and Social Relations* H.R. Wagner (ed) Chicago: University of Chicago Press.

Scott, M, and Lyman, S. (1968) 'Accounts' *American Sociological Review* 32, 46–62.

Scott, R. (1970) 'The Construction of Stigma by Professional Experts' in J.D. Douglas (ed) *Deviance and Respectability* New York: Basic Books.

Seale, C. (1999) *The Quality of Qualitative Research* London: Sage.

Shattuck, R. (1986) 'Catching up with the avant-garde' *New York Review of Books* 18(December), 66–74.

Shaw, M. (1972) 'The coming crisis of radical sociology' in R. Blackburn (ed) *Ideology in Social Science: Readings in Critical Social Theory* London: Fontana.

Shem, S. (1980) *House of God* London: Corgi.

Shils, E. (1980) 'Tradition, Ecology and Institution in the History of Sociology' in E. Shils *The Calling of Sociology* Chicago: University of Chicago Press.

Shryock, R. (1979 [1936]) *The Development of Modern Medicine* Madison: University of Wisconsin Press.

Silverman, D. (1981) 'The child as a social object: Down's Syndrome children in a paediatric cardiology clinic' *Sociology of Health and Illness* 3, 253–74.

Silverman, D. (1984) 'Going private: ceremonial forms in a private oncology clinic' *Sociology* 18, 191–204.

Silverman, D. (1987) *Communication and Medical Practice* London: Sage.

Silverman, D. (2000) *Doing Qualitative Research: a practical handbook* London: Sage

Social Services Committee of the House of Commons (1987) *Problems Associated with AIDS: Minutes of Evidence* London: Her Majesty's Stationary Office 1, 182, i–xv.

Sorenson, J.R. (1973) *Genetic Counselling* (Newsletter) 1, 5.

Sorokin, P. (1956) *Fads and Foibles in Modern Sociology* Chicago: Henry Regnery.

Spencer, J. *et al.* (1970) 'Some Problems of Statistical Consultancy' *Journal of the Royal Statistical Society* Series A, 133, Part 2.

Spurling, H. (1977) *Handbook to Anthony Powell's Music of Time* London: Heinemann.

Starr, P. (1982) *The Social Transformation of American Medicine* New York: Basic Books.

Steiner, G. (1971) *Bluebeard's Castle: Some Notes Towards the Redefinition of Culture* London: Faber and Faber.

Steiner, G. (1978) 'The Distribution of Discourse' in G. Steiner *On Difficulty* London: Oxford University Press.

Stimson, G. (1977) 'Social care and the role of the general practitioner' *Social Science & Medicine* 11, 485.

Stimson, G.V. and Webb, B. (1975) *Going to See the Doctor* London: Routledge & Kegan Paul.

Straus R. (1957) 'Nature and status of medical sociology' *American Sociological Review* 22(2), 200–204.

Strong, P.M. (1977) 'Medical errands' in A. Davis and G. Horobin (eds) *Medical Encounters* London: Croom Helm.

268   *Sociology and Medicine*

Strong, P. (1978) 'The alcoholic, the sick role and bourgeois medicine' Mimeo.

Strong, P.M. (1979a) *The Ceremonial Order of the Clinic: Parents, Doctors and Medical Bureaucracies* London: Routledge & Kegan Paul.

Strong, P. (1979b) 'Sociological Imperialism and the Profession of Medicine' *Social Science and Medicine* 13A, 199–215.

Strong, P. (1979c) 'Materialism and medical interaction' *Social Science & Medicine* 13A. 613–19.

Strong, P.M. (1982) 'Review of "Erving Goffman *Forms of Talk*" *Sociology* 16, 453–5.

Strong, P.M. (1983a) 'The importance of being Erving: Erving Goffman 1922–1982' *Sociology of Health and Illness* 5(3), 345–55.

Strong, P.M. (1983b) 'The Rivals: an essay on the sociological trades' in R. Dingwall and P. Lewis (eds) *The Sociology of the Professions: Law, Medicine and Others* London: Macmillan.

Strong, P.M. (1986) 'Issues in micro-interactionist sociology: identities, formats, methods and inter-disciplinary relations' Milton Keynes: Open University; unpublished essay, submitted in part requirement for PhD.

Strong, P.M. (1988) 'Minor courtesies and macro structures' in P. Drew and A. Wootton (eds) (1988) *Erving Goffman: Exploring the Interaction Order.* Oxford: Polity Press.

Strong, P. (1992) 'What do professional ethicists do? A sociological study of parliamentary witness on AIDS' a paper given at the 'International Symposium on Ethical Issues in Social and Biomedical Research in Community Settings', Brunel University, West London, 13–14 April.

Strong, P. and Berridge, V. (1990) 'No one knew anything: some issues in British AIDS policy' in P. Aggleton, G. Hart and P. Davies, (eds) *AIDS: Individual, Cultural and Policy Dimensions* Basingstoke: Falmer.

Strong, P. and Dingwall, R. (1983) 'The limits of negotiation in formal organizations' in N. Gilbert and P. Abell (eds) *Accounts and Action* Aldershot: Gower.

Strong, P.M. and Davis, A.G. (1976) 'The Management of a Therapeutic Encounter' in M. Wadsworth and D. Robinson (eds) *The Sociology of Everyday Medical Life* London: Martin Robertson.

Sudnow, D. (1972) 'Temporal Parameters of Interpersonal Observation' in D. Sudnow (ed) *Studies in Social Interaction* New York, Free Press.

Susser M. (1974) 'Introduction to the theme: a critical review of sociology in health' *International Journal of Health Services* 4, 408.

Susser M. (1975) 'Prevention and health maintenance revisited' *Bulletin of the New York Academy of Medicine* 51, 1.

Sykes, G. and Matza, D. (1957) 'Techniques of Neutralisation', *American Sociological Review,* 32, 667–69.

Szasz, T. (1970) *The Manufacture of Madness* New York: Harper & Row

Taber, M. *et al.* (1968) 'Disease ideology and mental health research' *Social Problems* 116, 349.

Tate, H. *et al.* (I 979) 'Randomized Comparative Studies in the Treatment of Cancers in the U.K. – room for improvement?' *The Lancet* 2 Sep., 623–5.

Taylor, C. (1964) *The Explanation of Behaviour* London: Routledge & Kegan Paul.

Taylor, C. (1967) 'Neutrality in political science' in P. Laslett and W.G. Runciman (eds) *Philosophy, Politics and Society* Oxford: Blackwell.

Thomas, D. (1979) *Naturalism and Social Science: A Post Empiricist Philosophy of Social Science* Cambridge: Cambridge University Press.

Thomas, K.B. (1978) 'The consultation and the therapeutic illusion' *British Medical Journal* 1328.

Timpanaro, S. (1980) *On Materialism* London: Verso.

Touraine, A. (1969) *La Revolution du Mai ou Le Communisme Utopique* Paris: Editions du Seuil.

Trilling, L. (1972) *Sincerity and Authority* London: Oxford University Press.

Turner, E.S. (1958) *Call the Doctor: A Social History of Medical Men* London: Michael Joseph.

Turner, J.H. (1988) *A Theory of Social Interaction* Oxford: Polity Press.

von Cranach, M. *et al* (1979) *Human Ethology: Claims and Limits of a New Discipline* Cambridge: Cambridge University Press.

Voysey, M. (1975) *A Constant Burden* Routledge and Kegan Paul, London.

Waitzkin, H.K. and Waterman, B. (1974) '*The· Exploitation of Illness in Capitalist Society* Indianapolis: Bobbs-Merrill.

Weber, J. and Goldmeier, D. (1983) 'Medicine and the media' *British Medical Journal* 287, 420.

Weeks, J. (1989) 'AIDS: the intellectual agenda' in P. Aggleton, G. Hart, and P. Davies (eds) *AIDS: Social Representations, Social Practices* Basingstoke: Falmer Press.

Wenglinsky, M. (1973) 'Errands' in A. Birenbaum and E. Sagarin (eds) *People in Places: the Sociology of the Familiar* London: Nelson.

Whyte, W.F. (1966) *Street Corner Society: the social structure of an Italian slum* 2nd edn. Chicago: University of Chicago Press.

Williams, R. (1986) 'Understanding Goffman's methods' in P. Drew and A. Wootton (eds) *Erving Goffman: Exploring the Interaction Order* Cambridge: Polity.

Witts, L. (1971) 'The Medical Professorial Unit' (The Harveian Oration) *British Medical Journal* 6 Nov., 319–23.

Wolfe, T. (1975) *The New Journalism* London: Picador.

Wolman, D. (1976) 'Quality control and the community physician in England: an American perspective' *International Journal of Health Services* 6, 79.

Woodruff, M. (1977) *On Science and Surgery,* Edinburgh: Edinburgh University Press.

Wuthnow, R. (1992) 'Introduction: new directions m the empirical study of cultural codes' in R. Wuthnow (ed) *Vocabularies of Public Life: Empirical Essays in Symbolic Structure* London: Routledge.

Wyngaarden, J.B. (1979) 'The Clinical Investigator as an Endangered Species' *New England Journal of Medicine* 301, 1254–9.

Yorkshire Television (1978) 'A crisis in the family' in the series *A Change of Mind* February 28.

Zola, I.K. (1972) 'Medicine as institution of social control' *Sociological Review* 20(4), 487–504.

Zola I.K. (1975) 'In the name of health and illness: on some sociopolitical consequences of medical influence' *Social Science & Medicine* 9(2), 83–7.

Zola I.K. (1977) 'Healthism and disabling medicalisation' *in* I. Illich, (ed) *Disabling Professions* London: Marion Boyars.

Zola I.K. and Miller S.J. (1973) 'The erosion of medicine from within' in E. Freidson (ed) *The Professions and Their Prospects* New York: Sage.

Index

Italics are used to indicate titles of documents. Footnotes are indicated by n after the page number